"I salute my friend Kirsten Powers for boldly and eloquently breaking the spiral of silence on silencing. That someone who identifies as a liberal is courageously drawing attention to the ugly new intolerance among us will give Americans of every political stripe hope and joy for our common future."

—Eric Metaxas, *New York Times* bestselling author of *Miracles* and *Bonhoeffer*

"Tolerance and free expression are founding values of our republic and yet they're under attack from the extreme wings of the American political spectrum. Shining a harsh light on the 'illiberal left,' Kirsten Powers exposes a grim campaign to silence speech. This is an important book."

—Ron Fournier, senior political columnist and editorial director of *National Journal*

"In this examination of the multiplying attacks on freedom of speech, Kirsten Powers casts a cool eye on the damages done to politics, academia, and civic discourse by the aggressive assertion of a perverse new entitlement. It is the postulated right to pass through life without being disturbed, annoyed, offended, or discomposed by the expression of anyone else's thoughts."

—George F. Will, Pulitzer Prize–winning syndicated columnist and author of the *New York Times* bestseller *A Nice Little Place on the North Side*

THE SILENCING

THE SILENCING

HOW THE LEFT IS KILLING FREE SPEECH

KIRSTEN POWERS

REGNERY
PUBLISHING
A Division of Salem Media Group

Regnery® is a registered trademark of Salem Communications Holding Corporation

Library of Congress Cataloging-in-Publication Data

Powers, Kirsten.
   The silencing : how the left is killing free speech / Kirsten Powers.
      pages cm
   ISBN 978-1-62157-370-8 (hardback)
   1. Liberalism--United States. 2. Right and left (Political science)--United States. 3. Freedom of speech--United States. I. Title.
   JC574.2.U6P68 2015
   323.44'30973--dc23
                                        2015011565

Published in the United States by
Regnery Publishing
A Division of Salem Media Group
300 New Jersey Ave NW
Washington, DC 20001
www.Regnery.com

Manufactured in the United States of America

10 9 8 7 6 5 4 3 2 1

Books are available in quantity for promotional or premium use. For information on discounts and terms, please visit our website: www.Regnery.com.

Distributed to the trade by
Perseus Distribution
250 West 57th Street
New York, NY 10107

To my father

CONTENTS

INTRODUCTION

I grew up during the 1970s with a feminist mother who was trailblazing her way across Alaska as one of the country's few female archaeologists. She and my father, also an archaeologist, had set out for the "Last Frontier" on an adventure after earning their Ph.D.s at the University of Wisconsin–Madison. Although they divorced a few years later, my parents continued as colleagues at the University of Alaska-Fairbanks for three decades.

The campus was a haven to the few liberals in Fairbanks, an otherwise overwhelmingly conservative town located in the center of the state. It was at my hippy day care center Enep'ut (the Yup'ik Eskimo word for "our house") that I sat in front of a fuzzy black and white television to cheer with dozens of toddlers as Richard Nixon resigned. That triumph of right over wrong was my first taste of politics—and I was hooked. Mine was one of a few little hands that went up in favor of Jimmy Carter in 1976 when my teacher asked which nominee we supported for president—a trend that continued through every presidential campaign until I graduated from high school. It's unlikely many of my friends' mothers were sobbing the night Carter lost to Ronald Reagan, as was mine.

My political education occurred at the dinner table. Whether at my mother or father's house, the topic invariably would be politics. It was there I was also taught how to defend my views. We viewed this as a necessary survival skill, as our family was surrounded by people who believed liberalism was the root of all evil. At my tiny Jesuit high school, I would debate my conservative classmates on issue after issue, whether it was feminism or caring for the poor. My friends' parents were uniformly small-government conservatives, and their children followed suit. Ronald Reagan, their patron saint, was president. He could do no wrong.

At my house, however, there was a very different storyline on the president. The Democratic roots in our family ran deep, as both my parents hailed from Irish Democratic stock. My father's tribe was a mix of working class Catholics and Protestants. On my mother's side was an army of Massachusetts-born Irish Catholic Democrats who idolized John F. Kennedy. The allegiance to the Democratic Party had been cemented generations before, when family members reached the shores of America. I was constantly reminded that the Democratic Party stood up for working people, for families like ours, and those that came later, and not just from Ireland.

Despite this background, I can't remember anyone ever suggesting that conservative views were illegitimate and unworthy of debate. I first encountered that attitude when I moved to New York City much later, where bumping into a conservative was less likely than spotting a unicorn. That unfamiliarity ultimately bred contempt.

It was easy to stereotype conservatives because I no longer knew any beyond my childhood friends, whom I rarely saw. I had already been happily ideologically cocooned for much of my twenties as I worked as a political appointee in the Clinton administration. This isolation grew when I moved to New York in my early thirties and became enmeshed in

Democratic politics there, including working on Andrew Cuomo's first race for governor and consulting for the New York State Democratic Committee, among other things. Even the few Republicans I knew were basically liberal.

Two experiences unexpectedly put me in a regular relationship with conservatives: working as a contributor at Fox News and a later in life conversion to Christianity. The more I got to know actual conservative and religious people, the harder it was to justify the stereotypes I had so carelessly embraced. In my early days at Fox, I can remember trying to convince a conservative there that George Bush's nomination of Harriet Miers to the Supreme Court didn't really count as a female appointment because she was conservative and an evangelical Christian. He was horrified. I was confused as to why he would be horrified.

I'm now embarrassed that I ever thought such a thing, let alone said it aloud. Such a prejudiced view was only able to take root because of the lack of ideological, political, and religious diversity in my world.

But I wasn't alone in my prejudice.

A 2007 study of faculty on college campuses found that 53 percent of university professors had "cool" or negative feelings toward evangelicals.[1] This raises serious questions about how Christian students can expect to be treated on secular campuses. Sadly, at the time this study was performed, I would have likely been among that 53 percent—even though I didn't know a single evangelical.

Another study, released in 2012, found that 82 percent of liberal social psychologists surveyed said they would be at least a little prejudiced against a conservative applicant for a job in their department.[2]

Here's the problem: disagreement is fine; discrimination is not. Liberals are supposed to believe in diversity, which should include diversity of thought and belief. Instead, an alarming level of intolerance emanates from the left side of the political spectrum toward people who express views that don't hew to the "settled" liberal worldview. The passion for silencing isn't reserved for conservatives or orthodox Christians. Moderate Democrats, independent minded liberals, and the ideologically agnostic become targets if they deviate on liberal sacred cow issues.

This intolerance is not a passive matter of opinion. It's an aggressive, illiberal impulse to silence people. This conduct has become an existential threat to those who hold orthodox religious beliefs. But increasingly I hear from people across the political spectrum who are fearful not only of expressing their views, but also as to where all of this is heading. I've followed this trend closely as a columnist with growing concern. It's become clear that the attempts—too often successful—to silence dissent from the liberal worldview aren't isolated outbursts. They are part of a bigger story. This book is that story.

ONE

REPRESSIVE TOLERANCE

*Who ever knew Truth put to the wors[e] in a free and
open encounter?*

—JOHN MILTON

I n the fall of 2014, the historic all-women's Smith College held an
alumnae event to explore the place of free speech within the liberal
arts tradition. Smith president Kathleen McCartney introduced a
four-person panel that included three graduates of the prestigious university with the exhortation, "We want to have fearless encounter with
new ideas. I think that's what is truly at the heart of a liberal arts education."

The panel was gamely titled, "Challenging the Ideological Echo Chamber: Free Speech, Civil Discourse and the Liberal Arts."[1] Wendy Kaminer,
an alumna and liberal feminist First Amendment expert, dove right in to
condemn the proliferation of campus speech codes that prohibit language
that makes people uncomfortable. The former long time American Civil
Liberties Union (ACLU) board member raised the issue of Mark Twain's
The Adventures of Huckleberry Finn, which some have argued should be
banned from classrooms for its use of racial epithets. Panelist Jaime

Estrada, a recent Smith grad working for the University of Pennsylvania Press, interjected, "But it has the n-word, and some people are sensitive to that."

Kaminer replied, "Well, let's talk about the n-word. Let's talk about the growing lexicon of words that can only be known by their initials. I mean, when I say, 'n-word,' or when Jaime says 'n-word,' what word do you all hear in your head?" Members of the audience replied by saying the full word. Kaminer said, "You all hear the word n--ger in your head? See, I said that, nothing horrible happened." Estrada disagreed: "I mean, it depends on who you are in the audience, something horrible happened in their head." The event continued seemingly without incident, and the panelists disagreed civilly, including Kaminer and Estrada.[2]

This is how the discussion was reported in the *Mount Holyoke News*: "Students, faculty and alumnae of Smith College were shocked this past week to find out that a Smith graduate made racist remarks when speaking at an alumnae panel in New York City on Sept. 22."[3] The *Smith Sophian*, the campus paper, ran a story headlined, "Backlash Follows Use of Racial Slur at NYC Panel." The paper also published a transcript of the event, which, lest we forget, was comprised of alumnae and staff of Smith College, not members of the Ku Klux Klan, that blared at the top: "Trigger/Content Warnings: Racism/racial slurs, ableist slurs, antisemitic language, anti-Muslim/Islamophobic language, anti-immigrant language, sexist/misogynistic slurs, references to race-based violence, references to antisemitic violence." It's not clear why the warning was necessary, as the newspaper censored the transcript so that any word that could potentially offend the fair ladies of Smith was removed. At one point, the transcript reads, "Kathleen McCartney: . . . We're just wild and [ableist slur], aren't we?" Yes, the word "crazy" was censored.[4]

Smith students protested. Someone wrote "Impeach Kathy" on the sidewalk outside the Smith president's home in chalk. Coeds donned black and observed a moment of silence on the campus lawn to take a stance against "racialized violence, criminalization of black bodies, failed institutional memory, microaggressions, and the vast and even unnamable issues that work against people of color every day." One student compared Kaminer's comments to a 2012 incident when a student of color received a hate note slipped under her door. Smith responded to the outcry over Kaminer's attempt to explain how free speech works by holding a panel on anti-blackness.[5] The Student Government Association put out a letter asserting that, "If Smith is unsafe for one student, it is unsafe for all students."[6]

Jordan Houston, the *Smith Sophian*'s opinions editor, accused McCartney of blithely sitting on a panel that turned into an "explicit act of racial violence" and complained that Kaminer was allowed to speak "uncensored." Houston quoted from a statement by the Social Justice & Equity Committee '14–'15, saying McCartney's behavior "implicitly suggested that hate speech is permissible at Smith" and she failed in her "responsibility to speak up when another white person says something racist."[7] Never mind that the New York City panel didn't even occur at Smith—which is located in Massachusetts—nor was it geared to students. Most importantly: nothing racist was uttered.

Certainly people may disagree about whether Kaminer should have used such provocative language to make her point. But to portray her comments as "hate speech" or "racialized violence" or as having made even one person "unsafe" is not just absurd. It's a chilling attempt to silence free speech. So much for the "fearless encounter with new ideas" McCartney advocated.

The repurposing of Kaminer's comments into an act of violence should not be dismissed as a one-off incident from bizarro land. Casting disagreement as a physical attack or "hate speech," or any host of socially taboo behaviors, has become a central tactic in an ever expanding campaign to silence speech. Kaminer's real crime was to vigorously challenge the alarming trend toward censorship on campuses. Rather than arguing with her on the merits, her opponents set about the process of delegitimizing her by tarring her as a racist.

Who were her opponents? Many think they were liberals. That's partly right. The people who cast Kaminer as a modern-day Bull Connor were almost definitely ideologically liberal. But most likely the majority of the attendees and participants at the Smith alumnae event were liberal as well, the difference being that they were able to disagree without demonizing.

The people who smeared Kaminer as a racist and who routinely demonize those who express the "wrong" views, are what I call the "illiberal left." They are most prevalent on college campuses and in the media—not insignificant perches from which to be quashing debate and dissent—but their tentacles are expanding into every sector of society. They consider themselves liberals, but act in direct contradiction to the fundamental liberal values of free speech, debate, and dissent. What distinguishes them from mainstream liberals and your average Democrat (who shares many of the illiberal left's policy inclinations) is not so much *what* they believe, but *how* they believe it. Most people who reside on the left side of the political spectrum can tolerate difference of opinion without turning into authoritarian speech police. They can either engage or ignore people with whom they disagree. They are not moved to, for example, call for jail time for their ideological opponents as environmentalist Robert F. Kennedy Jr. did for the Koch brothers. More on that later.

The illiberal left, on the other hand, believes that people who express ideological, philosophical, or political views that don't line up with their preferences should be completely silenced. Instead of using persuasion and rhetoric to make a positive case for their causes and views, they work to delegitimize the person making the argument through character assassination, demonization, and dehumanizing tactics. These are the self-appointed overlords—activists, university administrators, journalists, and politicians—who have determined what views are acceptable to express. So, shut up—or else.

Left-leaning writer Fredrik deBoer has called it the "We Are All Already Decided" phenomenon. It "presumes that the offense is not just in thinking the wrong thing you think but in not realizing that We Are All

Already Decided that the thing you think is deeply ridiculous," he wrote in April 2014. "This is the form of argument…that takes as its presumption that all good and decent people are already agreed on the issue in question."[8] It goes without saying that "good and decent people" are politically and ideologically liberal. The illiberal left hunts down heretics, dissidents, and run-of-the mill dissenters to not only silence them, but make examples of them for the rest of society.

Dissent from liberal orthodoxy is cast as racism, misogyny, bigotry, phobia, and, as we've seen, even violence. If you criticize the lack of due process for male college students accused of rape, you are a "rape apologist." End of conversation. After all, who wants to listen to a rape lover? People who are anti–abortion rights don't care about the unborn; they are misogynists who want to control women. Those who oppose same-sex marriage don't have rational, traditional views about marriage that deserve respect or debate; they are bigots and homophobes. When conservatives opposed the Affordable Care Act's "contraception mandate" it wasn't due to a differing philosophy about the role of government. No, they were waging a "War on Women."

With no sense of irony or shame, the illiberal left will engage in racist, sexist, misogynist, and homophobic attacks of their own in an effort to delegitimize people who dissent from the "already decided" worldview. Non-white conservatives are called sellouts and race traitors. Conservative women are treated as dim-witted, self-loathing puppets of the patriarchy, or nefarious gender traitors. Men who express the wrong political or ideological view are demonized as hostile interlopers into the public debate. The illiberal left sees its bullying and squelching of free speech as a righteous act.

This illiberal effort relies on an arsenal of delegitimizing terms. The mushrooming silencing lexicon now includes the terms "mansplaining," "whitesplaining," and "microaggression." The 99.9 percent of humanity that identifies with the gender identity, male or female, assigned at birth are derided as "cisgendered." These various terms are meant to silence any person who labors under the defect of "privilege," a moving target that seems to apply to whomever the illiberal left is up to demonizing that day. While the favored targets have been mostly conservatives and orthodox Christians, the illiberal left has been branching out. Just ask Bill Maher, who flipped in an instant from liberal darling to hate-filled bigot when he expressed a fraction of the disdain for Islam that he's routinely demonstrated toward Christianity.

On campuses there are speech codes, so-called "free speech zones," and a host of "anti-discrimination" policies that discriminate against people who dissent from lefty groupthink. Christian and conservative groups have been denied official university status by student government organizations for holding views not in line with liberal dogma. The illiberal left's attempts to control the public debate are frequently buttressed by a parade of childish grievances. They portray life's vagaries as violations of their basic human rights and demand the world stop traumatizing them with facts and ideological views that challenge their belief system. They insist colleges provide "trigger warnings" on syllabi to prevent them from stumbling upon a piece of literature that might deal with controversial or difficult issues that could upset them. Frequently, the illiberal left will invoke the symptoms of post-traumatic stress disorder (PTSD), a devastating and serious illness, to characterize reading or hearing something they find upsetting or offensive. They've described such disparate experiences as reading *The Great Gatsby*, seeing a statue of an underwear-clad man, or passing an anti-abortion demonstration as potentially lethal to their psychological well-being.

The illiberal left yearns for a world sanitized of information that offends them. So why not just tune out the views they don't like? They can't. They are authoritarians at heart; they know what Americans should think and what information they should consume. So they launch petitions to have particular views censored from newspapers.[9] They try to get columnists fired for expressing the wrong views.[10] The illiberal left has maniacally maneuvered to delegitimize the Fox News Channel, unable to abide the existence of *one* news network critical of the president. High-ranking White House officials were the face of this effort, telling anyone who would listen that Fox News was "not really a news station" and not "legitimate."[11] These top government officials were joined in their illiberal campaign by the progressive nonprofit Media Matters for America (MMFA), which enjoys the support of some of the Democratic Party's top donors.[12] At one point, Media Matters' CEO David Brock told *Politico* that the organization's ninety-person staff and $10 million annual budget was dedicated to the purpose of waging "guerrilla warfare and sabotage"[13] against Fox News. A leaked MMFA memo for liberal donors detailed a strategy to destroy Fox that included plans to assemble opposition research on Fox News employees.[14]

In 2014, the outside world got a peek at the illiberal left's staging area—academia—with a spate of high-profile 2014 commencement speech cancelations and forced withdrawals. These were spurred by the protests of lefty students and professors outraged that someone who held views with which they disagreed, such as support for the Iraq War or capitalism, would be allowed to deliver a commencement address. According to the Foundation for Individual Rights in Education (FIRE), college campuses are becoming ever more intolerant of opposing views. FIRE found that during the twenty-two years between 1987 and through 2008, 138 protests of planned campus speeches led to 62 incidents of an invited guest not speaking. Yet in just six years—2009 through 2014—151 protests have caused the cancelation of 62 speeches on campuses across the country. Since 2000, conservative speakers were targeted with nearly twice the frequency as liberal speakers (141 vs. 73 attempts respectively).[15]

"The fact that conservatives are the focus of so many dis-invitation efforts is made far more striking by the fact that—especially when it comes to commencement addresses—conservatives are far less likely to be invited to deliver speeches in the first place,"[16] wrote FIRE President Greg Luki-anoff, himself a liberal, in his book *Freedom from Speech*. When the mob is unsuccessful in pressuring campus administrators into canceling a speech, or shaming the speaker into withdrawing, then they utilize the "heckler's veto" to harass and intimidate, sometimes to the point that those in attendance can't hear the speaker.

The illiberal left's silencing campaign smacks of "repressive tolerance," philosopher Herbert Marcuse's theory that curbing freedom of expression in pursuit of left-wing ideological goals is both necessary and defensible. Marcuse wrote, "Suppression of...regressive [policies]...is a prerequisite for the strengthening of the progressive ones." If this sounds familiar, it's because you've heard one of the illiberals casting a sexist, dehumanizing attack against a conservative woman as a defense of "women's rights." Their misogyny and authoritarianism is all for the greater good.

The illiberal left knows that delegitimization works. It's their strongest weapon in a country with unparalleled free speech protections. If you can't suppress views you don't like with repressive laws, then delegitimize the people expressing them. Even advocates of "hate speech" laws, such as New York University law professor Jeremy Waldron have admitted it's unlikely that such legislation "will ever pass constitutional muster in America." That's true today, but whether it will hold true in the future depends on what conception of the First Amendment liberal jurists—who are being influenced by the illiberal left's contempt of free speech—bring to the bench.

In the meantime, delegitimization through demonizing and intimidation remains the illiberal left's most effective tactic. In a burst of refreshing honesty, Mary Frances Berry, an African American and former chairwoman of the U.S. Commission on Civil Rights under President Bill Clinton, wrote in a *Politico* online discussion: "Tainting the tea party movement with the charge of racism is proving to be an effective strategy for Democrats." Berry, a professor at the University of Pennsylvania, added, "There is no evidence that tea party adherents are any more racist than other Republicans, and indeed many other Americans. But getting them to spend their time purging their ranks and having candidates distance themselves should help Democrats win in November. Having one's opponent rebut charges of racism is far better than discussing joblessness."[17]

The illiberal left's campaign of conformity is distinct and notably different from the routine politicking in which both parties engage. This is not about political parties enforcing ideological or partisan purity within their own ranks of elected officials, as detrimental to society as that may be. It's not about harsh criticism, or a plea for civility. Searing critiques can and should be a part of a robust public debate, and no person engaging in that debate should be off limits from such accountability. But what the illiberal left does cannot reasonably be called debate. Ad hominem character assassinations are not arguments. Nor are they reflective of a liberal impulse.

This is not to suggest that conservatives don't ever engage in such behaviors. Of course they do. Though if you are a liberal and "conservatives do it too" is your best defense for left-wing intolerance and hostility to free speech, then it might be time for some soul-searching. There is also a serious quantitative difference between left and right attempts to silence people. Conservatives simply do not control the primary institutions where free speech is most under assault: the media and academia. That's not to say they never have or never will again, something that liberals might want to consider.

The people who are prosecuting many of these delegitimization campaigns are not fringe characters. They include Nancy Pelosi, Harry Reid, Debbie Wasserman Schultz, senior White House aides, administrators and professors of major public and private universities, and the president of the United States. Major media figures and major liberal activist groups consistently carry water for the illiberal left. These are all people who call themselves liberal, and who claim to believe in tolerance, while behaving in the most illiberal manner imaginable.

Toleration and free expression have been central to modern liberalism, stemming from a proud tradition tracing its roots to the writings of Thomas Jefferson and John Stuart Mill. While watching the illiberal left in action, it's easy to forget that it was the political left that championed free speech in America. During the Vietnam War era, the targeting of left-wing anti-war activists at the University of California-Berkeley for their dissent launched what came to be known as the "Free Speech Movement." As *Reason* magazine's Matt Welch wrote, "Back then the people using the conspiratorial slur 'outside agitators' to denigrate campus activists were...conservative politicians disgusted to see antiwar sentiment at publicly funded universities. In 1965, Bay Area Assemblyman Don Mulford...introduced anti-outsider legislation to (in his words) 'remove from the campus the professional agitators, the beatniks, the mentally ill, the untouchables, the unwashed.' The bill sailed into law." Today, the "outside agitators" are Americans who stray on even one issue that the illiberal left has deemed settled.

Amidst the hysteria following Bill Maher's debate on Islam with Ben Affleck, a group of UC Berkeley students sought to revoke the HBO host's invitation to offer a commencement address that fell on the fiftieth anniversary of the "Free Speech Movement," because they disapproved of his views on Islam. They failed in the effort because, as Bill Maher told his *Real Time* audience, "The university has come down on my side, saying what I hoped they would say all along, which is that we're liberals, we're supposed to like free speech!"[18]

In an interview with CNN's Sally Kohn for *Vanity Fair*, Maher said his message to the protesting students was, "You know, I'm a liberal. My message is: be a liberal. Find out what liberalism means and join up. Liberalism certainly should not mean squelching free speech...And I would just say to all liberals: we should own the First Amendment the way the right-wingers own the Second."[19]

When one thinks of suppressing speech and engaging in ideological witch hunts, Republican Senator Joseph McCarthy is the name that comes to mind. McCarthy's ruthless campaign to root out those he believed to be disloyal to the United States spawned the term "McCarthyism" to refer to the practice of making false accusations against political or ideological enemies in an effort to delegitimize and silence them. In addition to his anti-Communist crusades, McCarthy worked to expel from government positions people whom he accused, or threatened to publicly accuse, of homosexuality. How ironic that today there is a left-wing crusade to expel from positions of authority anyone who opposes same-sex marriage. The McCarthyite impulse has come full circle.

In March 2014, pioneering Internet company Mozilla announced the appointment of co-founder Brendan Eich as CEO.[20] That same day, a Twitter mob exploded with criticism of Eich.[21] Gay rights supporters were angry about a six-year-old donation of $1,000 to the "Yes on 8" campaign, which sought to ban same-sex marriage in California in 2008.[22] It's okay to be angry about Eich's donation. Screaming for Eich's head on a pike for his failure to conform to Mozilla's majority view on same-sex marriage is not. Liberals are supposed to believe in protecting minority views, even when they disapprove of those views.

Instead an online mob of presumably "liberal" people tweeted about Eich's donation,[23] many calling him a bigot and homophobe for supporting Prop 8. Remember, this proposition passed the same year Senator Barack Obama sat in Rick Warren's church to explain his religious based opposition to same-sex marriage. Eich took the time to address the criticisms. On his blog he wrote, "I am committed to ensuring that Mozilla is, and will remain, a place that includes and supports everyone, regardless of sexual orientation, gender identity, age, race, ethnicity, economic status, or religion."[24] Such assurances proved inadequate, however. Almost seventy thousand people signed a petition organized at CredoAction, a progressive social change organization, telling Eich to renounce his beliefs or resign as Mozilla's CEO. They accused him of "advocat[ing] for inequality and hate" and ordered Mozilla to fire him if he refused to resign.[25]

Finally, just over a week after his appointment, Mozilla announced that Eich would be stepping down as CEO. "While painful," wrote Executive Chairwoman Mitchell Baker, "the events of the last week show exactly why we need the Web. So all of us can engage freely in the tough conversations we need to make the world better."[26]

It's not necessary to support Eich's donation to recognize something deeply disturbing occurred here. Pushing someone out of his job for dissenting on an issue that has nothing to do with the mission of the company and then portraying the purge as a "free" conversation that boosted humanity is creepily Orwellian. The writer Andrew Sullivan—who is gay and was one of the earliest public advocates of same-sex marriage[27]—wrote at the time of Eich's ouster, "When people's lives and careers are subject to litmus tests, and fired if they do not publicly renounce what may well be their sincere conviction, we have crossed a line. This is McCarthyism applied by civil actors. This is the definition of intolerance."[28]

Sullivan correctly acknowledged that Mozilla had not violated any laws in punishing Eich for his opposition to same-sex marriage and that they had the right to take the actions they did. But that didn't make what they did consistent with the liberal values Mozilla claimed to embrace. In discussion of the controversy on ABC's *This Week*, Democratic strategist Donna Brazile concurred with Sullivan, saying, "We have to be very careful that we are not practicing a new McCarthyism." Yet, this is exactly what the illiberal left is regularly doing right under everyone's noses. They don't have the force of the government behind them (though some would like it in the form of "hate speech" laws), but they don't need it. Because of the outsized influence this crowd enjoys in today's culture—along with the ubiquity and reach of social media—reputations and livelihoods can be destroyed with the push of a button.

KILLING THE HABITS OF THE HEART

Because many of the silencing tactics employed by the illiberal left do not involve the government—though some do, particularly at public universities—the illiberal left will often claim they are not infringing on anybody's right to free speech. This willfully misses the point.

Freedom requires more than the "structures" of freedom such as a liberal Constitution and a just legal system. It requires the "spirit" of freedom, which is passed from generation to generation.[29] This insight, which comes from the eighteenth century philosopher Montesquieu, was famously applied to the United States by Alexis de Tocqueville in his book *Democracy in America*, in which he observed that America owes its freedom not so much to the law as to the "habits of the heart"[30] of freedom-loving American citizens.

The illiberal left is eradicating these "habits of the heart" so Americans won't even remember what it was like to be able to speak freely without fear of retaliation from a silencing mob or a few disgruntled lefties. "Mankind ought to have a rational assurance that all objections have been satisfactorily answered; and how are they to be answered if that which requires to be answered is not spoken?" asked British philosopher John Stuart Mill in *On Liberty*. "Or how can the answer be known to be satisfactory, if the objectors have no opportunity of showing that it is unsatisfactory?"

The more success the illiberal left has in terrorizing people who express dissenting views, the fewer objections there will be. Most people understandably just want to do their jobs and support their families. Given the choice between being shunned by their peers or losing their job for a personal view, they will almost always choose silence over confrontation. Because of this, society should always err on the side of respecting people's right to determine their own beliefs and express them without fear of official or unofficial retribution. Debate and persuasion should be the reflexive response to disagreement and even harmful propositions, not an authoritarian impulse to silence. It should be so not only because it is just, but because no society can flourish without the clash of ideas.

Harvard psychology professor and bestselling author Steven Pinker invoked the critical role free speech plays in a democratic system in a 2014 speech. We acquire knowledge through a "process that Karl Popper called conjecture and refutation," said Pinker. "We come up with ideas about the nature of reality, and test them against that reality, allowing the world to falsify the mistaken ones. The 'conjecture' part of this formula, of course, presupposes the exercise of free speech. We offer conjectures without any prior assurance they are correct. It is only by bruiting ideas and seeing which ones withstand attempts to refute them that we acquire knowledge."

The illiberal left seeks to short-circuit this process. They don't want to defend their views, nor do they want to allow forums for other people to present views that are at odds with the conclusions they have drawn on an array of issues. Sometimes, the mere suggestion of holding a debate is cast as an offense.[31]

Pinker singled out university campuses for their hostility to free speech, likening them to the worst authoritarian regimes in history. "It may seem outlandish to link American campus freedom—which by historical and global standards is still admirably high—to the world's brutal regimes," Pinker said.

"But I'm here to tell you that the connection is not that far-fetched. This morning I woke up in Oslo, after having addressed the Oslo Freedom Forum, a kind of TED for political dissidents. I met people who escaped from North Korea by walking across the Gobi desert in winter; people who were jailed for a single tweet; people whose families were thrown in prison because of their own political activity. These stories put the relatively minor restrictions on campus speech in perspective. But the American commitment to unfettered speech, unrivaled even by our democratic allies in Europe, stands as a beacon of inspiration to the world's dissidents, one of the few features of the American brand that still commands global admiration. At least one speaker at the Forum singled out speech codes and other restrictions on expression in the United States as a worrisome development."[32]

The behavior of the illiberal left flies in the face of decades of jurisprudence forged by liberal Supreme Court Justices who argued for an expansive view of the First Amendment and treated free speech as a precious commodity to be guarded jealously. "Those who won our independence believed...that freedom to think as you will and to speak as you think are means indispensable to the discovery and spread of political truth," wrote Supreme Court Justice Louis D. Brandeis in 1927. "The path of safety lies in the opportunity to discuss freely supposed grievances and proposed remedies; and that the fitting remedy for evil counsels is good ones."[33] This does not become less true outside of Uncle Sam's shadow. Supreme Court Justice William Brennan Jr.—a liberal lion known for his outspoken progressive views—was perhaps the strongest First Amendment advocate of the modern era. Appointed in 1956, Brennan participated in 252 free speech cases during his thirty-four-year tenure on the Court. In 88 percent of these cases, Brennan sided with the free speech claim.[34] In *New York Times v. Sullivan*, likely Brennan's most well-known free speech opinion, he wrote: "We consider this case against the background of a profound national commitment to the principle that debate on public issues should be uninhibited, robust, and wide-open…"[35]

The illiberal left does not share this commitment. Their burgeoning philosophy in favor of government power to curtail freedom of thought, speech, and conscience is troubling. Environmentalist Robert F. Kennedy Jr.—a graduate of one of the nation's most elite law schools, the University of Virginia—said in a September 2014 interview of those who deny climate change, "I wish that there were a law you could punish them under."[36] Accusing the libertarian Koch brothers of "treason" for disagreeing with his view of climate change, he said they should be "at the Hague with all the other war criminals." He asked rhetorically, "Do I think the Koch brothers should be tried for reckless endangerment? Absolutely, that is a criminal offense and they ought to be serving time for it." Kennedy's penchant for arguing for state action against those who do not share his view of climate change is not new. In 2007, he said in a speech at Live Earth that politicians who are "corporate toadies for companies like Exxon and Southern Company" had committed treason and needed to be treated as traitors.[37] In 2009, he deemed certain coal companies "criminal enterprises" and declared that one company's CEO "should be in jail…for all of eternity."[38]

In a 2014 speech, Floyd Abrams, one of the nation's top First Amendment scholars, himself a lifelong liberal, noted, "It stuns me how many people—educated people, including scholars—seem to believe that the First Amendment should be interpreted as nothing but an extension and embodiment of their generally liberal political views."[39] He told me in an interview, "It is accurate to say that…conservative jurists have moved strongly in the direction of more First Amendment protection and liberal jurists have moved markedly in the other direction." Abrams founded the Floyd Abrams Institute for Freedom of Expression at Yale Law School and noted that of the liberal legal scholars who come to his center, most view the First Amendment as an impediment to progressive policy goals. He says, "Their definition of liberalism is so imbued with their devotion to egalitarianism that they are willing to pay some First Amendment prices to get there."

Cornell Law School professor Steven H. Shiffrin is a leading scholar of the First Amendment and co-author of a widely used First Amendment casebook.[40] He is also an evangelist for the new progressive view of the First Amendment. Shiffrin gave a 2014 lecture called "The Dark Side of the First Amendment" in which he proclaimed, "The First Amendment is at odds with human dignity" and complained that racist speech was protected despite "its undermining of racial equality."[41] University of Chicago Law School professor Eric Posner expressed a similar contempt for free speech when he wrote in *Slate*, "For the left, the [First] amendment today is like a dear old uncle who enacted heroic deeds in his youth but on occasion says embarrassing things about taboo subjects in his decline." The time had come to put the nutty uncle back in the attic. Posner was writing in the wake of the riots in the Middle East attributed to a YouTube video. He expressed dismay that the U.S. government was prevented by U.S. law "from restricting the distribution of a video that causes violence abroad and damages America's reputation." As he wrote, "The rest of the world— and not just Muslims—see no sense in the First Amendment."[42]

Posner and Shiffrin are influential legal scholars and they are not alone in their views. Their intolerance of free speech that leads to what they deem the wrong policy conclusions or offends the wrong people is frankly typical of the illiberal left. Today's progressive legal policy is less likely to treat the First Amendment as a bulwark against government infringement on the free expression of Americans than a roadblock to a progressive ideological agenda. "What's coming up through the pipeline should have everyone who cares about freedom of speech very concerned," FIRE's president Greg Lukianoff, a graduate of Stanford Law School, told me in an interview. "I'm afraid that a lot of these more tenuous theories that law schools have come up with—that have grown up on campuses—that allow them to punish speech they dislike, while protecting speech they like are going to have increasing presence on the bench at every level and, I'm afraid, eventually on the Supreme Court."

The more suppressive view of free speech seems to be gaining currency more broadly, especially among younger Americans. According to the 2013 First Amendment Center annual survey, "This year there was a significant increase in those who claimed that the First Amendment goes too far in protecting individual rights." The older you are, the less likely it is that you believe the First Amendment's protections are too robust. Only 23 percent of people over sixty and 24 percent of those between forty-six and sixty hold that sentiment. But an astonishing 47 percent of eighteen- to thirty-year-olds say the First Amendment goes too far, and 44 percent of thirty-one- to forty-five-year-olds agree.[43]

If younger Americans are that accepting of government interference in speech, then how much more tolerant will they be of unofficial silencing?

AGE OF UN-ENLIGHTENMENT

The illiberal left isn't just ruining reputations and lives with their campaigns of delegitimization and disparagement. They are harming all of society by silencing important debates, denying people the right to draw their own conclusions, and derailing reporting and research that is important to our understanding of the world. They are robbing culture of the diversity of thought that is so central to learning and discovery.

It's sadly ironic that so many of the illiberal left view themselves as rational, intellectual, fact-based thinkers and yet have fully embraced a dogmatic form of un-enlightenment. Deviating from lefty ideology is equated to heresy and academic inquiry is too often secondary to ideological agendas. The illiberal left insert ideologically driven statistics into the media and academic bloodstream and then accuse anyone who questions them of diabolical motives. When researchers make discoveries supporting the wrong ideological conclusion, the character assassination and intimidation begin.

In a 2011 speech, then-University of Virginia social psychologist Jonathan Haidt, who describes himself politically as a "liberal turned centrist," explained, "If a group circles around sacred values, they'll evolve into a tribal-moral community. They'll embrace science whenever it supports their sacred values, but they'll ditch it or distort it as soon as it threatens a sacred value." The illiberal left likes to accuse conservatives and religious people of doing this, but ignores the central role it plays in their own determination to reinforce their ideological beliefs. Haidt pointed to Daniel Patrick Moynihan who was labeled a racist for a 1965 report he produced as assistant secretary of Labor in the Kennedy administration. The report rang alarm bells about the rise of unmarried parenthood among African Americans, and called for government policies to address the issue. "Open-minded inquiry into the problems of the Black family was shut down for decades, precisely the decades in which it was most urgently needed," Haidt said. "Only in the last few years have sociologists begun to acknowledge that Moynihan was right all along. Sacralizing distorts thinking. Sacred values bind teams together, and then blind them to the truth. That's fine if you are a religious community...but this is not fine for scientists...."[44]

Haidt believes that the fact that conservatives are underrepresented by "a ratio of two or three hundred to one" in social psychology "is evidence that we are a tribal moral community that actively discourages conservatives from entering." Allowing for more diversity of ideological thought would lead to "better science and freer thinking," concluded Haidt. This argument doesn't just apply to academia. It applies to any facet of society where non-liberal views are deemed out of bounds.

When people are afraid to express their opinions because they've seen other people treated as deviants deserving of public shaming or worse, they will be less likely to speak freely. This already happens in newsrooms and academia, where people hide their religious or political views in water cooler conversation for fear of discrimination, or ultimately just opt out of the hostile work environments altogether. "We are hurting ourselves when we deprive ourselves of critics, of people who are as committed to science as we are, but who ask different questions, and make different background assumptions," Haidt noted.

In preparing for his speech, Haidt searched for conservative social psychologists to interview, and was only able to find two, both of them graduate students, who came close to fitting the bill. "Both of them said they are not conservative, but neither are they liberal, and because they are not liberal, they feel pressure to keep quiet," Haidt reported, noting that one of the not-liberal social scientists was in the room as a participant in the conference. Haidt shared an e-mail from one of the heretics: "Given what I've read of the literature, I am certain any research I conducted in political psychology would provide contrary findings and, thereby, go unpublished. Although I think I could make a substantial contribution to the knowledge base, and would be excited to do so, I will not." These stories are commonplace, as is the desire for the academics to remain unnamed. Conservative and orthodox Christian professors have told me chilling stories of intimidation, harassment, discrimination, denial of tenure, and more, but they are not included in this book because all were too fearful to go on the record lest it further alienate them from the members of the illiberal left who hold their academic and professional futures in their hands.

This is not the kind of world we want. Educated people, noted Pinker in extolling the virtues of free speech, "should be acutely aware of human fallibility, most notably their own, and appreciate that people who disagree with them are not necessarily stupid or evil. Accordingly, they should appreciate the value of trying to change minds by persuasion rather than intimidation or demagoguery."[45]

But as this book will demonstrate, the left's commitment to free speech is collapsing. In its place, the illiberal left is executing a campaign of coercion and intimidation. I call it "The Silencing."

TWO

DELEGITIMIZING DISSENT

He that filches from me my good name
Robs me of that which not enriches him
And makes me poor indeed.

—IAGO, SHAKESPEARE'S *OTHELLO*

I n the illiberal attack on free speech, victory is silence. Any person who dissents from the illiberal left's settled dogma is viewed as an enemy to be delegitimized, demonized, and dismissed. Once political and ideological opponents are viewed through the lens of a "take no prisoners" mentality then no type of character assassination is off limits.

Former CNN host and NBC *Weekend Today* co-anchor Campbell Brown experienced this firsthand. An accomplished journalist for two decades, Brown won widespread acclaim and an Emmy as part of a team covering Hurricane Katrina. After leaving journalism, she became an education reform advocate, founding the nonprofit Partnership for Educational Justice in 2014 to challenge teacher tenure rules that protect underperforming educators.[1]

Teachers unions and their illiberal left allies quickly deemed Brown public enemy number one. Rather than debating Brown and challenging her arguments, the illiberal left began a delegitimization campaign. Brown was no longer an accomplished woman, nor was her desire to improve the education system sincere. No, she was a nefarious right-wing bimbo under the control of conservative men lurking in the background. It started in 2012, when Brown wrote an article in the *Wall Street Journal* criticizing teachers unions for protecting teachers guilty of sexual misconduct from getting fired.[2] In a Twitter exchange, Brown asked president of the American Federation of Teachers Randi Weingarten about the issue. Weingarten responded and ultimately accused Brown of having a secret agenda. "Campbell did not want to be balanced. She's married to Romney advisor Dan Senor," Weingarten tweeted.[3] In other words, Brown was a mindless parrot who adopted her Republican husband's political views. As Campbell responded, "Wow, no sexism here. Sad."

The teachers union–affiliated Alliance for Quality Education set up a website (RealCampbellBrown.com) depicting Brown as a stringed puppet holding a GOP sign and wearing a "1%" button. The tagline below her image read, "Right wing. Elitist. Wrong about Public Schools." The website also claimed she was a registered Republican.

Brown told me she has donated to five political campaigns, all Democrat. She explained that she was a political independent throughout her journalistic career. To vote in the New York City primary, she registered as a Democrat, then later as a Republican to vote in a different primary. In their attempt to portray Brown's organization as a front for the Republican Party, the illiberal left ignored not only her publicly accessible donations to Democratic campaigns, but also that Brown had recruited notable Democrats, including former Obama White House Press Secretary Robert Gibbs and former Obama campaign spokesperson Ben LaBolt, to work for her organization.[4] Then there was the inconvenient fact that the organization's chairman was David Boies, who represented Al Gore in *Bush v. Gore*.[5]

Diane Ravitch, an education historian and professor at New York University, invoked a favorite delegitimization tactic by chauvinistically dismissing Brown for her beauty and portrayed her as an empty-headed interloper into the education debate. "[Brown] is a good media figure because of her looks, but she doesn't seem to know or understand anything about teaching and why tenure matters," Ravitch told the *Washington Post*. "I know it sounds sexist to say that she is pretty, but that makes her telegenic, even if what she has to say is total nonsense."[6] Never mind that Boies, Gibbs, and LaBolt all believed that same "nonsense."

The voices portraying a professional woman as a bimbo and appendage of her husband belong to liberals who are supposed to be advocates for human dignity, respecters of women, and protectors of free speech. They chose to drag an accomplished journalist and earnest advocate through the mud. Infuriated by her audacity to question policy darlings like teacher tenure, they used sexist and dishonest labels to try to shut her up.

Opponents of Brown's new endeavor saw her as the "new Michelle Rhee," the former Washington, D.C., schools chancellor whose dedication to reforming failing schools led her to support vouchers and other reform efforts opposed by teachers unions. "As a lifelong Democrat I was adamantly against vouchers," Rhee explained in a Daily Beast piece called "My Break with the Democrats." When the *Washington Post* asked about her position on renewing a D.C. voucher program, she knew that "as a good Democrat," she was supposed to say "no." Instead, she decided to talk directly to parents in an effort to make a fully informed decision. "After my listening tour of families, and hearing so many parents plead for an immediate solution to their desire for a quality education, I came out in favor of the voucher program," she said. "People went nuts. Democrats chastised me for going against the party, but the most vocal detractors were my biggest supporters."[7] It's normal for political parties to close ranks when one of their members deviates from a key policy position. This doesn't make it right, but it's not unique to liberals or Democrats. What sets the illiberal left apart are their campaigns to delegitimize people who deviate on even one issue by openly engaging in racist and sexist attacks, all the while presenting themselves as the protectors and representatives of all women and non-white people.

The delegitimization campaign against Rhee seemed to be the blueprint of what would later happen to Brown. Richard Whitmire, the author of a book about Rhee's reform efforts in the nation's capital, characterized reactions to Rhee as "virulent" and "extreme," with a marked tendency to personal attacks such as "Rhee's a terrible mother!"[8] Whitmire noted in his *Education Week* piece "What Is Behind the Discrediting of Michelle Rhee?" that her "critics come from left-wing, not right-wing, politics." He also explained "this core group of critics—well represented in any online discussion of Rhee and usually writing under disguised identities—seems to have limited interest in debating the school reform decisions Rhee made. Rather, their goal is 'proving' Rhee is a flat-out fraud."[9] In other words, the illiberal left chooses to make dehumanizing attacks on Rhee, such as blasting her as an "Asian bitch," as Florida teacher Ceresta Smith did at a 2013 "Occupy DOE 2.0" protest.[10] This is easier than engaging in a rigorous debate about the best way forward for education.

Another Rhee critic insinuated the avowed Democrat was a conservative and called her an "education Ann Coulter."[11] In an article for Salon. com nearly two years later, the same man called Brown a "Rhee-placement" in a piece called "Education 'reform's' new Ann Coulter: A reeling Michelle Rhee passes the lead to Campbell Brown."[12] Like Brown, Rhee had her own union-funded attack site—RheeFirst.com.[13]

The sexist and racist character assassinations of Campbell Brown and Michelle Rhee demonstrate the great lengths the illiberal left will go to label and demonize opponents and avoid contending against alternative ideas in the public square. It doesn't matter if the label has any connection to reality. It only matters that it sticks. Since they can't win the argument on the merits, the illiberal left instead attacks the people who make the arguments, trying to cast doubt on their abilities, their intentions, even their value as a person.

TACTIC #1: DEHUMANIZING

In *Less than Human: Why We Demean, Enslave, and Exterminate Others*, social philosopher and psychologist David Livingstone Smith explores the enduring practice of dehumanizing individuals we don't like or with whom we disagree. He shows how ancient cultures and modern societies operate similarly in that groups that seek to maintain or expand their power base will often systematically question and attack the very core of their enemies' human identities.

New York University law professor Jeremy Waldron has even highlighted the harm of dehumanization as a justification to ban certain kinds of speech. In an article for the *New York Times*, Waldron argued that hate speech harms the dignity of those at whom it is directed. He defines dignity as "a person's basic social status, his or her being treated as an ordinary member of society in good standing, his or her being included in the ordinary business of society. A person's dignity is damaged, then, when he or she is publicly defamed or dehumanized, or when he or she is perceived as belonging to a group, all of whose members are defamed or dehumanized."[14]

Waldron is right about the harm of dehumanizing, but wrong about the solution. Laws that limit what a person can say, even when what they say is depraved, are illiberal and authoritarian. But if someone like Waldron, a liberal, believes that dehumanizing attacks are terrible enough to justify creating a legal cause of action for the targets of such language, then perhaps people who call themselves liberal should stop using dehumanizing smears to delegitimize their opponents.

If Waldron's theory was put into practice, we'd be slapping the cuffs on a who's who of the illiberal elite. When they aren't besmirching dissenters from their worldview as racist, sexist, and misogynist, the illiberal left are hurling racist, sexist, and misogynist attacks against those they wish to delegitimize in the public square. It's a sad irony that those who claim to stand against racism or sexism turn into unrepentant bigots if it will help delegitimize their ideological or political opponents. In the illiberal silencing campaign, liberal principles are perpetual casualties.

These attacks are fueled by the determinist assumption that certain groups of people, because of their race or sex, must support liberal policies and vote for Democrats. If the heretics deviate from the paternalistic pre-ordained script, they are treated as self-loathing sub-humans. The illiberal left denies women and non-white members of society the right to choose which political party or ideological positions they may support. That's only for white men (who, if they're not Democrats, are presumed to be racist and sexist anyway). The rest of America is expected to line up behind liberals and the Democratic Party and if they don't, the delegitimization commences.

Supreme Court justice Clarence Thomas is often called an "Uncle Tom" who acts only to please white people. The illiberal left claim his conservative views derive from self-loathing or hate. As Democratic Congressman Bennie Thompson of Mississippi said, "it's almost to the point saying this man doesn't like black people, he doesn't like being black."[15] African American Republican Ron Christie, who worked for both President George W. Bush and Vice President Dick Cheney, was told by African American California Democrat Congresswoman Maxine Waters that he was a "sellout to [his] race" and that black Republicans are "Uncle Toms." Christie noted in an article that this kind of treatment, "is all too familiar to black conservatives who dare to express views that are out of the liberal mainstream."[16]

The epithet "Uncle Tom" is derived from Harriet Beecher Stowe's abolitionist novel *Uncle Tom's Cabin*. The insult suggests black submissiveness to a white agenda. "Short of dropping the n-bomb on someone, there are few things more insulting to many African Americans than being called an 'Uncle Tom,'" wrote journalist Dexter Mullins at the African American news website theGrio.com.[17] Though there are variations on the theme. Condoleeza Rice was called an "Aunt Jemima" while working for the Bush administration.[18]

Raffi Williams, a young black conservative who works as the deputy press secretary for the Republican National Committee, told me he regularly gets Facebook comments or tweets from supposed liberals calling him an "Uncle Tom," "house n-word,"[19] race traitor, and sellout.[20] Audience members at a 2002 gubernatorial debate threw Oreos at then-Lieutenant Governor Michael Steele, he told me. This sent a message that he was "black on the outside and white inside," reported the *Baltimore Sun*.[21] He has also been called a "token negro" and "a white man with black skin" whose appointment as the head of the Republican National Committee "was propaganda to convince America the Republican party wasn't run by racists since they'd appointed a Negro to their top position."[22] Former Fox Sports columnist Jason Whitlock compared Thomas Sowell to a reviled "house negro" character in the Quentin Tarantino film *Django Unchained*.[23]

The website "ThyBlackMan"—which describes itself as a place to remind black men "of our brotherhood and value as men in this society"— wrote without irony of conservative black man and commentator Larry Elder, "His coaches at the Republican Party always send in their white men in black skin whenever they need to check Obama for scoring too many points. And since they promote from within Elder probably will be coaching his own team of self haters pretty soon."[24] They've also made sport of dehumanizing and demonizing the African American commentator Deneen Borelli. In the same piece, Borelli was accused of hating "herself so much she gets her pictures photo shopped in order to look more European friendly," and was ranked #9 on a list of "SAMBOs"—a SAMBO was described as a "white person trapped inside a black body."[25] Rather than accepting that Borelli might legitimately be conservative, she was accused of "demonizing her own people" to enrich herself financially.[26]

The illiberal left loves to call Republicans racist for not having enough black and brown people representing them, but as soon as one is elected, the delegitimizing commences. They aren't "real black or brown people" or they are self-hating sellouts and traitors. In 2015, Arsalan Iftikhar, a liberal human rights lawyer and media commentator, told MSNBC's Alex Wagner that Louisiana Governor Bobby Jindal was "trying…to scrub some of the brown off his skin as he runs to the right in a Republican presidential exploratory bid."[27] This is a double whammy: Jindal is portrayed as self-loathing and GOP voters as racists who will only like him if he isn't brown. When Haitian-American Mia Love made history in 2014 as the first black female Republican to be elected to the U.S. House of Representatives, the Huffington Post ran a story headlined, "She Looks Black, but Her Politics Are Red." Her values were not her own, but were instead "grounded in a white, male, Christian context." Love is apparently just a mindless puppet to her white male overlords. The writer—an assistant professor at Wichita State University—alleged that Love was "allowed to pass through [the halls of power] in her black, female body with the understanding that she must not see, speak or openly advocate for anything related to race or gender—an unholy compromise."[28] This echoed a post at the liberal website *Gawker*, in which Hamilton Nolan wrote "the only reason Mia Love has been so lovingly shepherded to the national podium to deliver this message is because of her own race...."[29] There isn't a shred of evidence to support this contention, but if there was, one would think that Nolan would be cheering. Don't liberals support affirmative action?

Love was further portrayed in the Huffington Post article as "window dressing" and a useful idiot playing into the "pattern of using blacks to further white interests" comparing her position as a member of the U.S. House of Representatives to slavery. In the end, the Huffington Post writer concluded that Love's "accomplishment is quite dangerous for people of color."[30] This kind of treatment unfortunately wasn't new for Love. Following her August 2012 appearance at the Republican National Convention, Love's Wikipedia page was vandalized with vile racist and sexist slurs. The page was altered to refer to Love as a "house n--ger" and a "dirty, worthless whore who sold out her soul in the name of big business."[31] The vandals also called her a "total sell-out to the Right Wing Hate Machine and the greedy bigots who control the GOP."[32] But who are the haters and bigots here?

Love's treatment was not unlike what met Republican Tim Scott, who was elected in 2014 to be one of three African American members of the U.S. Senate. In a January 2014 speech at Zion Baptist Church in Columbia, South Carolina, North Carolina's NAACP chapter president, the Reverend

William Barber, referred to Scott as a Republican pawn. "A ventriloquist can always find a good dummy," he told the gathering of three hundred.[33] Barber refused to apologize.[34] House Assistant Democratic Leader Congressman James Clyburn told the *Washington Post* upon Scott's historic election, "If you call progress electing a person with the pigmentation that he has, who votes against the interest and aspirations of 95 percent of the black people in South Carolina, then I guess that's progress."[35] University of Pennsylvania Professor Adolph Reed wrote in a *New York Times* op-ed shortly after Scott's appointment to the Senate that Scott was one of the GOP's "cynical tokens."[36]

Conservative columnist Michelle Malkin, a Filipino-American, is a frequent target of racist attacks from so-called liberals. After Malkin called actor Alec Baldwin a "Hollyweirdo" on Twitter in 2011 he responded by mobilizing his presumably liberal followers to "go all Town Hall on" Malkin because she was a "crypto fascist hater." The responses to Malkin were unfortunately predictable. One said, "Don't you realize the white wingers you look up to. Only [sic] see you as someone who should be doing manicures for their wife." She was called an "Aunty Tom" and a "sellout Asian bitch." Another of Baldwin's followers wrote, "This stir-fry noodle believes she matters. You'll always be the chink inferior to the Aryan conservatives."[37]

The same tactic is applied to Hispanic conservatives who oppose liberal policies. When conservative Gabriel Gomez was running for a U.S. Senate seat in Massachusetts in 2013, a columnist labeled him a "LINO," which stands for "Latino in name only."[38] When New Mexican gubernatorial candidate and Democrat Gary King wanted to attack his opponent, Republican Governor Susana Martinez, he didn't open a dialogue on why she opposes drivers' licenses for undocumented workers or vetoed an increase to the minimum wage. No, he commented that Martinez "does not have a Latino heart."[39] They seem to agree with Democratic Senator Harry Reid of Nevada, who in 2010, while he was Senate majority leader, said, "I don't know how anyone of Hispanic heritage could be a Republican."[40]

Racist delegitimization isn't just for conservatives. Fox News political analyst Juan Williams—a lifelong Democrat—has experienced "rank intimidation" from "the ideological and rigid Left," he told me in an interview. He is asked, "'Why are you working [at Fox]? You can't be a good black person and work at Fox.'" While he's received racist e-mails during the 2008 and 2012 campaigns from both sides of the ideological spectrum, he says that with the left, "the idea is you have to choose a side and choose your army." To do otherwise is to invite the worst kind of delegitimizing, or "muzzling" as Williams labeled the phenomena in his 2012 book, *Muzzled: The Assault on Honest Debate*.[41] If he offers a sincere critique of Obama or Democrats, Williams told me, "The response from the Left is, 'You're a sellout. You're attacking our president because Fox gives you a paycheck.' Or that I'm performing sex acts on white men at Fox in order to get my check." Illiberal left silencing of Williams cost him his job at National Public Radio where he had been a correspondent for a decade. NPR fired him ostensibly for what they deemed racist comments about Muslims. But according to Williams, the firing came after consistent pressure on the network from at least one senior Obama White House staffer unhappy that an African American liberal was appearing on Fox.

Women who don't stick to the illiberal left's scripts are subject to the same kind of delegitimization. Conservative women in particular are deemed fair game for misogynistic attacks that would normally have the illiberal left screaming "War on Women." Republican women are dehumanized as fake women, "female impersonators,"[42] or "uninflected by the experience of the female body" (whatever that means).[43] Alternatively, they are treated as sex objects with no brains or will of their own. When Senator Joni Ernst—a GOP rising star—delivered the State of the Union response in 2015, MSNBC host Ronan Farrow compared the U.S. senator to a flight attendant.[44] This echoed comments made by then-Senator Tom Harkin during Ernst's campaign for the Senate that described her as just a pretty face, comparable to the then twenty-four-year-old singer and actress Taylor Swift.[45]

Liberal MSNBC host Ed Schultz once said on his radio show that Sarah Palin set off his "bimbo alert"[46] and called conservative radio host and bestselling author Laura Ingraham a "right-wing slut."[47] He even called me a "bimbo" for accurately quoting him in a column. It's so much easier to insult a woman than to actually engage on the issue she raises. While still sitting atop the MSNBC heap, television host Keith Olbermann wished conservative S. E. Cupp had been aborted by her parents[48] and called conservative pundit Michelle Malkin a "mashed-up bag of meat with lipstick."[49] Bill Maher dismissed Minnesota Congresswoman Michele Bachmann as a "bimbo" and called Sarah Palin the c-word and a "dumb twat."[50] What is it that makes liberal men think they can get away with treating dissenting women in the most callous possible way? It's as if being "pro-choice" on abortion gives them carte blanche to mistreat, mischaracterize, and verbally abuse any woman with views contrary to their own. Liberals should know better, shouldn't they? "Even mild sexism—a focus on hair and makeup—is a very lethal tool," noted Siobhan Bennett, Women's Campaign Fund president, to the magazine *Mother Jones*. "It can make a woman [running for office] drop 10 points [in the polls]."[51]

I didn't support the campaigns of Bachmann or Palin, but sexist dehumanizing should be off limits regardless of how much one might disagree with the politics of a female candidate or politician. These words are used specifically to attack their identity as women, and when they are used, they degrade all women. When Rush Limbaugh called law student and contraceptive mandate activist Sandra Fluke a "slut," I was very critical of him, but found it odd that some of the same people who were lobbying for him to lose his radio show for this one comment not only never called for Maher to lose his show, but were frequent guests.[52] Gloria Steinem, Jane Fonda, and Robin Morgan found Limbaugh's remarks too much to bear, writing at CNN that the FCC should deny his show a license in order to serve the public interest.[53] Prior to Limbaugh's comments, Steinem had happily appeared as Maher's guest with nary a word about his well-chronicled misogynistic outbursts.[54] It was left to Ann Coulter to confront Maher, telling him flat out on his show that he was a misogynist. I too have criticized Maher for his misogyny, but have never suggested he lose his show. It's the illiberal left that wants to run their ideological enemies out of business under the false pretense of being the protectors of women—and then turns around and attacks their female opponents in the most demeaning, sexist ways.

Illiberal feminists are perhaps the most ferocious warriors among the illiberal left. They deny conservative men the right to speak on any issue that affects women, and they are utterly intolerant of any dissenting women, even disallowing them their right to state their own opinions in their own words as when MSNBC host Andrea Mitchell told Republican strategist Juleanna Glover to refer to herself not as "pro-life" but "anti-abortion."[55]

Liberal writer Nina Burleigh profiled conservative women as "baby Palins" in a 2011 *Elle* magazine article. In addition to infantilizing conservative women, Burleigh portrayed her subjects as ungrateful traitors to their sex. "The young women I interviewed for this article share almost every goal of feminism. They want to be—and in many cases, already believe themselves to be—'empowered': educationally, financially, sexually," Burleigh wrote. "But they resist any effort to put advancing their fellow women front and center. That means opposing everything from gender-based affirmative action, such as government-mandated quotas for female athletes under Title IX, to equal-pay-for-equal-work laws."[56] Somehow it escapes the illiberal left that it is possible to sincerely believe that conservative policies are best for all people, including women. Is it really so hard to understand that people can have differing yet reasonable opinions on these issues?

TACTIC #2: DEMONIZING

Demonizing is another favored tactic utilized by the illiberal left to delegitimize opponents. They simultaneously make racist and misogynist attacks against opponents *and* accuse opponents of being racists, bigots, misogynists, rape apologists, traitors, and homophobes. As we saw with Campbell Brown and Michelle Rhee, for any Democrat, liberal, or ideological agnostic who questions the sanctioned illiberal line, there's another tactic: accusing dissenters of being closet conservatives.

The purpose of demonizing opponents is to make them radioactive to the broader culture. The illiberal left uses character assassination to ensure their opponents won't be treated as sincere or thoughtful contributors to the national conversation. The illiberal left doesn't desire debate, it wants a monologue on one side and silence on the other.

ALL DISSENT IS RACIST

The illiberal left's inability to treat differing viewpoints as valid leads them to demonize disagreement as racism. In September 2009, during a speech at Emory University, former President Jimmy Carter said that racist attitudes were driving criticism of President Obama. It wasn't the first time he'd made such comments. The day before, Carter told NBC's *Nightly News*, "I think an overwhelming portion of the intensely demonstrated animosity toward President Barack Obama is based on the fact that he is a black man, that he's African-American."[57] Actor and liberal activist Robert Redford echoed Carter's sentiments, saying that GOP congressional members want to "paralyze the system. I think what sits underneath it, unfortunately, is there's probably some racism involved, which is really awful."[58] This line of argument depends on the fallacy that President Obama has endured uniquely hostile treatment while in the White House. In this alternate universe, no president has ever been harshly criticized by members of the opposing party or had their signature efforts opposed by Congress. We are asked to forget that Bill Clinton had his attempt at healthcare reform demonized and destroyed by strident Republican opposition. Or that he was accused of having approved the killing of one of his best friends, Vince Foster, whose death was ruled a suicide. Indiana Republican

Congressman Dan Burton, who ran the House inquiry into Foster's death, said in 1998 of Clinton, "If I could prove 10 percent of what I believe happened [regarding the death of Vincent Foster], he'd be gone. This guy's a scumbag. That's why I'm after him."[59] An e-mail that circulated widely starting in 1998 accused Bill Clinton of being responsible for more than fifty suspicious deaths. It became such an urban legend that the website Snopes.com had to investigate and rule it "false." There is also the fact that Clinton was one of only two presidents in American history to be impeached.

Still, the notion that racism is the only possible reason Republicans would oppose President Obama has become such conventional wisdom that baseball legend Hank Aaron compared Republican opposition to President Obama to the KKK, telling an interviewer, "When you look at a black president, President Obama is left with his foot stuck in the mud from all of the Republicans with the way he's treated. We have moved in the right direction, and there have been improvements, but we still have a long ways to go in the country. The bigger difference is that back then they had hoods. Now they have neckties and starched shirts."[60] By late 2013, MSNBC host Chris Matthews had labeled Obama's critics racists at least twenty times on the air.[61] In 2014, U.S. Senator Mary Landrieu of Louisiana said that Obama's unpopularity in the state was due to the fact that "the South has not always been the friendliest place for African-Americans."[62]

Isn't it possible that conservatives oppose Obama because they oppose his *policies*? And isn't it also true that the South is one of the more conservative parts of the country? It would have been more accurate for Landrieu to say that the South has not lately been the friendliest place for *Democrats*.[63] When she made her claim, Landrieu was the only Democrat representing the Deep South in the Senate,[64] And there was only one white Southern Democrat serving in the House: Georgia Congressman John Barrow, a pro-gun, fiscally conservative Democrat, running for his sixth term. Both Landrieu and Barrow ended up losing their elections in 2014, while the voters of South Carolina elected Republican African American Tim Scott to the U.S. Senate.[65]

Almost needless to say, those who opposed the Affordable Care Act (also known as Obamacare) were labeled racists. Louisiana Democratic Party Chair and State Senator Karen Carter Peterson stood on the floor of the state senate and announced that opposition to the Affordable Care Act stemmed from "the race of this African-American president.... It comes down to the race of the president of the U.S., which causes people to disconnect and step away from the substance of the bill."[66] In 2014, Congressman Bennie Thompson of Mississippi walked the same road by claiming that his state's governor opposed Obamacare "just because a black man created it."[67] In May 2014, West Virginia Democratic Senator Jay Rockefeller accused the GOP of opposing Obamacare because the president is "the wrong color" in a Commerce Committee meeting.[68] Earlier that same month, he said some lawmakers "don't want anything good to happen under this president, because he's the wrong color," in a Senate Finance Committee hearing on transportation funding.[69] Robert Scheer, contributing editor to the *Nation* and editor of Truthdig.com, attributed Republican governors' rejection of Obamacare to a racist strategy "to deny healthcare" to "a working poor population that skews disproportionately black in the South."[70] Scheer neglected to account for the motivations of the few Democratic governors who refused to set up state healthcare exchanges to participate in Obamacare.[71]

I supported Obamacare, but to think that Republicans and conservatives oppose it because the president is black is absurd. Just as with Bill Clinton's healthcare reform plan, conservatives and liberals have different ideas about the role of government. While there are obviously people who oppose President Obama and his policies because they are racist, demonizing opponents of his agenda as such is a dishonest and divisive attempt to delegitimize dissent from the left's worldview.

But to the illiberal left it's not just critics of the president who are "racist." While campaigning for Obama's reelection in 2013, DNC Chair

Debbie Wasserman Schultz cast Mitt Romney's positions on welfare reform and work requirements as racist, describing them as "a dog whistle for voters who consider race when casting their ballot."[72] MSNBC host Al Sharpton stated that critics of Attorney General Eric Holder were racists. Sharpton said that Republican Congressman Darrell Issa was applying the police tactic "stop and frisk" to Holder who "has been mishandled just like the young Black and Latino men (and women) who are demonized on our streets every day."[73]

While many may believe that Eric Holder was treated disrespectfully by Darrell Issa—count me among them—he wouldn't be the first member of a presidential administration to suffer that fate before a congressional committee. And unless Sharpton can point to actual racist comments, we can assume that Holder's treatment was driven far more by ideological and partisan differences than any racial prejudice (remember Republican animosity to President Bill Clinton's attorney general Janet Reno?). As with all these issues, members of the illiberal left prefer to smear people as racists rather than debating them on the merits.

Many people thought that with the election of the first African American president, racial animus would decline in America. The opposite seems to have occurred. The illiberal left has exploited this issue in an effort to gain political and ideological advantages and finds racism against the president lurking behind every bush. When Republican Congressman Paul Ryan of Wisconsin said in an interview with conservative radio host Bill Bennett that inner cities suffered from a "tailspin of culture...of men not working and just generations of men not even thinking about working or learning the value and the culture of work; and so there's a real culture problem here that has to be dealt with,"[74] Congresswoman Barbara Lee called it a "thinly veiled racial attack." *New York Times* columnist Paul Krugman accused Ryan of using a racist "dog whistle" and explained that the only reason Republicans opposed expanding Medicaid was because they were racist. He knew this because, as he asked rhetorically, "What do many Medicaid recipients look like—and I'm talking about the color of their skin, not the content of their character."[75] Ryan had been responding to a question about fatherhood—being a dad and having one. Krugman likes to cry "racist" in the most subtle ways. In a 2009 op-ed, he claimed that people who opposed Obama's proposals were "probably reacting less to what Mr. Obama is doing, or even to what they've heard about what he's doing, than to who he is," referencing cultural and "racial anxiety" in the next line.[76]

The illiberal left simply didn't know what to do with the Tea Party when it burst onto the scene, so they went with what usually works: they smeared them as a bunch of angry, uneducated racists.

Chris Matthews wondered aloud on his show *Hardball* of Tea Party members, "Do they still count blacks as 3/5ths?"[77] Iconic New York Congressman Charlie Rangel said that the Tea Party is made up of "mean, racist people" from former "slave-holding" states.[78] Keith Olbermann declared that, "If racism is not the whole of the Tea Party, it is in its heart."[79] Left-wing darling Representative Alan Grayson (D-FL) compared the Tea Party to the Ku Klux Klan. When Tea Party and Republican leaders complained, Grayson didn't back down, saying, "If the hood fits, wear it."[80] In the *Washington Post*, columnist Colbert King wrote, "But don't go looking for a group by the name of New Confederacy. They earned that handle from me because of their visceral animosity toward the federal government and their aversion to compassion for those unlike themselves. They respond, however, to the label 'tea party.' By thought, word and deed, they must be making Jefferson Davis proud today."[81] And so it went.

At one point, President Obama said in an interview that race was probably a "key component" in opposition to his presidency among the Tea Party.[82] It had been well chronicled that the Tea Party was born of frustration with Washington—both Republicans and Democrats—and was primarily fueled by economic worries. Yet Obama could only conceive of opposition that was driven by racism. *New York Times* reporter Kate Zernike reported on the Tea Party movement in a 2010 book, *Boiling Mad*. "What brought most people out for the tea party was real concern about the economy, about the [national] debt," Zernike told the *Christian Science Monitor*. "I think people need to understand the need to have a conversation around that issue. Also, these are people who feel like they have history and economic arguments on their side. So you need to understand what they are saying. [Those who want to argue with them] will need to [come prepared] to argue on the facts and the ideas."[83] Or you could just call them racist.

Instead of talking about hidden racist signals, or dog whistles, or smearing opponents, how about engaging them and arguing over the substance of welfare reform to figure out what works and what doesn't?

DISSENT IS MISOGYNIST

What used to be mere policy disagreements between Republicans and Democrats on abortion, equal pay, the minimum wage, and government funding of contraception are now described as being part of a "War on Women." According to the illiberal left, nobody opposes abortion out of a concern for the unborn. As the National Organization for Women and NARAL Pro Choice regularly tell us, "pro-life" Republicans are "right-wing extremists" and "anti-women." And if the "pro-life" Republicans are men, obviously their convictions stem from their desire to control women or a deep-seated misogyny. But think about that for a minute. If you think an unborn child has a right to life, that's hardly an "extreme" position or a misogynistic one. That's a difference of opinion on a very serious subject that deserves respect.

But that's rarely how it's treated by the illiberal left. House minority leader Nancy Pelosi intoned about the "War on Women" at a 2011 feminist event alleging that, "abortion is one issue [in the war] but contraception and family planning and birth control are opposed by [Republicans] too."[84] Never mind that opposing family planning or trying to keep women from buying birth control is not an agenda item for the GOP. The American Civil Liberties Union (ACLU) has an entire webpage devoted to the "War on Women," defined as "the legislative and rhetorical attacks on women and women's rights taking place across the nation." It's more than a little odd that an organization founded to protect free speech would characterize people expressing disagreement about abortion as "rhetorical attacks on women," that deserve to be demonized under the "War on Women" banner.

But the "War on Women" isn't just about abortion. It's a catchall tactic to portray everything conservatives do as akin to misogyny. Feminist writer Amanda Marcotte wrote in the *American Prospect* that watching the hit television show *Mad Men* felt "familiar" because Republicans are still trying to promote the sexist values of the 1960s.[85] Salon.com editor Joan Walsh warned in 2013 of the "GOP's economic war on women"[86] pointing to GOP positions on food stamps, the minimum wage, and mandatory paid sick leave and family leave. Democratic National Committee Chair Debbie Wasserman Schultz borrowed the terminology of domestic abuse to attack Republican Governor Scott Walker of Wisconsin. "Republican Tea Party extremists like Scott Walker … are grabbing us by the hair and pulling us back," she said. Wasserman Schultz also claimed "Walker has given women the back of his hand. I know that is stark…. But that is reality."[87] Disagreeing with Democrats is drastically different from hitting a woman or dragging one by her ponytail, even metaphorically. In the illiberal left paradigm, disagreement is violence. In this upside down world, a conservative Republican who is married and has five daughters, like former Virginia attorney general and gubernatorial candidate Ken Cuccinelli, can be dismissed by the likes of Al Sharpton as an "anti-woman crusader"[88] and by a writer at the *Daily Kos* as "notoriously anti-woman."[89] Really? The 54 percent of white women[90] who voted for Cuccinelli in his 2013 race against Terry McAuliffe for Virginia governor apparently didn't get that memo.

Though, as Cuccinelli's female voters weren't liberal, they too would be written off as "anti-woman." There's a special contempt reserved for conservative women for their alleged self-hating opposition to "women's rights." Ann Romney learned this when she wrote a *USA Today* op-ed for Mother's Day. *Newsweek*/Daily Beast columnist Michelle Goldberg told an MSNBC panel that Romney's cheerleading for motherhood (on Mother's Day no less) was "insufferable" and reminded her of Hitler and Stalin and authoritarian societies that gave awards to women who had big families. Goldberg later expanded on her views, saying "bombastic odes to traditional maternity have a sinister ring, especially when they come from people who want to curtail women's rights."[91]

The routine criticism of those serving in positions of influence is also frequently demonized as sexism when directed at a liberal woman. After Fox News host Bill O'Reilly said State Department spokesperson Jen Psaki "looks way out of her depth" and "doesn't look like she has the gravitas for the job," he was immediately labeled a sexist. Marie Harf, Psaki's deputy, fired back from the State Department podium, saying O'Reilly used "sexist, personally offensive language that I actually don't think [he] would ever use about a man."[92] Clearly, Harf doesn't watch O'Reilly's show because anyone who has seen it knows he is an equal opportunity critic. For example, Bill once called *Washington Post* columnist Dana Milbank "beneath contempt" and lamented that the paper "would employ a guy like that." My guess is that Harf knows this and is just invoking sexism to divert attention from the fact that O'Reilly's criticism hit a little too close to home.

Taking issue with the credibility of favored illiberal left "facts" all but guarantees one will end up on the receiving end of an illiberal smear campaign. Various professors and journalists—liberal, conservative, and in between—have been called "rape apologists" for bringing attention to questionable campus rape statistics and complaining about the lack of due process for men accused of rape on campus. In addition to having his job threatened, *Washington Post* columnist George Will was called a "rape apologist" for questioning whether college campus rapes are being handled in a way that is creating a culture that fuels false reporting.[93] Pointing out difficult truths can also invite the "rape apology" smear. Liberal *Slate* columnist Emily Yoffe ignited a firestorm with a piece advising college women not to drink to the point of incapacitation as a way to protect themselves from sexual assault.[94] "The post was predicated on the true-but-fraught fact that some rape takes place in drunkenness that wouldn't have taken place in sobriety, in that more than 80 percent of sexual assaults on campuses involve alcohol," reported the *Atlantic*'s James Hamblin. "Yoffe's writing was described in *Feministing* as 'a rape denialism manifesto' and distilled in the *Daily Mail* to banal victim-blaming: 'Don't drink if you don't want to get raped.'"[95]

Yale criminal law school professor Jed Rubenfeld wrote a *New York Times* op-ed questioning the ability of university administrators to adjudicate rape. He also noted the obvious fact that false rape accusations are a serious problem that can destroy people's lives.[96] Gloria Steinem protégé Jessica Valenti attacked Rubenfield as a rape apologist and victim-blamer in the *Guardian*. Blasting Valenti for her unhinged smear campaign, *Reason*'s Robby Soave wrote that Valenti "established that critics of her liberal feminist view are not opponents in a public policy debate—they are the enemies of rape victims. This is totally unjustified demagoguery. She might as well be saying, 'You're with me or you're with the terrorists.'"[97]

If the illiberal left has such an airtight case regarding their claims about campus rape, then they should make them without trying to delegitimize people who make reasonable, thoughtful arguments against their narrative. Instead, they seek to silence anyone who points out flaws in their claims. They know from experience that they can shut down debate with smear campaigns, so they do.

Rather than apologizing, Emily Yoffe responded to her critics. "As I was working on this story, several of my friends counseled me not do [sic] it," she said. "Talking about things women can do to protect themselves from rape is the third rail, they said. But why be a journalist unless you're willing to dig into difficult subjects and report your findings?"[98] Yoffe is one of the few brave journalists willing to face the inevitable illiberal onslaught in her quest to report the truth. But there are far more journalists like those who counseled Yoffe to not go off script. The silencing campaign is effective.

CLOSET CONSERVATIVE

One of the favored silencing tactics is to accuse those who refuse to sing from the illiberal song sheet of being secret conservatives. We saw this with lifelong Democrat Michelle Rhee and the self-identified independent Campbell Brown. This tactic is most often used on journalists who investigate Democratic politicians or express views at odds with liberal orthodoxy. The uber-bully in this regard is Media Matters, a non-profit organization funded by some of the Democratic Party's most influential donors. Its mission has been explained variously as an attempt to root out conservative misinformation in the media and to wage "guerrilla warfare and sabotage"[99] against Fox News. Media Matters works in tandem with other illiberal left media outlets, which treat their propaganda as actual news. One of their favorite tactics is to "out" mainstream journalists as conservatives when they start down the wrong trail of reporting. It's done to delegitimize journalists who file stories that could damage the Democratic Party or the left's collective credibility.

The treatment of Sharyl Attkisson's resignation and book, *Stonewalled: My Fight for Truth Against the Forces of Obstruction, Intimidation, and Harassment in Obama's Washington* is Exhibit A of this tactic. Attkisson is an award-winning journalist who worked as an anchor for CNN from 1990 to 1993 and as an investigative reporter at CBS from 1993 to 2014. She won a prestigious Edward R. Murrow award and five Emmy awards for her investigative work and was one of the first journalists to fly with combat missions over Kosovo. She became a target of the illiberal left due to her investigative efforts into the Obama administration, from the Fast and Furious gun scandal to the controversy over the Benghazi attack that killed an American ambassador to the administration's failed green-energy investments.

Suddenly, a tough reporter who had exposed fraud and corruption on both sides of the aisle was transformed by the illiberal left into a secret conservative who couldn't be trusted.

In a piece headlined "Was Reporter Sharyl Attkisson Too Right-Wing for CBS?" Lloyd Grove quoted a former CBS News colleague making the anonymous accusation, "'She is definitely not being truthful about being non-partisan. She has an agenda and a political bent.'"[100] This is eerily familiar to the claims the teachers unions made about Campbell Brown— all of which turned out to be false. A gigantic fly in the ointment for the illiberal left is Attkisson's history of investigating both Democrats and Republicans. If she had a conservative agenda it's hard to explain her investigative work on Republican fundraising and uncovering fraud around Halliburton's contracts in Iraq. One of Attkisson's Emmys was awarded for an investigative series titled, "Bush Administration's Bait and Switch on TARP and the Bank Bailout." These inconvenient facts are deliberately ignored because they would undermine the campaign to delegitimize Attkisson, who was simply doing the job that other reporters neglected to do in holding the Obama administration accountable for its actions.

Media Matters posted a piece about Attkisson that claimed she might be promoting a political (read: conservative) agenda because Republican Congressman Darrell Issa of California toasted her at a party for her book. Case closed. "She left CBS amid claims from colleagues that her work, which often focused on trumped-up claims of Obama administration misdeeds, had a 'political agenda,'" Media Matters' Matt Gertz wrote, "'leading network executives to doubt the impartiality of her reporting.'" Gertz based his accusations on quotes from anonymous sources cited in a post by another news outlet.[101] The claims were directly at odds with everything Attkisson had said publicly about her departure.

MSNBC's Chris Hayes recorded an interview with Attkisson ostensibly to discuss her book. When the segment aired, he introduced it by portraying his guest—who could not respond to his allegations since she was not there—as a suspicious character. He intoned, "Attkisson departed CBS News amid criticism over her reporting on Benghazi, Fast and Furious and other alleged scandals being pursued by conservatives and Republicans." Who criticized her? What appeared on the screen as Hayes made this claim was a screenshot of the same piece that Media Matters cited. Never mind that all the sources were anonymous. Hayes continued, "While CBS executives reportedly came to doubt the impartiality of her reporting, conservative groups honored Attkisson as a mainstream media ally." Translation: if conservatives applaud your reporting and think you are "mainstream" then you must be a right-wing mole. When liberals think a reporter does good work, that's "mainstream."

The interview had Hayes asking Attkisson, "People are watching you like, 'Are we going to see you as a Fox News contributor or writing for a conservative outlet next'; can you tell me right here that this is not the way this is going?"[102] When journalists work for media networks known to be liberal it proves absolutely nothing. But if you go to Fox News, which Attkisson did not, then in Hayes's book you are not legitimate. (He learned this from the Obama White House.) Hayes later sneered, "You're like the toast of the town over at Fox News."

If Attkisson needed someone to commiserate with, she could always talk with Peter Boyer. During his career, he has worked for many of the most respected names in journalism—including eighteen years as a staff writer for the New Yorker. Boyer's resume also includes such names as PBS, NPR, Vanity Fair, the New York Times, and a stint as senior correspondent for the merged Newsweek and the Daily Beast. He now serves as editor-at-large for Fox News, an unpardonable sin to many liberals.

But long before he landed at Fox News, illiberal left busybodies were busy smearing a great journalist for being too fair-minded. Matt Yglesias at the American Prospect wrote that "Boyer appears to have made something of a career for himself as a conservative interloper at otherwise liberal media outlets."[103] His proof? Boyer's Vanity Fair profile of Rush Limbaugh "drew praise from the conservative Media Research Center as being 'fair.'"[104] His complaint speaks volumes. Yglesias believes that treating conservatives fairly is proof that you are not a real journalist, when the opposite should be true. The notion of a "fair" journalist doesn't belong in the illiberal left lexicon; a journalist is either with them or he or she is a secret conservative, by which they mean traitor to the properly left-wing media. Yglesias also complained about Boyer's numerous investigative segments on the Clinton administration scandals as a PBS *Frontline* correspondent. He took particular issue with the fact that a few of the segments focused on scandals where the accused was exonerated.

So, a reporter doing an investigative piece into accusations makes him a bad journalist and undercover ideologue if the subject is later exonerated. What does that mean then for the armies of journalists who were the judge, jury, and executioner for Scooter Libby who they "knew" leaked Valerie Plame's name? The illiberal left didn't investigate Scooter Libby, they obsessively harassed and accused a person who ended up not being the leaker. Anyone who questioned their attack was smeared as well. When it was revealed that Colin Powell's chief of staff leaked Plame's name, nobody in the media stepped up to take responsibility or apologize. Yglesias has no problem with that, but smears a journalist for doing investigations into the Clinton administration, as if investigating presidential administrations isn't the job of a reporter.

In a post that would have made Joe McCarthy proud, a Media Matters headline blared "Who Is Fox News' Peter Boyer?" Like Yglesias, Media Matters found Boyer very suspicious because there are conservatives who don't hate him. Media Matters breathlessly recounted that Rush Limbaugh once called Peter Boyer a "great, great guy," and Sean Hannity thought that Boyer's *Newsweek* profile of Sarah Palin was "actually somewhat favorable."[105] Media Matters acknowledged that Boyer had an "impressive resume" but insinuated he was hired by Fox News because he wrote a 2011 *New Yorker* profile of Roger Ailes that didn't depict the Fox News CEO as Satan (Media Matters' preferred storyline). Their cherry-picked facts from a nearly forty-year career in journalism were presented as an open-and-shut case against Boyer.[106]

Ron Fournier, editorial director of the *National Journal*, previously worked at the Associated Press for two decades and won the White House Correspondents' Association Merriam Smith Award four times. His credentials suddenly meant nothing when he dared to write pieces about liberals and Democrats that were less than glowing. During the 2008 election when he was AP's Washington bureau chief, Fournier wrote that then-Senator Barack Obama was "bordering on arrogance." He quoted several of the candidate's statements, such as Obama's belief that he would overtake Senator Hillary Clinton's lead in the polls because, as the Illinois senator said, "to know me is to love me."[107]

"You'd think that writing a content-free hit piece like that would mean that the writer is a friend of the Clinton campaign. Not so much," read a post at the progressive news site Firedoglake. "This guy has an agenda in play, and he is not on our side. He wasn't on our side when he took a bat to Edwards' kneecaps, he wasn't on our side when he went after Hillary, and it's not on our behalf that he's concerned about Obama's character."[108] Why would a journalist at the Associated Press be presumed to be on the "liberal side"? Probably because most journalists are liberals and many aren't great at hiding their bias. But there are a handful of journalists who aren't partisan or ideologically aligned with either side. There are also reporters who do have a bias, but are diligent about checking that bias in their effort to provide fair-minded reporting. It would be more accurate to say that fair-minded reporting is what Fournier produces.

Still, Media Matters' Eric Boehlert accused Fournier's reporting of aiding Senator John McCain's presidential campaign in 2008.[109] A *Daily Kos* diarist called Fournier an "AP Conservative shill"[110] who needed to be "stopped" in a piece called "No Excuses: Ron Fournier Needs to Be Recused or Fired."[111]

MoveOn.org mobilized an e-mail campaign for people to contact AP to "stop the anti-Democrat, pro-McCain bias,"[112] while Firedoglake's similar campaign[113] to e-mail Fournier's then-boss, Kathleen Carroll, simply said "Remove Ron Fournier."[114]

Most recently, Fournier has outraged the left by writing in the *National Journal* about Obama's failure to break Washington gridlock ("What If Obama Can't Lead?")[115] and for a piece titled "Why I'm Getting Sick of Defending Obamacare."[116] The impact of the illiberal left's desire to delegitimize him and smear his reputation is most clearly illustrated in a hit piece by Tom Kludt at the liberal website Talking Points Memo. Kludt insinuated that Fournier was a conservative because the *National Journal* editor critiques Obama's leadership, his columns are regularly aggregated by Matt Drudge, he's admired by conservative MSNBC host Joe Scarborough, and as a reporter for the Associated Press, he "had an email correspondence with Karl Rove that was a bit too friendly."[117]

Reporters, commentators, and fair-minded liberals beware: if you relay facts that the illiberal left doesn't like, you'll be labeled a biased, bitter, agenda-driven conservative who should be ignored if not outright shunned or fired from your job.

THREE

ILLIBERAL INTOLERANCE AND INTIMIDATION

We had other freedoms, the really important ones, that are denied the youth of today. We could say what we liked; they can't.... We could, and did, differ from fashionable opinion with impunity, and would have laughed [political correctness] to scorn, had our society been weak and stupid enough to let it exist.

—GEORGE MACDONALD FRASER

In the summer of 2012, Chick-fil-A president Dan Cathy told an interviewer for a religious magazine that he supported the traditional family. The illiberal left swiftly launched a vicious smear campaign against Cathy and the popular fifty-five-year-old fast food restaurant.[1] Protesters descended on Chick-fil-A restaurants across the country to condemn the chain's alleged "bigotry" and "intolerance." To the illiberal left, any opposition to same-sex marriage translates into hatred of gay people. At Salon.com, Cathy was called an "unapologetic homophobe"[2] and the *Village Voice* deemed him a "homophobic chicken peddler."[3] At the feminist website Jezebel, readers were warned, "Don't eat at Chick-fil-A. Not only are the owners bigoted jerks, if you get sexually assaulted in the parking lot, you'll have to marry the guy. It's the biblical way."[4] At *Slate* Cathy's position opposing same-sex marriage was characterized as the equivalent of racism: "Racism persists, but at least racists have been formally politically defanged. Homophobes, meanwhile, have not," complained the writer.[5]

One protestor, Adam Smith—a senior executive at a medical supplies manufacturing company—set out to do some defanging. Video recording himself as he waited in a Tucson, Arizona, Chick-fil-A drive-through, Smith explained that he was there for a free water and to "say a few things." As he waited, Smith noted that the people in cars ahead of him, "have to have their Chick-fil-A anti-gay breakfast sandwich. It always tastes better when it's full of hate." When Smith finally reached the drive-through window he began berating a young woman named Rachel as though she was employed by the Ku Klux Klan. He accused her of working for a "hateful corporation" and said, "I don't know how you live with yourself and work here. I don't understand it. This is a horrible corporation with horrible values." Throughout the abuse, the fast food worker calmly murmured, "I disagree," and assured him, "We don't treat any of our customers differently." She tried to deflect his attempts to start an argument and explained she preferred to keep her personal views out of the workplace.

As Smith nastily condescended to Rachel, she was kind. "It's my pleasure to serve you always," she said. Rachel told Smith she was uncomfortable with being taped, but he didn't stop. Despite his disrespect, she remained respectful, saying "It's my pleasure to serve you always." As Smith departed she said, "I hope you have a really nice day." Mr. Tolerance was so pleased with himself that he posted a video of a woman saying she didn't want to be recorded on YouTube.[6] In this story, we are expected to believe the woman working the drive-through is the intolerant one.

After Smith's company fired him from his CFO position for verbally accosting a young woman, he posted a YouTube apology.[7] In an interview, Rachel said she forgave him and felt it was unfair for him to be dragged through the mud any more. "I'm Christian and God tells us to love thy neighbor," she said.[8]

Chick-fil-A was considered so evil that college students started petitions to have the restaurant kicked off their campuses.[9] Emory University ejected the restaurant from its on-campus food court[10] after the administration felt it necessary to release a public statement censuring the company,[11] and Davidson College announced it would no longer serve the chain's food at student activities.[12] Duke University announced that Chick-fil-A was not going to be readmitted to their student union when they finished renovations. Larry Moneta, Duke's vice president of Student Affairs said, in explanation, "Duke University seeks to eliminate discrimination and promote equality for the LGBT and all our communities in all our endeavors."[13]

To be clear, Chick-fil-A had not been accused of discriminating against gay customers or employees. The company was targeted because its Christian owner reiterated an orthodox, and until recently unremarkable, Christian belief in an interview. It's the same view held by Pope Francis.[14] Think about that for a minute, and think about what it says for the tolerance of the illiberal left and its commitment to freedom of thought and speech.

Debate and persuasion should be the default response when someone encounters a person who does not share their view, not demands that the other person change their position or be pushed to the margins of polite society. Still, illiberal left mayors across the country threatened to discriminate against a company for not sharing their beliefs about marriage. Boston mayor Tom Menino said of Chick-fil-A, "If they need licenses in the city, it will be very difficult."[15] In other words, cities have a right to discriminate against Christian-owned businesses if their owners have opinions that don't jibe with the illiberal left. Chicago mayor and former White House chief-of-staff Rahm Emanuel joined the crusade, discouraging any expansion by the restaurant in Chicago because, "Chick-fil-A values are not Chicago values."[16]

Interestingly, Emanuel's former boss, President Barack Obama, had publicly professed the same "values" as Cathy on marriage until barely two months before, when the president announced he had "evolved" into supporting same-sex marriage.[17] No matter. Following Emanuel's statement, Chicago Alderman Joe Moreno quickly announced, "Because of [Cathy's] ignorance, I will now be denying Chick-fil-A's permit to open a restaurant in the 1st Ward."[18] San Francisco Mayor Edwin M. Lee tweeted, "Very disappointed #ChickFilA doesn't share San Francisco's values & strong commitment to equality for everyone" and then added, "Closest #Chick-FilA to San Francisco is 40 miles away & I strongly recommend that they not try to come any closer."[19]

How would the illiberal left react if companies led by people who supported same-sex marriage were told by conservative Christian mayors that they would be denied permits to operate due to their beliefs not being in sync with local values? There would be justified screams of "bigotry" and "homophobia" within seconds.

The illiberal left reserves a special strain of strident wrath for manifestations or protections of Christian belief in America. Resistance to same-sex marriage is arguably the belief the illiberal left finds most offensive. It's certainly one of the primary battlefields on which the war on free speech is being waged. The illiberal left has worked hard to convince Americans that opposing same-sex marriage is so inherently immoral that the opposition must be brutally suppressed.

Demonizing is their favorite tactic for silencing disagreement with their position. The illiberal left justifies this demonizing by comparing people who oppose same-sex marriage to segregationists. But dehumanizing and hating black people went hand in hand with segregation. This is not true of opposing same-sex marriage. As we've seen with Pope Francis, it is more than possible to hold an orthodox view of homosexuality and respect and love gay people. If the illiberal left spent more time with orthodox Christians they would understand that Pope Francis is not an outlier. It's easier for the illiberal left to demonize their opponents and sanctify themselves as higher moral beings than treat differences of opinion respectfully. The goal is to make their opponents' view illegitimate. It's a tried-and-true debate-ending tactic.

In discussing same-sex marriage, Mark Joseph Stern at *Slate* asked, "Can a person oppose equal rights for gay people and not be, in some fundamental way, a homophobe? The answer seems to me to be a pretty obvious no."[20] John Shore of the Not All Like That Christians Project wrote at the Huffington Post, "If you vote against gay marriage or gay rights you are a bigot, as surely as anyone who voted against civil rights in the '60s was a bigot. If you preach against gay rights, you are a bigot.... If, in private, you intimate to your dearest friend that you don't think gay people should be allowed to get married, you are a bigot."[21]

If that is true, then hundreds of millions, if not a billion, of the world's 2.2 billion Christians are bigots. It means that Bill and Hillary Clinton and Barack Obama were public bigots for most of their lives, as was virtually every Democrat holding elected office until a few years ago. As late as 2008, Barack Obama told Rick Warren that "I believe that marriage is the union between a man and a woman. Now, for me as a Christian... it is also a sacred union. God's in the mix."[22] But the illiberal left didn't call him a homophobe or a bigot; he was their savior.

I am a longtime vocal supporter of same-sex marriage. At no point in my life have I not supported it. I readily acknowledge that some people oppose same-sex marriage for the wrong reasons—they are, indeed, prejudiced against gay people. But in my experience, most people who don't share my opinion—which included, until recently, scores of Democrats—are not bigots but people with sincere and respectable beliefs, often based in a Christian worldview that I otherwise largely share. In either case, authoritarian demands for intellectual conformity and the relentless demonizing of people who don't support same-sex marriage are inherently illiberal and wrong.

Matthew Vines, the author of *God and the Gay Christian* is gay and a strong advocate for gay and lesbian rights in the Christian Church. He told me in an interview, "I strongly disagree with those who think same-sex relationships are wrong, but I don't think the vast majority of them are hateful. I always start by finding what beliefs and values I have in common with someone and affirming those things. That typically helps to create a climate of mutual respect when we discuss the things we don't agree about."

The illiberal thought police view it differently. The executive editor of the Huffington Post's Religion section, Paul Raushenbush, has asserted, "Let's just be very clear here—if you are against marriage equality you are anti-gay. Done."[23] Camille Beredjick wrote at Patheos, "Stop sugar-coating it. If you're against marriage equality, you're…against LGBT people."[24] Salon.com ran a story under the headline, "The Bigots Finally Go Down: How Anti-Gay Haters Officially Lost the Marriage Fight."[25] At the *Think-Progress* blog hosted by the Center for American Progress, a Democratic think tank founded by former Obama advisor and President Clinton's former chief of staff John Podesta, Zach Ford explained that it was right to call those who oppose marriage equality anti-gay and bigots. These are "accurate terms [that] can reinforce that positions against LGBT equality should be treated as taboo, rather than as understandable or defensible."[26] Liberal writer Lindsay Beyerstein has written that "Opposing gay marriage is the moral equivalent of supporting anti-miscegenation laws" and explained that, "By definition, bigots are people with unshakable *baseless* prejudices. There is absolutely no reason, besides blind prejudice, to deny same sex couples the right to civil marriage."[27] Examples of this sort of illiberal left "logic" are innumerable.[28]

The relentless stereotyping and demonizing of people who oppose same-sex marriage has paid enormous dividends for the illiberal left. Their views have seeped into the culture to the point that many people think that denying same-sex marriage opponents the right to speak about their views is acceptable. In 2014, an instructor in a philosophy class at Marquette University, a Catholic school, let it be known that opposition to same-sex marriage was unworthy of discussion.[29] In a conversation recorded by a student following the class, instructor Cheryl Abbate explained "there are some opinions that are not appropriate, that are harmful" and compared questioning same-sex marriage to sexism and racism. Abbate went on to say that no one should express views that might be "offensive" to any gay student. Abbate told the student, who opposed same-sex marriage, "You don't have a right in this class…to make homophobic comments" and said the student could drop the class. The student complained, but the university took no action against the instructor.[30]

Marquette political science associate professor John McAdams wrote a blog post criticizing Abbate for refusing to allow criticism of same-sex marriage in class discussions and quoted the conversation Abbate had with the student.[31] He then found himself the object of illiberal scrutiny. Inside Higher Ed's Colleen Flaherty wrote that University of South Carolina associate professor Justin Weinberg argued that McAdams had made Abbate the "target of a political attack,"[32] likely stemming from "sexism."[33] Louisiana State University French studies professor John Protevi posted an open letter of support[34] of Abbate on his blog blasting McAdams's "one-sided public attack."[35] Abbate characterized McAdams's post as "cyberbullying and harassment" and noted, "It is astounding to me that the university has not created some sort of policy that would prohibit this behavior which undoubtedly leads to a toxic environment for both students and faculty."[36]

Just to be clear here: the illiberal left considers the victim in this story to be the professor who preemptively silenced a student and compared his views to racism and sexism. Disagreement expressed by McAdams, in an academic environment where rigorous debate should be encouraged, was cast as a bullying attack. Rather than his motivation being reasonably interpreted as wanting to expose illiberal silencing on a campus, McAdams was accused of being motivated by sexism. This is all standard fare for the illiberal left. Why make a substantive argument when it's just as easy to smear dissenters as sexist bullies?

While the university brushed off the student's complaints of being silenced, the administration became vigorously engaged when the illiberal left complained about McAdams's post. Incredibly, the dean of the College of Arts and Sciences sent McAdams a letter[37] informing him he was "relieved of all teaching duties and all other faculty activities, including, but not limited to, advising, committee work, faculty meetings and any activity that would involve your interaction with Marquette students, faculty and staff." He was ordered to stay off campus while he was being investigated for an unnamed transgression. Enclosed was a copy of Marquette's harassment policy, which appears to be modeled on Chairman Mao's *Little Red Book*. According to the Foundation for Individual Rights in Education (FIRE), screenshots of a faculty training session on the policy include "a slide about hypothetical peers Becky and Maria, who 'have been talking about their opposition to same-sex marriage.' Hans overhears the conversations, is offended, and reports the two for harassment. Hans's action is condoned."[38]

It's hard to imagine a more intellectually chilling policy than one that turns students and faculty into informants and punishes them for discussing issues in a manner not sanctioned by university authorities.

When a reporter inquired about the investigation against McAdams, a Marquette spokesperson straight out of Orwell's *1984* asserted that McAdams had violated the university's "Guiding Values to which all faculty and staff are required to adhere, and in which the dignity and worth of each member of our community is respected, especially students." Clearly Marquette's "Guiding Values" don't apply to students who oppose same-sex marriage. Marquette was also violating its expressed commitment to free speech in its official handbook, which states, "It is clearly inevitable, and indeed essential, that the spirit of inquiry and challenge that the university seeks to encourage will produce many conflicts of ideas, opinions and proposals for action."[39]

Due process was also out the window. McAdams was not informed of his offense, nor was he given an opportunity to defend himself. This treatment blatantly violates another one of Marquette's show documents, the faculty handbook, which states[40] that the university protects professors' "full and free enjoyment of legitimate personal or academic freedoms of thought, doctrine, discourse, association, advocacy, or action." Apparently, Marquette's professed commitments to their students and professors are trumped by their enigmatic and creepy "Guiding Values." One might also note the irony of an orthodox Catholic position on marriage being ruled as outside the bounds of legitimate discussion at a Catholic university at the hands of the illiberal left who dominate or run so many college and university campuses.

With the illiberal left in charge, even favored academics can go from victor to villain in an instant if they adopt the wrong perspective. University of Virginia law professor Douglas Laycock was well-respected on the left for his work on liberal causes such as defending a Muslim prisoner's right to grow a beard while incarcerated in an Arkansas prison and co-writing an amicus brief in *United States v. Windsor* arguing in favor of same-sex marriage. But Laycock's support took a hit when his interpretation of the Constitution led to what the illiberal left considered the wrong conclusions. In the lightning-rod Supreme Court case *Sebelius v. Hobby Lobby Stores, Inc.*, Laycock supported Hobby Lobby, arguing in an amicus brief that the government should not force corporations to provide health insurance covering birth control against their religious beliefs. Laycock also organized a letter to Arizona Governor Jan Brewer, cosigned by ten professors at other law schools and sent on University of Virginia School of Law letterhead, arguing that a controversial proposed Arizona law (SB 1062) that would allow businesses to deny service to gays and lesbians based on religious conviction was a necessary and constitutionally sound strengthening of the law to protect religious freedom. I vigorously and publicly disagreed with Laycock's interpretation in this case but never felt the need to try to delegitimize him as a scholar. Two University of Virginia student activists, Gregory Lewis and Stephanie Montenegro were less tolerant of Laycock's conclusions that didn't support their worldview. The duo released an open letter addressed[41] to Laycock expressing concern with work he had done which they believed was aiding opponents of LGBT rights and those who were resisting providing contraception under the Affordable Care Act (also known as "Obamacare"). They argued that they wanted "professors to fully understand the implications of their academic work," as if Laycock should always interpret the Constitution in a way that supports left-wing ideological preferences. The students were not remotely self-conscious about nakedly admitting to supporting some of Laycock's academic conclusions (the ones that fit with their activist agenda) but not those that didn't support their views. At no point did the students make a legal argument that undermined Laycock's conclusions, or any legal argument at all. They merely insisted that Laycock change his interpretation of the Constitution because they didn't like it.

Then, chillingly, they made an argument that has become increasingly common among the illiberal left: liberal political orthodoxy trumps academic freedom. "While academic freedom has immense value within the walls of the classroom," they wrote, "[we] invite you into a dialogue with UVA students who are negatively impacted by your work. It is vitally important to balance the collective work of our academic community with the collective impact of that work in communities across the country." They expressed a desire to start a "dialogue" with Laycock and then filed a Freedom of Information Act (FOIA) request demanding, among other things, university-funded travel expenses and cell phone records for the past two-and-a-half years. The students asserted that they wanted "a full, transparent accounting of the resources used by Professor Laycock which may be going towards halting the progress of the LGBT community and to erode the reproductive rights of women across the country."[42] As UCLA law professor Stephen Bainbridge pointed out at the time, "You don't start a dialogue with FOIA requests."[43]

No, you don't. Unless you have invented another definition for the word, which is precisely what the illiberal left has done. A "dialogue" with the illiberal left is one in which they inform you of the "right" way to think. Resistance to their demands will result in your being stuck with labels like bigot, misogynist, homophobe, racist, sexist, or some other toxic moniker that's alienating to the rest of society.

In 2014 a group of prominent religious leaders sent a letter to the White House asking for a religious exemption to a White House executive order that would prohibit federal contractors from discriminating against LGBT persons in recruitment, hiring, and training.[44] At issue was whether religious organizations, which sometimes contract with the federal government—

for instance, in helping with disaster relief—would be barred by the executive order from accepting federal contracts and, if they did accept them, be at risk of anti-discrimination lawsuits. Signers of the letter asking for a religious exemption included the chief executive of Catholic Charities USA, mega-church pastor Rick Warren, and the executive editor of *Christianity Today*. But it was no conservative manifesto. Former Obama staffer Michael Wear rounded up the signatories, which also included pastor Joel Hunter, who prays regularly with the president, and Stephen Schneck, co-chair of Catholics for Obama in 2012.[45]

An exemption was predictably opposed by the illiberal left—not because they respectfully disagreed with the religious organizations' position, but because they cast them as bigots. "This would be a catastrophic erosion of non-discrimination protections," said Kate Kendell of the National Center for Lesbian Rights. "We *must* tell President Obama loud and clear: no special rights for religious bigotry!!!" wrote activist John Becker. Rachel Maddow asserted on her MSNBC show that the letter was just part of "the floodgates...already opening" from the Supreme Court's Hobby Lobby decision. The genesis of the letter, she said, was about conservatives grabbing "every other conceivable advantage...by calling what they want to do that's otherwise against the law a variety of religious freedom."[46] Members of the illiberal left—from *ThinkProgress* to *Daily Kos*— echoed the claim that the Hobby Lobby decision had ushered in Armageddon for gay rights.[47]

Instead, what seems most at risk is the freedom of religious organizations to participate in public life when religious beliefs are deemed "bigotry." As same-sex marriage and civil unions have become legal in more states, the new legal structure has been utilized to attack religious charities with government contracts. In places like Illinois, Massachusetts, and the District of Columbia, for example, Catholic Charities has been forced to shut down their adoption and foster care services because the state demanded they place children with same-sex couples in violation of Catholic teaching on marriage and the family.[48]

"The new intolerance is an everybody problem...because it penalizes people who are a clear net plus for society, people who spend their days helping the poor, clothing the naked, feeding the hungry, caring for the cast-off, and otherwise trying to live out the Judeo-Christian code of social justice," writer Mary Eberstadt said in a 2014 *First Things* lecture. "More and more, those people are also witnesses to a terrible truth: the new intolerance makes it harder to help the poor and needy."

Bethany Christian Services is America's largest adoption agency with approximately 115 offices across thirty-six states. It was founded in 1944 and has had government contracts to provide foster care and adoption programs for more than sixty years. As a Christian organization, Bethany was able to save the government hundreds of thousands of dollars because it could provide services with the help of volunteers, donated financial capital, and less bureaucracy.

Bethany, however, has recently found itself in a contentious situation. When facilitating private adoptions, Bethany will only place children into two-parent families with a mother and a father. When LGBT couples come to Bethany to adopt children, the organization refers them to other agencies that can help them. Bethany does not prevent LGBT couples from adopting children; as an organization it only asks that it be allowed to follow its orthodox Christian belief system by placing children in two-parent families that have a mother and a father.

But such freedom to practice the organization's Christian beliefs, while being a government contractor, is in jeopardy. William J. Blacquiere, president and CEO of Bethany, said in an interview, "From the perspective of Bethany, we see the government as a partner. We've had contracts with state governments since the 1960s. During that time we had respect for the state's laws and they respected us. It definitely feels like that respect is disappearing."

While the illiberal left seems to hold a special animosity to Christianity, it is strangely protective of Islam, despite the fact that orthodox Muslims also oppose same-sex marriage. Nonetheless, the illiberal left labels the religion's critics as "Islamophobes" suggesting some sort of mental illness or "phobia" is behind any difference of opinion. Liberal firebrand Bill Maher learned this the hard way. In 2014, the host of HBO's *Politically Incorrect* got into a heated agreement with actor Ben Affleck about Islam. After atheist writer Sam Harris called Islam, "the motherlode of bad ideas," Maher added that Islam is "the only religion that acts like the mafia, that will f*cking kill you if you say the wrong thing, draw the wrong picture, or write the wrong book." Affleck was furious. He pushed back, arguing that Islam was being painted with too broad a brush. Maher cited a Pew poll finding that a large majority of Egyptians felt that if you leave Islam, death was the appropriate retaliation. Maher asked, "If 90 percent of Catholics in Brazil felt the appropriate response to leaving Catholicism was death, wouldn't that be a slightly bigger story?"

Affleck's rebuttal to these claims amounted to this: Maher and Harris were "gross" and "racist," which was enough to make Affleck a hero among the illiberal left. On the *View*, Rosie O'Donnell wanted "Affleck for President!"[49] Over at MSNBC, Chris Matthews declared, "I'm with Affleck because knocking someone's religion is the way to start or escalate a fight. It's no way to cool one."[50] MSNBC host Krystal Ball said, "I have such a liberal crush now on Ben Affleck. I thought he was so amazing throughout that show, and so strong there."[51] MSNBC host Chris Hayes echoed Affleck's claims that Maher and Harris were saying things that were "gross and racist" because their conversation didn't include any actual Muslims.[52] Michael Eric Dyson, guest-hosting the *Ed Show* on MSNBC, called Maher a "patron saint of liberals," but said his argument against Islamic illiberalism reinforced bigotry.[53]

Maher's contempt for Christianity is well known, yet it has barely elicited a peep from the illiberal left. Maher has called the God of the Bible a "d-ck," a "psychotic mass murderer," and a "tyrant,"[54] and said, "If we were a dog and God owned us, the cops would come and take us away." The illiberal left is fine with such anti-Christian broadsides, because it accepts, and even promotes, the idea that Christianity is bigoted, but it condemns as off-limits and racist any discussion of Islamic illiberalism.

Maher's comments led a student at the University of California-Berkeley—the birthplace of the "Free Speech Movement"—to start a Change.org petition[55] demanding the school cancel Maher's scheduled commencement speech. The petition claimed the school had a "responsibility…to protect all students…." It called Maher's comments "racist" and "bigoted" and characterized his comments about Islam and religion as "hate speech." The petition garnered nearly six thousand signatures. The student committee responsible for selecting commencement speakers reconvened without inviting Berkeley administrators and decided to rescind the invitation.[56] The students' attempt to punish Maher as a liberal apostate failed after the chancellor stepped in, citing the university's support for Maher's right to free speech.

Maher's treatment demonstrated how little tolerance the illiberal left has for critics of Islam. This includes people who were raised in the faith, such as Ayaan Hirsi Ali, who should be a hero to liberals. Hirsi Ali is a survivor of genital mutilation who escaped a forced marriage to become a member of the Netherlands parliament. She's an advocate for women and a courageous proponent of free speech, with a price on her head for speaking out about the illiberalism of Islam. Now a naturalized U.S. citizen, Hirsi Ali is a fellow at Harvard University's Kennedy School of Government, and in 2005 was named by *Time* magazine as one of the "100 most influential people in the world." Given this impressive list of accomplishments, one might assume that liberals would be heralding her as the ultimate success story—a woman overcoming insurmountable odds and challenging the patriarchal religion she says oppressed her and other women. Instead, many of the illiberal left have demeaned her, dismissed her, and attempted to silence her for the heresy of having a negative opinion about Islam, the religion of her upbringing.

"It may be naive, stupid, irrational, but I'm [speaking out against Islam] because I think that if I do, there'll be less honor killings, fewer little girls undergoing female genital mutilation like I did,"[57] Hirsi Ali told the *Washington Post*. Yet Jessica Mack on her blog *Gender Across Borders:*

A Global Feminist Blog, was of the opinion that it would be better for Hirsi Ali to work within the system of Islam. She criticized her for "speaking out against Islam... and enduring constant death threats (and consequent 24-hour security). This isolates her in a way, cuts her off in her activism. She is not a woman of the people."[58] So, it's Hirsi Ali's fault a bunch of male Muslim fanatics want to kill her. "Above all else, Hirsi Ali's story is one of an individual's dogged pursuit of personal freedom. This individual happens to be a woman, and so some of the hardships she endures are unique in that way. But somehow she doesn't connect these intense personal experiences to the larger feminist project,"[59] Mack wrote.

The illiberal left's protectiveness of a patriarchal religion may seem confusing to an impartial observer, but Hirsi Ali thinks she understands. She explained in an interview with the *Washington Examiner*'s Ashe Schow. "Liberals, she said, protect Islamic extremists partly because the Left has no idea what really goes on in Muslim countries," Schow wrote. "'I think if I adopt the position in good faith to multiculturalists and leftists, I would say [they take the position they do] because they see [Muslims] as victims. They see them as victims of the white man and so they think: 'Let's protect them from the white man. Let's protect them from capitalism.'... That is misguided at best and malicious at worst,'"[60] Hirsi Ali said.

In their effort to delegitimize Hirsi Ali as a valid critic, she is portrayed as a pathological provocateur, not a women's advocate fighting to lift the oppression of Muslim women. The liberal *Guardian* columnist Emma Brockes complained in an article about Hirsi Ali that "when she writes that 'violence is an integral part' of Islamic social discipline, or says in our interview that 'Muhammad's example is terrible, don't follow it', it is deliberately, almost narcissistically provocative.... To Hirsi Ali, the act of speaking out, of saying what no one else will say, seems at this stage to be almost a pathology...."[61]

Hirsi Ali picked the wrong religion about which to have a negative opinion. Contrast the character assassination of Hirsi Ali as a pathological narcissist to Brockes's glowing profile of author Anne Rice after Rice wrote on her Facebook page that she was quitting "Christianity and being a Christian" because she refused to be "anti-feminist...anti-artificial birth control...anti-Democrat...anti-secular humanism...anti-science and anti-life." Brockes asked rhetorically, "Given the unchanging nature of the Catholic church, the obvious question is, what took [Rice] so long?" Brockes criticized Hirsi Ali because the "phrasing she uses [in discussing Islam] is startlingly direct." Yet Brockes praises Rice for her direct criticism of Catholicism: "[I] began to really study [Catholicism] and I found that it was not an honorable religion, that it was not honest." Brockes's title blared: "Anne Rice: I thought the church was flat-out immoral. I had to leave."[62] So, the Catholic Church is condemned, broad brush. But to say, "Muhammad's example is terrible" crosses the line.

Maher and Hirsi Ali could fairly be characterized as anti-Islam. This doesn't mean they are in the grip of an irrational "phobia." Some of their comments are blisteringly critical, and yes, offensive to adherents of Islam. So what? There is a chasm of difference between critiquing a religious system and harboring bigotry against millions of that religion's adherents. To set one of the world's largest and most influential religions as out of bounds for discussion and criticism—including harsh criticism—is inherently illiberal. I'm a Christian, but I would never suggest that people should not be allowed to harshly criticize Christianity. Religion is a powerful force in society that can be misused to oppress. All religions should be put under the microscope and picked apart. The proper response to religious criticism is not to silence it; it is to disprove it through debate and example.

The writer and atheist evangelist Christopher Hitchens held Christianity—and all religions—in complete contempt. "Violent, irrational, intolerant, allied to racism and tribalism and bigotry, invested in ignorance and hostile to free inquiry, contemptuous of women and coercive toward children: organized religion ought to have a great deal on its conscience," he wrote in his book *God Is Not Great*. He once called Mother Teresa "a fanatic, a fundamentalist, and a fraud."[63] That didn't stop me from reading his work, nor would I have ever suggested he be kept from receiving an award or speaking at a university. In fact, I, along with hundreds of other Christians, attended debates where he harshly and derisively blasted Christianity. Bill Maher and Hirsi Ali are also critics of Christianity but the illiberal left doesn't characterize that as a "phobia," nor should they. To the illiberal left Islam cannot be criticized without recourse to bigotry; on the other hand, the illiberal left seems to regard Christianity as the very definition of bigotry.

EXCLUSIONARY DIVERSITY

The intensity of illiberal intolerance of orthodox Christianity is escalating and it's scary to project where it might end up. Michael Wear had a front row seat to the Obama administration's evolving views of religious tolerance. Wear worked on Obama's 2008 and 2012 presidential campaigns, promoted Obama to evangelical Christians, and served in the Obama White House office on faith-based initiatives. "In the 2008 campaign and during the president's first year or so, it was all about aspiration and all about open doors. There was not a constituency that the president did not want to reach or a vote we wanted to concede," Wear told me.

There were efforts designed to build bridges with conservative Christian leaders and groups who normally vote mostly Republican. During the 2008 campaign, Barack Obama and John McCain participated in the "Saddleback Civil Forum on the Presidency" hosted by pastor Rick Warren.[64] During his first term, Obama met privately with about thirty high-profile evangelical leaders in Chicago,[65] and with Billy Graham at the evangelist's home in North Carolina. He also decided to expand the faith-based initiatives office that President George W. Bush had created. During his first year as president, President Obama delivered a commencement speech at University of Notre Dame vowing to work with "pro-life" Catholics to "reduce the number of women seeking abortions."[66] Many of these actions inflamed members of his liberal base, like the American Civil Liberties Union[67] and Americans United for Separation of Church and

State, who renounced his efforts.[68] The *New York Times* ran an op-ed blasting Obama's continuance of an office of faith-based initiatives in the White House as "institutionaliz[ing] a bad idea."[69]

In 2008, president-elect Obama invited evangelical leader Rick Warren, who some were calling "America's pastor," to offer the benediction at the inaugural ceremony. This was especially significant because Warren had been a vocal supporter of California's Proposition 8, an anti–same-sex marriage initiative. Many liberals and LGBT activist groups protested the decision, but the president-elect defended the invitation. At a December 2008 press conference, Obama reiterated his support for "equality for gay and lesbian Americans." But he also said that he would not revoke Warren's invitation because of his desire "to create an atmosphere…where we can disagree without being disagreeable and then focus on those things that we hold in common as Americans."[70]

With a level of grace often absent in political spaces, Obama said, "During the course of the entire inaugural festivities, there are going to be a wide range of viewpoints that are presented. And that's how it should be, because that's what America's about…. And that's, hopefully, going to be a spirit that carries over into my administration."[71]

But that spirit was not to last. By the conclusion of President Obama's first term, it was clear to many White House advisors that working with political opponents wasn't a winning strategy. The events leading up to President Obama's second inaugural address proved that change had indeed taken place. This time, another evangelical pastor, Louie Giglio, was invited to give the benediction. Again liberals and LGBT groups protested the president's choice. The liberal political blog *ThinkProgress* published a sermon preached by Giglio in the mid-1990s condemning the "homosexual lifestyle" as sinful.[72] This time President Obama did not stand behind his invitation. Giglio bowed out, saying in a statement that his participation would "be dwarfed by those seeking to make their agenda the focal point of the inauguration."[73] Giglio had been chosen in the first place to bring awareness to fighting sex trafficking, an area where he has played a leadership role. But saving women and children from being sold into sex slavery didn't rank in the illiberal left's list of concerns. The Presidential Inaugural Committee released an official statement saying, "We were not aware of Pastor Giglio's past comments at the time of his selection and they don't reflect our desire to celebrate the strength and diversity of our country at this Inaugural.... As we now work to select someone to deliver the benediction, we will ensure their beliefs reflect this administration's vision of inclusion and acceptance for all Americans."[74]

Wear characterizes the second inaugural experience as "one of the saddest times of my political life." He noted that between the first and second inaugurals, "We went from diversity being the reason for inclusion to diversity being the reason for exclusion."

That is where the illiberal left's silencing of opponents is taking us: to the end of freedom of speech, thought, and debate, to uniformity—all in the in the name of diversity.

FOUR

INTOLERANCE 101

SHUTTING DOWN DEBATE

If liberty means anything at all, it means the right to tell
people what they do not want to hear.
—GEORGE ORWELL

I n March 2014, a feminist studies associate professor at the University of California-Santa Barbara physically attacked a sixteen-year-old girl who had been handing out anti-abortion literature in a public space on campus. The professor, Dr. Mireille Miller-Young, later told a police officer that she was justified in her attack because the literature and graphic abortion signs displayed by the anti–abortion rights group were "disturbing" and "offensive." She was particularly offended, she said, because she was pregnant and teaches reproductive rights.[1]

The police officer who interviewed Miller-Young asked what crimes she felt the anti–abortion rights group had committed.[2] Miller-Young told the officer that coming to campus and showing "graphic imagery" was insensitive to the community and claimed the "pro-life" group may have violated university policy. In fact, the group staged their demonstration in the campus "free speech area" as university policy dictated. Had they actually violated university policy, that still would not have made their actions criminal, or inviting of physical attack.

Nonetheless, throughout the police report, Miller-Young is unrepentant. The police report continues, "Miller-Young said that her actions today were in defense of her students and her own safety... Miller-Young also suggested that the group had violated her rights." The officer asked Miller-Young what right the group had violated, and she responded, "My personal right to go to work and not be in harm." But there was no harm done to Miller-Young. She just couldn't tolerate the expression of views with which she disagreed. So she attacked a teenage girl.

Miller-Young's behavior, while indefensible, is easily understood if one considers the ideological confines of the illiberal left. Seen through this intolerant and narrow lens, *disagreement is violence.* Offending them is akin to physical assault. They are so isolated from the marketplace of ideas, that when confronted with a view they don't like, they feel justified in doing whatever they can to silence that speech.

Campuses across the United States have become ground zero for silencing free speech. Universities founded to encourage diversity of thought and debate have become incubators of intolerance where non-sanctioned views are silenced through bullying, speech codes, "free speech zones," and other illiberal means.

Professor Miller-Young's assault is the headline of the incident, but what led up to the attack is equally alarming. According to Mairead McArdle, then a twenty-year-old student at nearby Thomas Aquinas College, the incident started when she approached Miller-Young and handed her an anti-abortion pamphlet. "As soon as she [saw it] she raised her voice and said, 'Oh so you are the people who use fear tactics to scare women. And is that your sign? Well let's go talk about that,'" McArdle recounted to me. "We then walked over to the sign [that depicted an aborted fetus]. From that point on she did not stop yelling at us. With her it never went back to a reasonable discussion. She was just mad. She said, 'You don't have the right to be here, you don't belong here, you don't go here.'"

So who was the person using "fear tactics" against women here? It seems it was Miller-Young. "She told us, 'You guys don't know what you are talking about," McArdle said. "She was cursing. She called us idiots. She was interrupting us nonstop, we barely got a word in. She threw the pamphlet at me. After awhile some of the other students gathered around, some of whom said they were Miller-Young's students. They started yelling at us. One of the girls kept coming up to me and saying, 'Can you please just be a decent human being and take [the sign] away?' And I told her that I understood it was hurtful to some people, but that we had a right to be there, and they could not just tell us to go away.'"

But this wasn't enough for Miller-Young. "The professor was inciting the mob. She was talking to them and walking between them and us. She was saying 'So, should we take away their signs? Should we do it for them? They don't have a right to be here. They are feeding you a bunch of [expletive],'" said McArdle. "She started a chant of 'tear down the sign.' The people in my group looked at each other and it was clear that everyone was scared. We tried to go in and talk to individual people to break up the [mob]. It was fifteen to twenty students. When we did go in to talk to people it worked for a minute or two. As soon as she realized her mob was breaking up she was muscling in between people saying 'No, they are just trying to break us up, we have to stick together.'"

Multiple students who were participating in the anti-abortion demonstration confirmed that when they were able to engage the students one on one, they would listen respectfully and engage. But then Miller-Young would intervene and try to stir them up. This kind of behavior—tyranny by someone holding a minority view in a group—is a theme that often emerges in stories involving the illiberal left's silencing campaign. All it takes is one or two people to claim grievance and start bullying everyone else to fall in line.

Eventually Miller-Young realized she had lost the students and upped the ante. McArdle recalls, "She was yelling and walking towards me and I backed up because I thought she was going to hit me. That's when she grabbed the sign. She asked a few students to help her and she carried it off. We were all shaken up. One of the girls was crying. A student with [Miller-Young] said, 'You better guard your other sign or we'll take that one too.'" In a video of the incident, the professor taunts the girls as she is walking away and says, "I may be a thief but you are a terrorist."

Thrin Short, the then-sixteen-year-old sister of one of the organizers of the demonstration, was frightened but realized they needed to retrieve the sign, as it was a focal point of their demonstration. She followed Miller-Young and her students—all the while filming them—and caught up with them at an elevator they had just boarded. Thrin recalled, "I was kind of scared to get in the elevator, but I figured that's what I would do." Miller-Young blocked the doorway and told her she couldn't get on. In the video, the professor repeatedly shoves Thrin, smirking the whole time. The video becomes blurry as Miller-Young grabs the girl.[3] According to Thrin, the professor was holding both of her wrists, and scratched her, in an effort to wrest the camera out of her hands. Pictures of her wounds were later posted on her group's website.[4]

The activists were not able to get their sign back. Miller-Young explained to the police officer that she and her students went to her office and destroyed the sign with scissors.[5] She said she had a "moral" right to have acted as she did. Even after the officer explained to her that a crime had occurred, she insisted she had set a good example for her students. She characterized all of her actions as those of a "conscientious objector." She described the sign used by the anti-abortion activists as "hate speech."

When the case went to trial, the jury took a different view of the situation, and Miller-Young was convicted of theft and battery.[6] Incredibly, she remains a professor at the University of California-Santa Barbara. She was never sanctioned for her behavior, at least not publicly. On the contrary, peers and university administrators robustly defended her. At least twelve university professors sent letters to the court attesting to her character[7] and describing her as an open-minded bridge-builder. She was treated as the victim in the case, and letter after letter complained of the critical press coverage her actions received, as though it was unmerited.

Dr. Stephanie Batiste, an associate professor in UCSB's Department of Black Studies and English, expressed sympathy with Miller-Young's reaction to the activists, reimagining the bullying that ended in a physical altercation as a simple and understandable outgrowth of Miller-Young's "kindness combined with her commitment to justice." She described Miller-Young as "a giving, sensitive person with a good heart" and said she was "instinctively kind."

Miller-Young is so "kind" that she has never directly apologized to the girl she attacked, or to the students she intimidated and mocked and attempted to silence. Instead, in a naked attempt to gain leniency, Miller-Young provided the court with a written apology. As the mother of the victim noted to the court, the apology "says nothing about her pushing, grabbing and scratching Thrin."[8] The letter also doesn't explain her lack of contrition with the police officer, or why a week after the incident she re-tweeted a tweet by one of her supporters who said she would stand with Miller-Young "until that whining little bigot eats her accusation with a barbed fork."

But really, whether she is kind or not is beside the point. No one has ever suggested that Miller-Young should be prevented from expressing disagreement, outrage, or even anger at the demonstration. The students were in fact happy to debate the topic with her. That was why they were there. What Miller-Young is not free to do, as a matter of law, is steal property or physically attack other people because she has been exposed to views that upset her. Separate from the law, it's alarming there is not broader agreement that a professor shouldn't abuse her power to intimidate young people in an attempt to silence their views. Even had she stayed on the right side of the law, Miller-Young should not have been considered innocent in the eyes of the university or her peers.

The academics defending Miller-Young pretend that she was held hostage and forced to look at images that offended her. Miller-Young was in possession of two legs that she quite easily could have used to walk away from the sign that she claims sent her over the edge. In her letter in support of Miller-Young, Erica Lorraine Williams, an assistant professor of anthropology at Spelman College, blasted the media's depictions of Miller-Young as a "crazed feminist studies professor who bullies and taunts young people." But that's exactly what she did. She proudly recounted it to a police officer and there is a video of it.

One can only imagine what would happen if a conservative professor who opposed abortion rights harassed, pushed, and scratched a pro–abortion rights activist and then stole and destroyed her sign. It would have led the evening newscasts under the "War on Women" banner and made the front page of the *New York Times*. The professor would have been fired within hours of the incident and escorted off the campus.

Yet the university—a publicly funded institution—never condemned or apologized for Miller-Young's behavior. When asked for a comment from the media, a UC Santa Barbara representative said the university didn't discuss personnel issues, but would confirm that the demonstrators were in the campus designated "free speech area" and thus had not been violating any campus rules.

Soon after the incident, Michael D. Young, vice chancellor for Student Affairs, sent a letter to students addressing the fact that "during the past few weeks, UCSB has been visited by various anti-abortion crusaders" and lamented that outsiders were coming on campus to create discord. He labeled them "the most recent generation of true believers, self-proclaimed prophets, and provocateurs." Miller-Young's actions were never mentioned. Instead, the chancellor created an "us-vs.-them" paradigm that assumed that every student at this public university shared his pro–abortion rights views. He wrote of how the UCSB community was being "tested" by "outsiders coming into our midst to provoke us, to taunt us and attempt to turn us against one another as they promote personal causes and agendas."[9] What a strange way to describe the expression of free speech on a university campus. How can someone demonstrating against abortion possibly be construed as attempting to "provoke" or to turn people against each other? Would the chancellor argue that a pro–abortion rights demonstration on a public campus was a hostile act? Unlikely.

While many people might think showing a picture of an aborted fetus is distasteful, the demonstrators told me they chose the image to draw attention to one of the realities of abortion. This was done in the same way one might show a picture of a starving child to show the reality of a famine. Young has no evidence that the activists were seeking to divide rather than inform. But this attitude is typical of the illiberal left. Real disagreement isn't tolerated. Activism against a liberal cause is construed as an attack. Which is probably why in Miller-Young's mind—and the minds of her defenders—she was justified in her actions.

It's easy to write Miller-Young off as an unstable kook, but by all accounts that would be wrong. The judge in the case expressed the belief that outside this event, she had "impeccable character."[10] Indeed, her letters of support attest that this woman is well liked and respected by people who share her worldview. There is little reason to doubt this. That is precisely the problem. Miller-Young, like many of her fellow illiberal left travelers, appears to be able to function perfectly as long as she is surrounded by people expressing ideas and beliefs she shares. She is isolated in a cocoon where she doesn't have to confront information or ideas that conflict with her worldview. This in itself is not unique. Many Americans have chosen to limit their interaction to people who are like them. Of course, most Americans aren't university professors who are supposed to be broad-minded and able to teach students with diverse views. University professors should, ideally, encourage debate. A campus should be a place where students are confronted with challenging and new ideas. College brochures and mission statements are laden with promises of free thinking and debate, precisely because there can be no rigorous education without these elements.

Most Americans also don't feel justified in harassing and intimidating people who hold beliefs with which they disagree. When someone expresses

a view they don't share, they don't label it "hate speech" as Miller-Young
called the anti-abortion demonstration. They lack the sense of entitlement
of the illiberal left, which believes that anyone who doesn't hold the "right"
views deserves to be ostracized. Most Americans, whether liberal, middle
of the road, or conservative, have learned to live with the tension of differing beliefs in a pluralistic society. They may not actually enjoy having to
hear the differing beliefs—which is why they often tune into forms of
media that will affirm what they already believe—but they aren't actively
trying to silence people with whom they disagree.

Thankfully, physical assault is not the preferred silencing tactic of the
illiberal left. Jail time isn't their goal: shutting people up is the mission. But
Miller-Young's case is instructive because of the terminology she chose to
defend herself. She was offended. The demonstrators were engaging in
"hate speech." The demonstration had caused her "harm." This language
appears repeatedly in cases where the illiberal left has worked to silence
their ideological opponents. Opposing points of view aren't legitimate:
they are malicious, vicious attacks that justify a host of silencing tech-
niques, including the kind of fierce intimidation exhibited by a university
authority figure like Miller-Young.

NO OFFENSE

The root of nearly every free speech infringement on campuses
across the country is that someone—almost always a liberal—has been
offended or has sniffed out a potential offense in the making. Then, the
silencing campaign begins. The offender must be punished, not just for
justice's sake, but also to send the message to anyone else on campus
that should he or she stray off the leftist script, they too might find
themselves investigated, harassed, ostracized, or even expelled. If the
left can preemptively silence opposing speakers or opposing groups—
such as getting a speech or event canceled, or denying campus recognition for a group—even better.

In a 2014 interview with *New York* magazine, comedian Chris Rock told journalist Frank Rich that he had stopped playing college campuses because of how easily the audiences were offended. Rock said he realized some time around 2006 that, "This is not as much fun as it used to be" and noted George Carlin had felt the same way before he died. Rock attributed it to, "Kids raised on a culture of 'We're not going to keep score in the game because we don't want anybody to lose.' Or just ignoring race to a fault. You can't say 'the black kid over there.' No, it's 'the guy with the red shoes.' You can't even be offensive on your way to being inoffensive." Sadly, Rock admitted that the climate of hypersensitivity had forced him and other comedians into self-censorship.

He said, "It is scary, because the thing about comedians is that you're the only ones who practice in front of a crowd. [T]here are a few guys good enough to write a perfect act and get onstage, but everybody else workshops it and workshops it, and it can get real messy. It can get downright offensive. Before everyone had a recording device...you'd say something that went too far, and you'd go, 'Oh, I went too far,' and you would just brush it off. But if you think you don't have room to make mistakes, it's going to lead to safer, gooier stand-up. You can't think the thoughts you want to think if you think you're being watched."

This Orwellian climate of intimidation and fear chills free speech and thought. On college campuses it is particularly insidious. Rock's description of developing comedy isn't dissimilar to how college students should develop their minds. Higher education should provide an environment to test new ideas, debate theories, encounter challenging information, and figure out what one believes. Campuses should be places where students are able to make mistakes without fear of retribution. If there is no margin for error, it is impossible to receive a meaningful education.

Instead, the politically correct university is a world of land mines, where faculty and students have no idea what innocuous comment might be seen as an offense. In December 2014, the president of Smith College, Kathleen McCartney, sent an e-mail to the student body in the wake of the outcry over two different grand juries failing to indict police officers who killed African American men. The subject heading read "All Lives Matter" and the e-mail opened with, "As members of the Smith community we are struggling, and we are hurting." She wrote, "We raise our voices in protest." She outlined campus actions that would be taken to "heal those in pain" and to "teach, learn and share what we know" and to "work for equity and justice."

Shortly thereafter, McCartney sent another e-mail. This one was to apologize for the first. What had she done? She explained she had been informed by students "the phrase/hashtag 'all lives matter' has been used by some to draw attention away from the focus on institutional violence against black people." She quoted two students, one of whom said, "The black students at this school deserve to have their specific struggles and pain recognized, not dissolved into the larger student body."[11] The *Daily Hampshire Gazette* reported that a Smith sophomore complained that by writing "All Lives Matter," "It felt like [McCartney] was invalidating the experience of black lives." Another Smith sophomore told the *Gazette*, "A lot of my news feed was negative remarks about her as a person." In her apology e-mail McCartney closed by affirming her commitment to "working as a white ally."[12]

McCartney clearly was trying to support the students and was sympathetic to their concerns and issues. Despite the best of intentions, she caused grievous offense. The result of a simple mistake was personal condemnation by students. If nefarious motives are imputed in this situation, it's not hard to extrapolate what would, and does, happen to actual critics who are not obsequiously affirming the illiberal left.

In an article in the *Atlantic*, Wendy Kaminer—a lawyer and free speech advocate—declared, "Academic freedom is declining. The belief that free speech rights don't include the right to speak offensively is now firmly entrenched on campuses and enforced by repressive speech or harassment codes. Campus censors don't generally riot in response to presumptively offensive speech, but they do steal[13] newspapers containing articles they don't like, vandalize[14] displays they find offensive, and dis-rupt[15] speeches they'd rather not hear. They insist that hate speech isn't free speech and that people who indulge in it should be punished. No one should be surprised when a professor at an elite university calls[16] for the arrest of 'Sam Bacile' [who made the YouTube video *The Innocence of Muslims*] while simultaneously claiming to value the First Amendment."[17]

Many of the conflicts that arise on university campuses involving intolerance of dissent don't involve constitutional claims. But when they do, they should be open and shut cases. Sadly, they aren't. The illiberal left act as though it is their job to "balance" the values of free speech and the complaint du jour. Legally, there are rare exceptions as to when the govern-ment—which includes state universities—can limit free speech, and those few exceptions unequivocally do not involve the petty grievances of hurt feelings, taking offense, or ideological disagreement. As for private univer-sities, they are not held to the same constitutional requirements as public universities,[18] but they still must reconcile their proclaimed values and mission statements that embrace diversity and freedom of thought with their illiberal crackdowns on free speech. Furthermore, some states have laws requiring private universities to guarantee free speech rights.[19]

But on today's campuses, left-leaning administrators, professors, and students are working overtime in their campaign of silencing dissent, and their *unofficial* tactics of ostracizing, smearing, and humiliation are highly effective. But what is even more chilling—and more far reaching—is the *official* power they abuse to ensure the silencing of views they don't like. They've invented a labyrinth of anti-free speech tools that include "speech codes," "free speech zones," censorship, investigations by campus "diver-sity and tolerance offices," and denial of due process. They craft "anti-harassment policies" and "anti-violence policies" that are speech codes in disguise. According to the Foundation for Individual Rights in Education's (FIRE) 2014 report on campus free speech, "Spotlight on Speech Codes," close to 60 percent of the four hundred–plus colleges they surveyed, "seri-ously infringe upon the free speech rights of students."[20] Only sixteen of the schools reviewed in 2014 had no policies restricting protected speech. Their 2015 report found that of the 437 schools they surveyed, "more than 55 percent maintain severely restrictive, 'red light' speech codes—policies that clearly and substantially prohibit protected speech." FIRE's Greg Lukianoff attributed the slight drop to outside pressure from free speech groups and lawsuits.[21]

For many Americans the term "speech code" sends shivers up the spine. Yet these noxious and un-American codes have become commonplace on college campuses across the United States. They are typically so broad that they could include literally anything and are subject to the interpretation of school administrators, who frequently fail to operate as honest brokers. In the hands of the illiberal left, the speech codes are weapons to silence anyone—professors, students, visiting speakers—who expresses a view that deviates from the left's worldview or ideology. Speech that offends them is redefined as "harassment" or "hate speech" both of which are barred by most campus speech codes. At Colorado College, a private liberal arts college, administrators invented a "violence" policy that was used to punish non-violent speech.[22] The consequences of violating a speech code are serious: it can often lead to public shaming, censoring, firings, suspensions, or expulsions, often with no due process.

Many of the incidents sound too absurd to be true. But true they are. Consider, for example, how Yale University put the kibosh on its Freshman Class Council's T-shirt designed for the Yale-Harvard football game. The problem? The shirt quoted F. Scott Fitzgerald's line from *This Side of Paradise*, that, "I think of all Harvard men as sissies."[23] The word "sissy" was deemed offensive to gay people. Or how about the Brandeis professor who was found guilty of racial harassment—with no formal hearing—for explaining, indeed criticizing, the word "wetbacks."[24] Simply saying the word was crime enough. Another professor, this time at the University of Central Florida, was suspended for making a joke in class equating his tough exam questions to a "killing spree."[25] A student reported the joke to the school's administration. The professor promptly received a letter suspending him from teaching and banning him from campus. He was reinstated after the case went public.[26]

The vaguely worded campus speech codes proliferating across the country turn every person with the ability to exercise his or her vocal chords into an offender in the making. New York University prohibits "insulting, teasing, mocking, degrading or ridiculing another person or group."[27] The College of the Holy Cross prohibits speech "causing emotional injury through careless or reckless behavior."[28] The University of Connecticut issued a "Policy Statement on Harassment" that bans "actions that intimidate, humiliate, or demean persons or groups, or that undermine their security or self-esteem."[29] Virginia State University's 2012–13 student handbook bars students from "offend[ing] ... a member of the University community."[30] But who decides what's "offensive"? The illiberal left, of course.

The list goes on and on. The University of Wisconsin-Stout at one point had an Information Technology policy prohibiting the distribution of messages that included offensive comments about a list of attributes including hair color.[31] Fordham University's policy prohibited using e-mail to "insult."[32] It gets worse: Lafayette College—a private university—instituted a "Bias Response Team" which exists to "respond to acts of intolerance." A "bias-related incident" was "any incident in which an action taken by a person or group is perceived to be malicious ... toward another person or group."[33] Is it really wise to have a policy that depends on the perception of offense by college-aged students?[34] Other schools have bias reporting programs encouraging students to report incidents.[35]

Speech codes create a chilling environment where all it takes is one accusation, true or not, to ruin someone's academic career. The intent or reputation or integrity of the accused is of little import. If someone "perceives" you have said or acted in a racist way, then the bar for guilt has been met. If a person claims you caused them "harm" by saying something that offended them, case closed.

Harvard raised eyebrows in 2011 by asking incoming students to sign a pledge upholding "civility," "inclusiveness," and "kindness." Signing was voluntary, until you considered that the pledges were hung in the dorms for all to see. So if you didn't sign the pledge, it would surely be noticed. What's wrong with asking students to be kind and inclusive? In another era, perhaps nothing. But today, these are loaded terms. Holding anti-abortion, pro-Republican, anti–same-sex marriage, and pro-gun views has been construed as bigoted (non-inclusive) on college campuses. Saying someone caused you "harm" or made you feel "unsafe" used to mean something. As we saw with professor Miller-Young, now these terms are used to describe situations where someone had to hear something with which they disagreed.

In November 2013, more than two dozen graduate students at UCLA entered the classroom of their professor and announced a protest against a "hostile and unsafe climate for Scholars of Color." The students had been the victims of racial "microaggression," a term invented in the 1970s that has been recently repurposed as a silencing tactic. A common definition cited is that racial microaggressions "are brief and commonplace daily verbal, behavioral, or environmental indignities, whether intentional or unintentional, that communicate hostile, derogatory, or negative racial slights and insults towards people of color." Like all these new categories, literally *anything* can be a microaggression.

According to the Facebook page of a Princeton group that tracks microaggressions on campus, "there are no objective definitions to words and phrases. The perspective and lived experiences of each individual contextualizes the world around them and thus places a particular meaning in words based on their distinct subjectivity. What counts as harmless banter to some may be emotionally triggering to others."[36] A frequent complaint posted in these forums transforms polite small talk into a racial attack. Here's the problem: sometimes white people ask people of color where they are from and they answer "California" or "Iowa" and then the white person says, "Where is your family from originally?" That is a racial microaggression. It's one I have engaged in more times than I can count. While the speech police believe that I was communicating a "hostile, derogatory, or racial slight" I was actually just interested in hearing about other cultures, and hearing about California or Iowa is decidedly less interesting than hearing about Korea or Egypt. I also frequently ask white people where their family originally came from, and am myself frequently asked that question. (It's Ireland.)

So what were the racial microaggressions that spawned the interruption of a class at the University of California at Los Angeles? One student alleged that when the professor changed her capitalization of the word "indigenous" to lowercase he was disrespecting her ideological point of view. Another proof point of racial animus was the professor's insistence that the students use the Chicago Manual of Style for citation format (the protesting students preferred the less formal American Psychological Association manual). After trying to speak with one male student from his class, the kindly seventy-nine-year-old professor was accused of battery for reaching out to touch him. The professor, Val Rust, a widely respected scholar in the field of comparative education, was hung out to dry by the UCLA administration, which treated a professor's stylistic changes to student papers as a racist attack. The school instructed Rust to stay off the Graduate School of Education and Information Services for one year.[37] In response to the various incidents, UCLA also commissioned an "Independent Investigative Report on Acts of Bias and Discrimination Involving Faculty at the University of California, Los Angeles." The report recommended investigations, saying that, "investigations might deter those who would engage in such conduct, even if their actions would likely not constitute a violation of university policy."[38]

(HAIR) TRIGGER WARNINGS

College students typically revel in satirical reviews. Not so among the illiberal left, if you choose the wrong target. University of Michigan student Omar Mahmood encountered the humorless speech police after he wrote a satirical column in late 2014 for the independent, student-run publication the *Michigan Review*. In a funny riff on political correctness on campuses, Mahmood—who describes himself as conservative and libertarian—wrote of his struggles as a man of color, having to face white privilege everywhere, including the "white snowflakes falling thick upon the autumn leaves, burying their colors." He wrote sarcastically of the indignities he faced for being left-handed and how his "humanity was reduced to my handydnyss." Mimicking the language of overwrought victimhood so prevalent among the illiberal left, he complained that, "the University of Michigan does literally nothing to combat the countless instances of violence we encounter every day. Whenever I walk into a classroom, I can hardly find a left-handyd desk to sit in. In big lecture halls, I'm met with countless stares as I walk up the aisle along the left-handyd column. The University cannot claim to be my school while it continues to oppress me."[39]

The column seemed to have hit too close to home. Mahmood, who also wrote for the campus newspaper the *Michigan Daily*, received a call from an editor there after his *Michigan Review* column ran. The editor informed Mahmood that his column created a "hostile environment" and that someone on the *Daily*'s editorial staff felt "threatened" by what he[40] wrote.[41] He was told he could only write for one of the two papers and, as a condition of staying on at the *Daily*—where they suspended his regular column—he would be required to write a letter of apology. Mahmood refused and FIRE intervened on his behalf. As of February 12, 2015, the paper had failed to reply to FIRE's inquiries.

Mahmood's column began with a "trigger warning," a phrase that is likely meaningless to anyone not schooled in the jargon of lefty university groupthink. He was wryly mocking the illiberal left's campaign in favor of "trigger warnings" on university syllabi so that students who might be "triggered" by certain content could opt out of completing assignments or attending classes that might upset them.

Oberlin College[42] found itself in the midst of a firestorm in 2014 after telling its professors that they should "avoid unnecessary triggers and provide trigger warnings." They defined a trigger as "something that recalls a traumatic event to an individual." Professors were urged to educate themselves about "racism, classism, sexism, heterosexism, cissexism, ableism, and other issues of privilege and oppression." The administrators explained, "Anything could be a trigger—a smell, song, scene, phrase, place, person, and so on. Some triggers cannot be anticipated, but many can."

How could any professor be expected to teach in such an environment? More importantly, why should they? Oberlin College administrators asserted that literally any topic could potentially "trigger" a student. The guidance continued, "Sometimes a work is too important to avoid. For example, Chinua Achebe's *Things Fall Apart* is a triumph of literature that everyone in the world should read. However, it may trigger readers who have experienced racism, colonialism, religious persecution, violence, suicide, and more." For such books, the university suggested professors issue a "trigger warning" because it would "show students that you care about their safety." Some professors had understandably expressed concern that trigger warnings would give away the plot of the assigned books. The university administrators were unmoved, arguing that "even if a trigger warning does contain a spoiler, experiencing a trigger is always, always worse than experiencing a spoiler."

Under these guidelines, it would be "unsafe" to assign most any book to most any student. Still, the professors were told to, "strongly consider developing a policy to make triggering material optional or offering students an alternative assignment using different materials. When possible, help students avoid having to choose between their academic success and their own wellbeing." These suggestions were met with concern and incredulity by many of the professors. Political science professor Marc Blecher told a reporter, "It would have a very chilling effect on what I say in class and on the syllabus." Meredith Raimondo, an associate dean who oversaw the committee[43] told the Associated Press that in response to protests from some faculty, the task force removed the controversial section and "plans to rewrite it with less 'emphatic-ness.'"

Echoing the concerns of the Oberlin administrators, an editor of George Washington University's student newspaper, Justin Peligri, wrote a 2014 column arguing for trigger warnings on syllabi as a "preventative measure" because the university "offers many politically-charged classes that explore controversial social issues."[44] Yes, that's generally the point of a college education. Over at Rutgers, student Philip Wythe asserted in a 2014 column in the campus newspaper that his university should also employ the use of trigger warnings.[45] Why? Because, he wrote, "literature courses often examine works with grotesque, disturbing and gruesome imagery within their narratives."

What kind of works did Wythe think pose a danger to his fellow students' mental health? He noted that, "F. Scott Fitzgerald's critically acclaimed novel, *The Great Gatsby*, possesses a variety of scenes that reference gory, abusive and misogynistic violence. Virginia Woolf's famous cerebral novel, *Mrs. Dalloway*, paints a disturbing narrative that examines the suicidal inclinations and post-traumatic experiences of an English war veteran. And Junot Díaz's critically acclaimed work, *This is How You Lose Her*, observes domestic violence and misogynistic culture in disturbing first-person narrations."

Thus Wythe helpfully suggested that *The Great Gatsby* might include the trigger warning: "TW: 'suicide,' 'domestic abuse' and 'graphic violence.'"

Is that what you think about when you read *The Great Gatsby*: suicide, domestic abuse, and graphic violence? Or might this classic novel tackle themes much larger than these bizarre "trigger warnings" suggest?

If a college student is going to be traumatized by *The Great Gatsby*, then they are going to find day-to-day life unbearable once they step outside the child-care programs that are passing for universities today. Rather than truly educate students, the illiberal left would rather "protect" students from some of the greatest works of American or world literature. Under these "trigger warning" rules, how would professors teach Dante or Shakespeare or just about any great book of literature beyond the narrowest politically correct confines?

In Lois Lowry's dystopian novel, *The Giver*, the author portrays an authoritarian society that has eradicated all bad memories from the world. People know nothing of racism, sexism, disease, or anything that might make them feel sad or uncomfortable. The world is left with unthinking robots with human skin. A character in the book explains why the government had to do this: "When people have the freedom to choose, they choose wrong." So, the illiberal left will choose for them.

The University of California-Santa Barbara is blazing the trigger warning trail. In March of 2014—the same month professor Miller-Young told the police officer that she attacked a student because she felt "triggered" by a demonstration[46]—the student government formally called on the university to mandate that all professors employ trigger warnings. "A Resolution to Mandate Warnings for Triggering Content in Academic Settings" demanded a policy that would require professors to alert students of potential triggering material and "allow...students to miss classes containing such material without losing course points."[47]

"Hypersensitivity to the trauma allegedly inflicted by listening to controversial ideas approaches a strange form of derangement—a disorder whose lethal spread in academia grows by the day," free speech advocate Harvey Silverglate noted in the *Wall Street Journal*. "What should be the object of derision, a focus for satire, is instead the subject of serious faux academic discussion and precautionary warnings. For this disorder there is no effective quarantine. A whole generation of students soon will have imbibed the warped notions of justice and entitlement now handed down as dogma in the universities."[48]

Students at Wellesley College employed the "triggering" concept to object to a statue of an underwear-clad man. One student started a Change. org petition insisting the statue be removed because it was "a source of apprehension, fear, and triggering thoughts regarding sexual assault."[49] Sruthi Narayanan, another offended student, posted a complaint that, "Our safe space—the only safe space for some of us—is being heavily compromised."[50] By a statue. Okay, a ridiculous statue. But if anything it deserved to be laughed at, not cast as a menacing threat. She lamented the "administration's decision to put up such a triggering statue without student consent." Another student, Megan Strait, complained that "not all students consented to this installation" and that due to the location students have no way to "opt out" of seeing the statue.

Do students think that once they graduate they will be able to "opt out" of anything they don't like? If colleges and universities encourage that attitude, they are not educating students; they are perpetuating their immaturity and fostering intolerance.

One voice of sanity responding to the petition to ban Wellesley's "Sleepwalker" statue was a student named Fani Ntavelou-Baum. She noted, "Reading this letter and the comments, I find what a student mentioned in one of my classes to be very true: 'In Wellesley you somehow have a position of power if you are the most offended person in the room.'"

We need to abandon the childish and illiberal idea that universities are meant to be emotionally "safe" places where students are never offended, never have to defend their beliefs, or never have to encounter a view or idea or fact they dislike. The goal of a college or university should be developing intellectual rigor that comes from the free clashing of ideas.

FIVE

INTOLERANCE 201

FREE SPEECH FOR ME BUT NOT FOR THEE

Shut up he explained.

—RING LARDNER

The phrase "free speech zone" should be jarring to any American. The entire country is, and should be, a free speech zone. Yet on many college campuses, the public expression of views is relegated to tiny spaces requiring university preapproval for use. According to the Foundation for Individual Rights in Education (FIRE), one in six of America's four hundred top colleges has so-called "free speech zones." The University of Cincinnati's (UC) free speech zone accounted for just 0.1 percent of the campus. Students were required to register ten days in advance of their planned expression of free speech, and if they failed to do so could be charged with trespassing.[1] The university abandoned their anti–free speech policy only after the campus branch of Young Americans for Liberty (YAL), a conservative student activist group, successfully sued the university with the help of FIRE.[2]

It seems absurd, except to the illiberal left, that on a college campus, sharing ideas, handing out flyers, even distributing copies of the Constitution, has to be relegated to a limited space controlled by university administrators.[3] Free speech zones ostensibly exist to create a "safe" environment for the expression and exchange of ideas. In reality, they serve as tools to regulate and discourage dissent and free speech. These bureaucratic roadblocks dissuade students from engaging in peaceful expression and protest, both of which should be regular occurrences on college campuses. According to FIRE "many students must wait five to ten business days to use a free speech zone." At many colleges, including Boston College, the dean of students has the authority to choose the time and place of any such demonstrations.[4] In 2014, students at the University of Central Florida noticed that their free speech zone, which previously included the entire patio in front of the Student Union, had been reduced to a tiny area of inclined grass.[5]

Courts have repeatedly held that a "free speech zone" on a public campus is unequivocally unconstitutional. Yet these zones continue to proliferate on the campuses of taxpayer-funded institutions like the University of Cincinnati, which had been warned beginning in 2007 that their speech regulations were unconstitutional. They changed their policy only after a court ordered them to cease from their violations of the First Amendment.[6] FIRE has determined that there are seventy schools in the United States that currently have unconstitutional "free speech zones." Greg Lukianoff, the Stanford Law School graduate who runs FIRE, says that sometimes it seems as though for every "free speech area" the courts strike down, another one pops up.[7]

Private universities are not *legally* barred from establishing "free speech areas," but you would think that institutions that brag about their openness to debate and the importance of diversity would shun the hypocrisy of free speech zones. But to the illiberal left, "debate" and "diversity" are not so broad as to include ideas with which they disagree.

Many of the incidents involving "free speech zones" would be funny if they weren't so chilling. A student[8] at Modesto Junior College in

California was denied the right to hand out copies of the U.S. Constitution on Constitution Day by campus police. He was informed by a clerical staffer in the Student Development office that there was no room in the "free speech area," which the staffer referred to as "that little cement area." Apparently two other students were expressing free speech that day and our budding free speech activist was informed the next available date for him to hand out U.S. Constitutions was several days hence, which obviously would no longer be Constitution Day.[9]

The U.S. Constitution seems to be a particular target of the illiberal left busybodies who dominate taxpayer-funded schools. In April 2014, two students sued the University of Hawaii at Hilo for preventing them from distributing the Constitution.[10] A few months later at Penn State, members of Young Americans for Freedom set up a table to hand out Constitutions.[11] The administration, which had violated its own previous commitment to dismantle the zones, told the YAF students that their use of a table to hand out material violated a university policy against unregistered structures.[12]

In 2014, at Miami-based Broward Community College, a conservative activist was ordered to go to the campus "free speech zone" by a campus security guard after asking a student if "big government sucks."[13] When the activist explained such zones were unconstitutional, the guard informed her, "If you just want to hang around I have a supervisor coming." The activist walked away, at which point the guard demanded to see her identification. She refused to provide it, because it is neither illegal to ask people questions nor is the United States yet the bureaucratic equivalent of East Germany. So what did the security guard do? He called the police, who showed up within minutes. The police politely asked her to leave, saying she was trespassing. Her group ultimately launched a Change.org petition asking Broward College to remove its "unconstitutional" free-speech zone.[14]

Unfortunately, if students want to exercise their right to free speech they often have to go to court against their own college or university. And it is not just students our colleges and universities aim to silence, it is anyone with an opposing point of view.

COMMENCEMENT SHAMING

It is becoming sadly predictable that whenever a prominent conservative, or even an insufficiently leftist liberal or moderate Democrat, is
invited to be a campus commencement speaker, that speaker is often forced
to withdraw because of student or faculty protests. I call it "commencement
shaming." What is intended to be an honor ends up in humiliation for the
invitee.

In 2014, for example, protests from lefty students and professors compelled two of the most accomplished women in the world—former U.S.
Secretary of State Condoleezza Rice and International Monetary Fund
chief Christine Lagarde—to withdraw from delivering commencement
speeches to Rutgers,[15] and Smith College, respectively.[16]

At Harvard's Graduate School of Education, students, alumni, and
faculty protested to demand the university rescind its commencement
invitation to Democratic State Senator Mike Johnston of Colorado, because
they disagreed with his policies on school reform. They questioned Johnston's claim to have been inspired by Dr. Martin Luther King Jr. and other
civil rights leaders and said they believed the Democratic senator's "vision
and policies have been informed far more by conservative economists…"[17]
Johnston saw what the students and faculty missed: an opportunity for
dialogue. He offered to meet with the protesters. Twenty-five protesting
students showed up for the meeting, and in the end his speech received a
standing ovation.[18]

Former New York City Mayor Michael Bloomberg, delivering the 2014
commencement speech to Harvard University, noted the alarming trend
on America's college campuses of silencing commencement speakers on
the basis of protests, often by a vocal minority. Bloomberg—who himself
had been the target of protests demanding his invitation to speak be with-
drawn—hit on the irony at the root of this phenomenon: it's "open-
minded" liberals who are leading the charge to limit the expression of
viewpoints on college campuses. He said, "In each case, liberals silenced a
voice [of] individuals they deemed politically objectionable. That is an

outrage." He added, "Today, on many college campuses, it is liberals trying to repress conservative ideas, even as conservative faculty members are at risk of becoming an endangered species."

Bloomberg continued: "Like other great universities, [Harvard] lies at the heart of the American experiment in democracy. Their purpose is not only to advance knowledge but to advance the ideals of our nation.... Tolerance for other people's ideas and the freedom to express your own are inseparable values at great universities," Bloomberg noted. "Joined together, they form a sacred trust that holds the basis of our democratic society. But that trust is perpetually vulnerable to the tyrannical tendencies of monarchs, mobs, and majorities. And lately, we've seen those tendencies manifest themselves too often both on college campuses and our society."

As explained in chapter one, the free-speech advocacy group FIRE has noted that in the six years from 2009 through 2014, the number of protests resulting in speech cancelations equals those from the previous twenty-two-year period at 62 instances each.[19] Clearly this is an accelerating trend. But liberals should not assume that they are safe from this roving campaign of intolerance. One of the 2014 commencement speakers felled by protesters was Robert J. Birgeneau, the former chancellor of the University of California-Berkeley—a man of impeccable liberal bona fides—who was invited to speak at Haverford College. But Haverford students and several professors complained about his leadership during a 2011 incident when UC police used force on students protesting college costs.[20] According to the *Philadelphia Inquirer*, Birgeneau received a letter stating that if he wanted to speak at the commencement, he must "meet nine conditions including publicly apologizing, supporting reparations for the victims, and writing a letter to Haverford students explaining his position on the events and 'what you learned from them.'"[21] Birgeneau understandably declined to meet their chilling demands and withdrew from providing the commencement speech.

The silencing isn't limited to commencement speeches. Even speeches meant to build bridges and tolerance for differing opinions are off limits.

Renowned Princeton professors Robert George and Cornel West have visited campuses to educate students on the importance of respectfully co-existing with people with whom you disagree. In 2014, they were invited to speak at Swarthmore College on the meaning of discourse. Known for their friendship despite their conflicting political views, they came to discuss topics such as, "What does it mean to communicate across differences regarding what is 'right' or 'wrong'?"

Many students at the famously liberal college protested that they did not want George, a conservative who opposes abortion and gay marriage, expressing his views on their campus. The event went forward. Afterwards, one student complained to the student newspaper that she was "really bothered" with "the whole idea...that at a liberal arts college we need to be hearing a diversity of opinion."[22] As ludicrous as that sounds, this view is far from an anomaly. This intolerant viewpoint is endemic among the illiberal left, which views opinions at odds with their ideological and political goals as illegitimate.

In October 2014, Scripps College canceled[23] a planned appearance by Pulitzer Prize–winning columnist George Will following protests over a column he wrote questioning the alleged epidemic of rape on college campuses. In it, he noted that, "when [colleges and universities] make victimhood a coveted status that confers privileges, victims proliferate."[24] He went on to question the validity of campus rape statistics. Women's groups and liberals in general were apoplectic. The controversy followed Will to Miami University in Ohio, where over one thousand students, faculty, and alumni signed an open letter requesting the university disinvite Will.[25] Another open letter from the university's Women's, Gender, and Sexuality Studies faculty asserted that in Will's column "he [was] engaging in hate speech as opposed to free speech" and accused him of "bullying" rather than seeking dialogue.[26]

Sorry, but Will's column, however upsetting it was to the Women's, Gender, and Sexuality Studies faculty, hardly registered as "hate speech." The faculty apparently missed the irony of trying to ban a columnist from speaking at their campus while condemning him for his alleged lack of interest in dialogue. Who is the bully here exactly?

One of the professors who objected to Will's appearance, Anita Mannur, director of the Women's, Gender, and Sexuality Studies program, told Media Matters, which was leading a harassment campaign against Will, "I am disappointed that a speaker who clearly does not respect women, or take the issue of sexual assault seriously, is being given a platform to speak, particularly because such inflammatory rhetoric has the potential to re-victimize and re-traumatize some of our students." Here again we are asked to believe that points of view skeptical of leftist assumptions, data, or campaign should be silenced because they might traumatize students. The final absurdity: Will was not even scheduled to speak to the Women's, Gender, and Sexuality Studies program, he was invited to lecture at Miami University's Farmer School of Business.

There was nothing in Will's column that implied he did not take sexual assault seriously, and certainly nothing that suggested he "does not respect women." But we see this tactic from the illiberal left all the time. Disagree with us, and we will smear you as a misogynist (or worse).

To their credit, Miami University's administration did not cave to the mob and the speech went forward. There were no reports of trauma units being overwhelmed at local hospitals following Will's lecture. But the controversy erupted again when Will was scheduled to be the graduation speaker at Michigan State University, along with documentary filmmaker Michael Moore, who of course has never said anything offensive about conservatives or anyone else. Despite protests, the university refused to cancel the speech, saying, "In any diverse community there are sure to be differences of opinion and perspective; something we celebrate as a learning community. We appreciate all views, and we hope and expect the MSU community will give the speaker the same respect."[27]

When Brandeis University was faced with the same kind of intolerant bullying of a prospective speaker, they chose appeasement over free speech. In 2014, after the historic university offered women's rights activist Ayaan

Hirsi Ali an honorary degree, they caved to student complaints and disinvited her. Hirsi Ali's unpardonable sin was her expression of fierce criticism of Islam, the religion of her birth and upbringing. It didn't matter that she was not being honored for any work related to Islam, the mere fact she was a critic was enough to delegitimize her. Hirsi Ali later complained that what was meant to be an honor had turned into a public shaming.

In 2013, Swarthmore alum and former president of the World Bank Robert Zoellick withdrew as the college's commencement speaker after students protested against him because he supported the Iraq War and served in George W. Bush's administration.[28] Prior to the withdrawal, a Swarthmore associate professor told a reporter that a "relatively small minority of students...have questioned Zoellick's appropriateness" but said most of the students were looking forward to his speech. Too bad for them: the minority mob won. That same year, Mayor Bloomberg's former police commissioner Ray Kelly was shouted down by students at Brown University and his speech had to be aborted after nearly thirty minutes of interruptions.[29]

Disrupting speeches has been a favorite tactic for the illiberal left if they are unsuccessful in getting the speech canceled in the first place. At the University of Chicago in 2009, former Israeli Prime Minister Ehud Olmert arrived to give what was meant to be a twenty-minute talk on leadership.[30] Thanks to protestors, who interrupted throughout, it took more than an hour.[31] A year later, the Israeli ambassador to the United States, Michael Oren, suffered through ten interruptions trying to deliver a speech at the University of California-Irvine.[32] At one point, Oren was forced to take a twenty-minute break mid-speech.[33]

In 2006, a series of speeches by anti-immigration reform leaders brought out the worst in liberal activists. Fire alarms were pulled to interrupt a speech by Republican Congressman Tom Tancredo at Michigan State's law school. The same tactic was used at Georgetown to disrupt a speech by Chris Simcox, a Minuteman Civil Defense Corps leader.[34] At Columbia, students rushed the stage, toppling tables and chairs and attacked Jim Gilchrist, the founder of the Minuteman Project, which works to keep illegal immigrants out of the United States. Marvin Stewart, an African American and a member of the Minuteman Project, who spoke with Gilchrist was booed by students who called him a racist, a sellout, and even a black supporter of white supremacy.[35]

The illiberal left often likes to invoke the importance of silencing people they claim have used "hate speech"—such as criticizing Islam or questioning rape statistics—when they demand bans on certain speakers. But as we can see, they have no problem using intimidation and hateful speech so long as it is directed at someone deviating from their worldview.

"THE WRONG KIND OF CHRISTIAN"

It's bad enough to have a speech canceled because illiberal malcontents have found something you've done offensive. What's worse is to have an entire organization forced off campus merely for adhering to their core values and religious beliefs.

In the fall of 2014, InterVarsity Christian Fellowship/USA was stripped of official recognition on the nineteen of twenty-three California State University (CSU) campuses where they had ministries. The Cal State system is the largest four-year college system in the United States, so this action was not insignificant. The cause of this de-recognition was an executive order by CSU Chancellor Charles Reed that included the requirement that "No campus shall recognize any fraternity, sorority, living group, honor society, or other student organization unless its membership and leadership are open to all currently enrolled students at that campus...."[36]

Referred to as an "all-comers policy" the executive order put InterVarsity, a multi-denominational student ministry that has maintained a presence on college campuses for more than seventy years, in an untenable position. They were being asked to choose between their faith and university policy. While InterVarsity welcomes all people—more than 25 percent of its participating students are non-Christians—they require their leaders to sign a statement of faith that they adhere to orthodox Christian doctrine.

CSU's lead attorney charged that InterVarsity would be engaging in discrimination rather than education if the group didn't allow atheists and others hostile to InterVarsity's beliefs to run for leadership positions in the organization.[37]

"It's an irony for us that, in the name of inclusion, they're eliminating religious groups because of their religious beliefs," InterVarsity's national field director Gregory Jao told the *Los Angeles Times*. "My understanding of an inclusive, welcoming university is to accept people based on their own beliefs. I'm inviting Cal State to live up to its best goals."[38]

In a statement expressing disappointment with CSU's decision, InterVarsity stated, "This new CSU policy does not allow us to require that our leaders be Christian. It is essentially asking InterVarsity chapters to change the core of our identity, and to change the way we operate in order to be an officially recognized student group. While we applaud inclusivity, we believe that faith-based communities like ours can only be led by people who clearly affirm historic Christian doctrine. And we do not believe it is appropriate for a government agency to dictate how religious organizations are led."

Cal State had told InterVarsity that they were compelled to institute this policy by a 1972 statute, according to InterVarsity head Alec Hill. Hill told me in a 2014 interview, "We haven't changed our national or local practice in 73 years. Cal State is now interpreting the statute in a new way. This whole experience has felt like it's Alice in Wonderland." When I asked Greg Lukianoff, the liberal atheist president of FIRE, whether there was any merit to the illiberal left's argument that the "all comers policies" were generic non-discrimination policies, he scoffed. "I've been doing this for 13 years and college after college that was specifically angry at evangelical groups for their position on gay rights…kept trying to figure out ways to keep them from being on-campus groups," he said.

In his 2012 book, *Unlearning Liberty*, Lukianoff wrote, "The fans of religious liberty for Muslims are often vehemently on the other side when the group in question is Christian. Between 2002 and 2009, dozens of colleges across the country threatened or derecognized Christian groups because of their refusal to say they would not 'discriminate' on the basis of belief. These colleges included, to name a few, Arizona State University, Brown University, California State University, Cornell University, Harvard University, Ohio State University, Pennsylvania State University, Princeton University, Purdue University, Rutgers University, Texas A&M University, Tufts University, the University of Arizona, the University of Florida, the University of Georgia, the University of Mary Washington, the University of New Mexico, the University of North Carolina at Chapel Hill, and Washington University."

Lukianoff told me, "University administrators have consistently targeted evangelical Christians, except in a few rare cases such as Louisiana State University where they went after a Muslim student group in 2003 for its position on homosexuality. In that case, when FIRE contacted LSU they quickly understood that they should not be telling a religious group what it should believe, but they seem to miss this lesson when it comes to evangelicals. When you look at these 'all comers' polices like the one in the Cal State System you need to understand that these are post hoc rationalizations for de-recognizing evangelical groups."[39]

Why is recognition important? A senior InterVarsity official told me, "Official recognition provides equal access to rooms on campus with other student clubs, participation in freshmen outreach with other clubs, and being on the university website clearly demonstrates that we are part of the academic community. Being unrecognized can create a stigma and may raise doubts about us in the eyes of students, parents, and the university community."

InterVarsity's concerns are often dismissed as paranoid delusion because, their critics argue, an atheist would never try to gain a position of leadership in their organization. Addressing this issue, First Amendment activist Harvey Silverglate, a liberal, wrote, "Given the heat that surrounds discussion of gay marriage and abortion, out-of-the-ordinary disruptive tactics—by either side against the other's organizations—are a realistic concern. This is one reason why in an earlier era beleaguered minority groups like the NAACP and gay-rights groups were most in need of, and usually received, official protection from those who would undermine them. In more recent years on college campuses the tables have turned, and religious groups that were once conventional now find themselves in need of protection."[40] Moreover, it's not remotely far-fetched to believe that a student in leadership who went away for the summer as a devout orthodox Christian could return as an atheist or even an adherent of another religion. InterVarsity reasonably sought to retain control over the decision of whether a leader who was contemptu-ous or even indifferent to their evangelical mission could be told to step down.

After Cal State decided to adopt the "all comers policy" InterVarsity tried to reach an accommodation with administrators. But in the end, they were granted only a one-year exemption. Cal State did give an exemption to fraternities and sororities, which were allowed to discriminate by sex, at least for now. That was a battle the university did not want to fight, as it might prove too unpopular with students and alumni. On college cam-puses, keg parties are not surprisingly more popular than Christian groups.

The list of campus Christian fellowship groups that have been stripped of official university status continues to grow, including, in recent years, groups at the State University of New York at Buffalo (SUNY), Tufts, Bow-doin, Rollins, and Vanderbilt, though SUNY at Buffalo later reversed itself.[41]

As the *New York Times*' Michael Paulson reported in June 2014, "For 40 years, evangelicals at Bowdoin College have gathered periodically to study the Bible together, to pray and to worship. They are a tiny minority on the liberal arts college campus, but they have been a part of the school's community, gathering in the chapel, the dining center, the dorms." But four decades of history with the school is of no concern to campus admin-istrators who demanded that the group open up its leadership elections to any student, including atheists.

Fourteen campus religious communities at Vanderbilt—comprising about 1,400 Catholic, evangelical, and Mormon students—lost their organizational status in 2012.[42] The *New York Times* reported that a university official asked a Christian student group to cut the words "personal commitment to Jesus Christ" from its list of qualifications for leadership.[43] The only commitment the illiberal left seems to tolerate is a commitment to progressive groupthink.

But even those who consider themselves progressive have learned that deviations from the illiberal left script is verboten. Tish Harrison Warren, the pastor running one of Vanderbilt's campus Christian organizations, bucked most orthodox Christian stereotypes. Warren wrote in *Christianity Today*, "I'm not a fundamentalist. My friends and I enjoy art, alcohol, and cultural engagement. We avoid spiritual clichés and buzzwords. We value authenticity, study, racial reconciliation, and social and environmental justice."[44] Warren discovered that no matter how progressive she was culturally—she's a woman pastor for crying out loud—if she held strong to religious values at odds with the dominant culture at Vanderbilt that made her "the wrong kind of Christian" as her piece was headlined. Her shared commitment to many important progressive political and policy issues was of no consequence to university administrators who had put campus Christian organizations in their crosshairs.

Warren had led the Graduate Christian Fellowship—a chapter of InterVarsity Christian Fellowship—for two years. The group, which consisted of Vanderbilt graduate students, had operated on campus for twelve years as an official student organization while requiring that leaders adhere to orthodox Christian doctrine. What changed? Warren attributes it to an incident where a student claimed he was kicked out of a Christian fraternity for being gay,[45] an allegation the fraternity denied.[46] Nonetheless, said Warren, the campus newspaper published the student's claim which naturally resulted in uproar. According to Warren, it was after this that Vanderbilt forbade campus groups from having any standards for those wanting to join or lead the group (except fraternities and sororities who were given an exemption to discriminate based on sex).

Warren tried to explain to Vanderbilt's administrators that the Christian group needed its student leaders to hold certain Christian doctrinal beliefs, but was told the group couldn't discriminate on the basis of anything [for leaders], including religious belief. At one point when she asked the administrators if they were really telling her that she couldn't require her Bible study leader to believe in the Trinity, they said that was exactly what they were telling her. On the one hand, it was dismissed as a silly issue because they said nobody would want to run a Bible study if they didn't believe in the Trinity.[47] (Warren pointed out that, actually, Unitarians reject the Trinity.) At the same time, she was told that having someone who didn't believe in the Trinity would be good because "It's important that many different views are represented and if a Jewish student wants to lead a Bible study, that's really good they're able to bring that perspective." She said that administrators would never address whether the gay rights groups should have to let a religious fundamentalist who opposed gay rights be a leader. It seems obvious, though, what the answer would be.

It also seems obvious that a Christian group should be allowed to have Christian leaders. "The function of campus ministry groups is devotional and proclamatory in that we have a specific message that we are proclaiming," Warren told me. "[Vanderbilt administrators] tried to make us about academic study or service or like a social group." Warren said the bottom line issue was they believed "that Christian groups were using doctrinal statements, even if they didn't mention sexuality (ours did not). They were worried that doctrinal statements (or creeds) were more or less a Trojan horse for discrimination against gay people. It's a real misunderstanding about religious faith and what drives religious people." Warren was being generous. It was beyond misunderstanding: it was astounding ignorance about one of the world's largest religions. One doesn't have to support InterVarsity's policy regarding leadership positions as it applies to gays and lesbians in committed relationships—I don't—to believe that the group should have a right to determine their own criteria for leadership. The same should be true of Muslim groups that share InterVarsity's orthodox view on sexuality.

As Vanderbilt was working to de-recognize the campus Christian groups, Warren said she heard from people in senior positions in the administration that if it were up to them the "all comers policy" would not go forward and they told her "I'm just doing my job and it's not worth losing my job over." There was a group of professors who penned an open letter against this policy, Warren recounted. But, said Warren, the professor leading the effort was warned by their department head "this could be career damaging for you." They pulled the letter at the eleventh hour.

The experience was painfully eye opening for Warren. "I was so surprised. [I]'ve never voted Republican. I'm not your stereotypical right-wing Christian," she said. While Warren described herself as "orthodox and evangelical" she was decidedly not fundamentalist, and yet that is how the university seemed to view her. "I had a lot of sorrow about the culture wars and the way Christians engaged in those," Warren said. "But I think I had an assumption that all the cultural warriors and all the fundamentalists were on the right. I realized through this process that they are on both sides." The difference of course is that Vanderbilt, like most secular universities, present themselves to the world as Enlightenment-bound, open-minded thinkers.

"Vanderbilt thinks they are operating out of a non-belief system but they are operating out of a belief system, and it's essentially [a kind of] progressive liberal theism... They repeatedly said how much they value religious groups on campus, but I think it's a certain kind of religious group. [They] want religious groups that are not orthodox in views of homosexuality," Warren told me. "Just come out and say it, put it in the flyer and let students know what they're getting into before they choose Vanderbilt... If [Vanderbilt] wants to be the Bob Jones or Liberty University of the Left, that's fine. The difference is that Bob Jones and Liberty are very honest about their preset positions and are very honest about who they are. [Vanderbilt should] say 'we don't like orthodox evangelical religious belief across the board.' Don't say, 'we love religious groups' and then gut our ability to self govern and practice in a meaningful way."

Warren's lament echoed that of the late Reverend Peter Gomes, the celebrated Harvard Divinity School theologian and Minister of Harvard's Memorial Church, who blasted the editors of the *Harvard Crimson* when they argued in 2003[48] that the Harvard Radcliffe Christian Fellowship (HRCF) should have been denied university recognition because of its "requirement that leadership believe in the holy spirit and resurrection of Jesus Christ." The editors alleged it violated Harvard's anti-discrimination policy. Gomes characterized this view as "foolish" and wrote that it "boggles the mind." Interestingly, Vanderbilt selected Gomes's book, *The Good Life* as required reading for Vanderbilt's freshman class of 2015 as part of an effort to teach them about ethics.[49] Perhaps they should make his scathing letter to the editor required reading as well.

In that letter, Gomes—himself a gay celibate man and also a vocal advocate for gays and lesbians[50] in the church—argued that opposing religious groups' right to discriminate based on doctrinal beliefs betrayed a "fundamental ignorance of the nature of religious belief, or a determination in the name of 'non-discrimination' to discriminate against a Christian student group which takes its Christian identity and principles seriously."[51] He explained what should have been obvious: "It does make an enormous difference to the integrity of a Christian club in the evangelical tradition if its leaders are unwilling to subscribe to the orthodox Christian beliefs to which the club is committed." He asked: "How can a profession of faith be irrelevant in the leadership of a faith-based group?" Gomes's frustration with the *Crimson*'s intolerant editorial was palpable throughout the letter, even though he himself did not embrace the orthodox view that homosexuality is a sin.[52]

He called the *Crimson*'s argument "not tolerant, neither is it pluralistic, nor inclusive. Let us call it what it is: hostile, rampantly secular, and overtly anti-Christian." He noted, "If there is any discrimination going on in this debate, it is the unseemly discrimination of *The Crimson* against an explicitly Christian student group, and the particulars of the faith which provides the basis of its identity."

Replace the *Crimson* with the names of a host of universities and colleges and all of the arguments are just as true today. The people who purport to believe in tolerance, diversity, and free speech in fact act like intolerant fundamentalists projecting their own narrow-mindedness onto Christian groups who merely want to be left alone to practice their faith and serve their campus communities.

TOLERANCE FOR ME, BUT NOT FOR THEE

While the illiberal left expects to be shielded from views they don't want to encounter, conservatives have to sit through classes with liberal professors in order to obtain a diploma. It's "hate speech" to hold an anti-abortion protest, but you can say pretty much whatever you want to a conservative without worrying about the long arm of campus justice coming down on you. Omar Mahmood, the Muslim student at the University of Michigan who wrote the satirical essay ridiculing political correctness that got him booted from the student newspaper, had his apartment vandalized after the column ran.[53] Mahmood told the *College Fix* that he considers himself a political conservative and holds views at odds with most other Muslims on campus. This can't be tolerated. According to the *College Fix*, "the vandalism posted on [his] apartment door stated 'you scum embarrass us,' 'you self-righteous d-ck,' 'you have no soul,' 'everyone hates you you violent pr-ck.'" There was also an image of the devil, and hot dogs and eggs had been thrown at his door.

If you are a conservative—or even a liberal who says something deemed conservative—your speech will get canceled or your award revoked for taking a view at odds with liberal dogma. Ayaan Hirsi Ali's honorary degree at Brandeis was yanked for slamming Islam, but nobody blinked when at a 2007 Smith Commencement address, Gloria Steinem compared people who oppose abortion and same-sex marriage to "Germany under fascism."[54] Moreover, there's no "trigger warning" for conservative students who are regularly confronted with ideological and philosophical views they find offensive or may even violate their religious beliefs. Nor have conservative students demanded them. It seems that what most non-left students desire is the simple right to determine their own views and express them freely without fear of retribution. This reasonable desire is a bridge too far for the illiberal left.

SIX

THE WAR ON FOX NEWS

*[Presidents] inherit traditions that make us greater than
the challenges we face. And one of those traditions is... a
free press that isn't afraid to ask questions, to examine
and to criticize.*[1]

—PRESIDENT BARACK OBAMA, APRIL 2012

S peaking at his first White House Correspondents' Dinner in 2009,
the new president of the United States opened with a joke to the
assembled media: "I am Barack Obama. Most of you covered me.
All of you voted for me. (Laughter and applause.) Apologies to the Fox
table. (Laughter.)"[2]

The president's light-hearted barb at Fox News was harmless on its face
and if it had been left at just a little tension between a White House and a
news organization, that would have been typical. Instead, it was a precursor to something much more ominous: a war on dissent by the White
House, starting with that outlier of the media, Fox News.

The president's joke evoked laughter because it hit on an underlying
truth: the media had been mostly in the tank for Obama during his historic
campaign for the White House, and had ushered the first African American president into Washington with glowing and fawning coverage. But
as compliant as the media corps had been, it wouldn't be enough for

President Obama or his White House. Instead, the president elected on a promise of unprecedented transparency would go down as one of the least transparent in history, drawing unflattering comparisons to President Richard Nixon. The media would ultimately grow frustrated and angry by their lack of access and the strong-arm tactics of Hope and Change, Inc.

The White House's obsession with delegitimizing Fox News was the canary in the coal mine. A mere seven months into his first term, President Obama complained to CNBC's John Harwood: "I've got one television station that is entirely devoted to attacking my administration.... You'd be hard pressed if you watched the entire day to find a positive story about me on that front."[3] Imagine for a moment that you were a Republican president, and you only had "one television station" attacking your administration. You'd be breaking out the champagne, not complaining about it.

Republicans accept as a well-documented fact of life that an overwhelming majority of the media is slanted against them.[4] They take critical media coverage for granted. The Obama administration does not. So much so that harsh criticism by a news outlet is viewed as intolerable dissent. Moreover, this broadside from the president of the United States was not buttressed by facts. Pew Research Center found that from September 8 through October 16 of the 2008 campaign—the heat of the election cycle—40 percent of Fox News stories on then-Senator Obama were negative as were 40 percent of the network's stories on Senator John McCain, Obama's Republican opponent. You can't get more fair and balanced than that. If you wanted to see bias against a candidate, CNN and MSNBC were better examples. Pew found that 61 percent of CNN's stories on John McCain were negative, compared to only 39 percent of their Obama stories. The disparity was even greater at MSNBC where a mere 14 percent of Obama stories were negative, compared to a whopping 73 percent of McCain stories (and only 10 percent of MSNBC's coverage of McCain was rated as positive). Overall, according to an October 2007 study of media coverage of the 2008 presidential campaign by the Project for Excellence in Journalism (funded by Pew) in collaboration with Harvard's Joan Shorenstein Center for Press, Politics and Public Policy, the press gave much more favorable coverage to Democratic candidates, noting, for example, that 46.7 percent of stories about Barack Obama had a positive tone, while only 12.4 percent of stories about John McCain did.[5] Obama should have been counting his blessings, not complaining about the one news television outlet that wouldn't fall in line. He had received, by some measures, the most laudatory press coverage of any senatorial or presidential candidate in recent history.[6]

It seemed that President Obama had come to expect nothing but media praise and ruled all criticism illegitimate. A few months after the president's interview with Harwood, the White House made an unprecedented effort to delegitimize a major news network. "What I think is fair to say about Fox—and certainly it's the way we view it—is that it really is more a wing of the Republican Party," said Anita Dunn, White House communications director, on CNN on October 11, 2009. "They take their talking points, put them on the air; take their opposition research, put them on the air. And that's fine. But let's not pretend they're a news network the way CNN is."[7] Dunn offered little evidence for what she said—nor did she apparently see any irony in a liberal administration, which should believe in freedom of the press, telling the American people which media outlets had government approval and which did not.

Evidence was not needed, of course, because it has long been a trope of the illiberal left that Fox News is a "right-wing mouthpiece," "isn't a legitimate news channel,"[8] and "should be treated as a right-wing misinformation network, not legitimized as a neutral source of news."[9] as MoveOn.org charged in 2007.[10] In 2007, left-wing blogger Matt Stoller penned an op-ed in *Politico* titled "Republican Propaganda Is Not News." He alleged that Fox News might be "controlled by the Republican Party itself" and warned against treating it as a "legitimate news channel."[11]

In September 2009, the White House had fired a warning shot, cutting veteran reporter and *Fox News Sunday* anchor Chris Wallace out of a round of interviews with the president on healthcare reform. White House Communications Director Anita Dunn conceded that CNN, NBC, ABC, and CBS were included, but Fox was excluded because the administration did not like the way Fox covered the administration.[12] Deputy White House Communications Director Dan Pfeiffer explained the snub to the *New York Times*: "We simply decided to stop abiding by the fiction, which is aided and abetted by the mainstream press, that Fox is a traditional news organization."[13]

Though some media outlets chortled at Obama's denunciation of a rival, others, to their credit, saw that something wasn't quite right. *Time* magazine's Michael Scherer, for instance, noted that the administration's "take-no-prisoners turn has come as a surprise to some in the press, considering the largely favorable coverage that candidate Obama received last fall and given the President's vows to lower the rhetorical temperature in Washington and not pay attention to cable hyperbole. Instead, the White House blog now issues regular denunciations of the Administration's critics, including a recent post that announced 'Fox lies' and suggested that the cable network was unpatriotic for criticizing Obama's 2016 Olympics effort."[14]

New York Times media reporter Brian Stelter followed up on October 11, 2009, stating that "Attacking the news media is a time-honored White House tactic but to an unusual degree, the Obama administration has narrowed its sights to one specific organization, the Fox News Channel, calling it, in essence, part of the political opposition."[15]

Despite some doubts in corners of the media, the Obama administration was unrepentant and continued their delegitimization campaign. On October 18, 2009, White House Senior Advisor David Axelrod said on ABC's *This Week* that the Fox News Channel is "not really a news station" and that much of its programming is "not really news."[16] Declared Axelrod, "The only argument [White House Communications Director] Anita [Dunn] was making is that they're not really a news station if you watch even—it's not just their commentators, but a lot of their news programming." Axelrod went on to inform ABC that when it came to Fox News, "It's really not news—it's pushing a point of view. And the bigger thing is that other news organizations like yours ought not to treat them that way, and we're not going to treat them that way." This echoed the message that White House Chief of Staff Rahm Emanuel delivered the same day to CNN. It wasn't just that Fox News was "not a news organization," Emanuel told John King on CNN's *State of the Union*, but, "more [important], is [to] not have the CNNs and the others in the world basically be led in following Fox, as if what they're trying to do is a legitimate news organization...."[17] This is an astounding statement for a government official to make.

No less astounding was the president himself weighing in, telling NBC News that his senior staff's attacks on Fox News were justified. "What our advisers have simply said is that we are going to take media as it comes. And if media is operating, basically, as a talk radio format, then that's one thing. And if it's operating as a news outlet, then that's another."[18] Of course, in reality, Fox is less given to "a talk radio format" than some of its rivals. A 2013 Pew study found, for instance, that on MSNBC opinion programming accounted for "fully 85% of the channel's airtime."[19] Only 15 percent of MSNBC's news coverage was "factual reporting." In contrast, Pew found that 55 percent of Fox News coverage was opinion and 45 percent was factual reporting.[20] But there was no administration war on MSNBC, because that network slants heavily to the left.

CBS Evening News anchor Katie Couric noted the administration's concentrated attack on Fox News, saying, "Politicians and the media have long had a contentious relationship. It's part of the American system. But we've never seen anything quite as intense as the feud between President Obama and the Fox News Channel."[21] But describing the coordinated attack on Fox News as a "feud" was misleading. Fox News was doing its job—reporting on, analyzing, and at times criticizing the administration. The administration was not, unless we think it is the job of the federal government to treat dissenting media voices as illegitimate. Veteran political reporter Jeff Greenfield, then at CBS, asked, "Why is the White House out to delegitimize Fox?" He concluded that the reason wasn't that Fox had opinion-based shows—so, after all, did MSNBC—but that Fox had hosts who were critical of Obama, and "Fox News is.... the most watched of the cable news networks, including a fair chunk of Democrats and independents."[22]

The administration's campaign received a boost from David Brock, CEO of Media Matters for America (MMFA). Media Matters is a nonprofit funded[23] by tax-deductible donations from major liberal donors.[24] Its stated mission is to monitor the media "for conservative misinformation."[25] Monitoring the media is obviously a good thing; the media should be held accountable, including Fox News. When Media Matters first launched I was supportive of them, and found some of their research helpful. But over time it became apparent that Media Matters was itself a vicious left-wing propaganda machine masquerading as a media monitoring operation. *New York Times* columnist Maureen Dowd noted in a 2015 column that David Brock—who previously aligned himself with right-wing politics—"has tried to discredit anyone who disagreed with his ideological hits.... And that's still the business he's in, simply on the other side as a Hillary [Clinton] zealot."[26]

On October 22, 2009, Brock sent a letter[27] to progressive organizations. In it, he cheered the administration's war on Fox. Brock wrote, "In recent days, a new level of scrutiny has been directed toward Fox News, in no small part due to statements from the White House, and from Media Matters, challenging its standing as a news organization."[28] Brock called Fox "lethal" and "too dangerous to ignore." He echoed the administration party line, complaining that, "Too many reporters and commentators have continued to treat Fox as a news organization."

In late October 2009, the Obama administration upped its war on Fox, by trying to bar Fox News reporters from interviewing the administration's "pay czar" Kenneth Feinberg. This was too much even for the pro-Obama media. The Washington bureau chiefs of ABC, CBS, NBC, and CNN refused to do their interviews with Feinberg unless Fox News was included.

The administration then relented and granted an interview to Fox News White House Correspondent Major Garrett.

When Fox News reported on the incident,[29] the Obama administration told reporters from other outlets that Fox News was making up the story.[30] The Associated Press reported that the administration denied excluding Fox News, saying instead that Fox News was excluded because they hadn't asked for an interview. Some journalists went along with the Obama party line. Christina Bellantoni—now the editor-in-chief of *Roll Call*—reported for Talking Points Memo DC that she had dug into "the version Fox has pushed all day"[31] and discovered that what really happened was the "Treasury [Department] called the White House pool crew and gave them the list of the networks who'd asked for the interview. The network pool crew noticed Fox wasn't on the list, was told that they hadn't asked and the crew said they needed to be included." She quoted a Treasury spokesperson saying, "There was no plot to exclude Fox News, and they had the same interview that their competitors did. Much ado about absolutely nothing."

The administration was lying to Bellantoni and the Associated Press. Internal e-mails obtained by Judicial Watch in 2011 revealed that on October 22, 2009, the White House director of broadcast media had e-mailed the Treasury department approving the inclusion of cable networks to interview Feinberg, but added, "We'd prefer if you skip Fox please."[32]

Contrary to the Obama administration's spin, many mainstream reporters knew exactly what had happened. Jeff Greenfield reported on *CBS Evening News*, "the Treasury Department tried to exclude Fox News from pool coverage of interviews with one of its key officials. It backed down after strong protests from the press." Then-CBS White House Correspondent Chip Reid noted that, "All the networks said, 'That's it, you've crossed the line.'"[33] CBS News D.C. Bureau Chief Christopher Isham, who served as the pool chair, told *Mediaite* that "he convened a conference call and all the bureau chiefs agreed they were not comfortable with excluding one of the members of the pool in a pool interview."[34]

Perhaps the White House didn't know that Fox News' then–Senior Vice President Michael Clemente had spent two years at CNN and twenty-seven at ABC News. It wasn't that hard to find out what had really happened.

In a January 2015 interview, Clemente told me, "I saw [White House Press Secretary Robert] Gibbs right after it happened and he said, 'It was a mistake, what can we do to put this behind us?' I said, 'We didn't start this, so just act normal and consider it over.' We shook hands and that was it."

Unfortunately, this wouldn't be the last time the White House cut Fox News out of briefings. Fox News host Greta Van Susteren noted that, "In the early days after Benghazi [when four Americans, including American ambassador to Libya, J. Christopher Stevens, were killed by terrorists] the State Department omitted only Fox News Channel from its conference call to all the media when it claimed to be answering questions about Benghazi for the media. Our friends in other media outlets were scandalized that Fox was not included and told us all about it. They were suspicious of the State Department forgetting us/Fox and courageous to tip us off. The State Department claimed it was [an] accident and not intentional. And then shortly thereafter, there was the CIA briefing about Benghazi at the CIA for all the networks—except one: Fox News Channel. The CIA would not let Fox News Channel attend."[35]

ABC's Jake Tapper queried White House Press Secretary Robert Gibbs about the administration's overt hostility to Fox News.[36]

> TAPPER: It's escaped none of our notice that the White House has decided in the last few weeks to declare one of our sister organizations "not a news organization" and to tell the rest of us not to treat them like a news organization. Can you explain why it's appropriate for the White House to decide that a news organization is not one—
> (Crosstalk)

GIBBS: Jake, we render, we render an opinion based on some of their coverage and the fairness that, the fairness of that coverage.

TAPPER: But that's a pretty sweeping declaration that they are "not a news organization." How are they any different from, say—

GIBBS: ABC—

TAPPER: ABC. MSNBC. Univision. I mean how are they any different?

GIBBS: You and I should watch sometime around 9 o'clock tonight. Or 5 o'clock this afternoon.

TAPPER: I'm not talking about their opinion programming or issues you have with certain reports. I'm talking about saying thousands of individuals who work for a media organization, do not work for a "news organization"—why is that appropriate for the White House to say?

GIBBS: That's our opinion.[37]

The administration continued to couch its assault on Fox News as a mere matter of "opinion" as if comments and actions by the White House press secretary, the White House chief of staff, and the president of the United States were akin to a college dorm room bull session. When I asked former Clinton White House Press Secretary Mike McCurry if it was appropriate for a White House to operate in this fashion, he said, "Fox [is] a member of the network pool. Trying to decide what represents legitimacy... is a very dangerous business because you run the risk of only speaking to the audiences that agree with you. If you are only narrowcasting to your own supporters you are never going to persuade people in the middle. That damages the country."

"We had plenty of people who were conservative [covering us]. I don't remember ever saying I'm not going to deal with you because you are illegitimate," McCurry noted. "Brit [Hume] was the ABC News White

House Reporter and was openly conservative. Brit would be doing a cross-word puzzle and I tried to spin something and he'd look up and say, 'Could you repeat that?' and I'd say, 'Damn, Brit caught me.'"[38]

He recalled how he had once dismissed a question from a reporter because she cited the Drudge Report. The reporter backed off, McCurry recalled, and following the briefing he was approached by other reporters who told him, "You can't decide what we get to ask" and "You don't get to decide what is a legitimate question." McCurry realized they were right. At another point he said, "Brit told me privately, 'You are the most political press secretary in history.' I actually took that to heart and I toned it down."[39]

McCurry realized that when a press secretary becomes too political it is degrading to the office. "Elected officials have to be accountable to people who are challenging them," McCurry told me in our interview. "I think the distinction has to be between dealing with those who are opinionated and those who are reporting. Even if [a reporter is the] only one pursuing this line of inquiry, as long as it's a reporter.... you have some obligation to deal with them."

GOOD NEWS, BAD NEWS

It might be instructive to consider what the White House considers "legitimate media." Obama granted a coveted post 2012 election interview to then twenty-nine-year-old zillionaire Chris Hughes, who had recently bought the *New Republic*. Hughes had also been a major Obama campaign donor and organizer who was featured on the cover of *Fast Company* with the headline, "The Kid Who Made Obama President." When Hughes and TNR editor-in-chief Franklin Foer sat down with Obama, the president took the opportunity to complain that more Republican members of Congress would work with Democrats if they were not "punished on Fox News." Fox News, in other words, is to be blamed for government gridlock. On the other hand, the mainstream media, as represented perhaps by the

New Republic, owned by his interviewer and supporter, was portrayed as a public good. "The more left-leaning media outlets recognize that compromise is not a dirty word," he said, and Democratic leaders are "willing to buck the more absolutist-wing elements in our party to try to get stuff done."[40] Of course, the *New Republic* did not challenge this baseless assertion, which a single night's viewing of MSNBC would disprove.

The administration, of course, has had no problem with MSNBC's former and current highly opinionated hosts Rachel Maddow, Keith Olbermann, or Ed Schultz. But the illiberal left condemns Fox News, which has plenty of straight news programming, purely because it has hosts who are conservative, *even if those hosts give air time to liberals.* I'm often challenged by liberals about working for the channel. Sometimes the challenge is a little less than friendly. In 2011 I was seated near Gloria Steinem at a luncheon. At one point, she turned to me and asked, "Why do you go on Fox?" She said my appearances came at "such a great cost." I was shocked, but said what I assumed every real liberal would say: it's important to debate ideas. She was unconvinced. When I told her she should go on the network, she disdainfully replied, "I would never go on Fox." But the fact is Fox is demonstrably fairer than its cable competition. A March 2014 *Columbia Journalism Review* article noted that, "Though MSNBC has a handful of moderate conservatives—namely *Morning Joe's* Joe Scarborough—Fox stands out for the prominence it awards its on-air naysayers, many of whom occupy regular roles on the network's most popular shows."[41] They noted, "While the liberal hosts of MSNBC often skewer conservatives, the debates happen with villains who are not in the studio: lambasted, by proxy, in news clips. At Fox, they happen in person, with a real-live liberal who is often on staff."

Not only does Fox give air time to people who are left of center, but a fair portion of its audience is comprised of Democrats and independents. Longtime Democratic strategist Joe Trippi, a Fox News contributor, told the *New Republic,* "My reading of the numbers is that more Democrats and independents watch Fox than CNN and MSNBC. Pew just did a study that showed that thirty percent of Fox's audience are Democrats." If you do the math, Trippi said, "Fox has two million people watching, and MSNBC has six hundred thousand. So for MSNBC to have more Democrats watching, every single person watching MSNBC would have to be a Democrat. So it never made much sense to not have people arguing the progressive side of things to that audience."[42]

When I discussed the obsession with delegitimizing Fox News with Trippi in 2015 he told me, "From a crass political standpoint it doesn't make sense. Which Democrats do you think are the persuadable Democrats you need to get your message to—those at Fox or MSNBC?" Clearly, people watching MSNBC are on board with the Democratic cause. They don't need a push. Trippi noted that in addition to the Democrats watching Fox News there are the independent moderates who are so critical to winning elections. "It's never made any sense to me that I wouldn't get my view to an audience this big and more diverse. The more people think through the arguments it doesn't make sense. Just going through polling data it's [clear Fox is] not this monolithic audience," Trippi said.

Obviously Democrats and liberals have access to the Pew data. They know that Democrats and independents are watching Fox, and that seems to be the problem.

How has Trippi found life at Fox? "No one at Fox has ever [gotten] . . . upset because I said something pro-Obama or pro-gay marriage," said Trippi. "[But] I have progressives who are mad at me for being at Fox. It's an ideological thing, because God forbid that I happen to agree with O'Reilly on something; that I might have an open enough mind to agree with him. You take more heat when that happens from progressives than from anybody at Fox. Nobody [at Fox] has ever told me to say anything."

In fact, Trippi—who was previously a contributor at CBS and MSNBC—told the *New Republic* that working as a Fox News contributor was the best media experience he had ever had. It's the best media experience I've ever had too.

Part of that is because, contra the Obama administration, Fox News is a serious news organization that open-minded liberals can respect. *Special Report with Bret Baier*, for instance, one of the best news shows on cable, "frequently beats the ABC or CBS newscasts in select markets, including Atlanta, St. Louis, and even Baltimore, a Democratic stronghold," according to the *New York Times*.[43] Left of center columnist Joe Klein, bemoaning how television news is turning away from covering politics and government, praised *Special Report* as the only "straight newscast" in its time slot.[44]

Fox News commentators and reporters include the likes of George Will and Charles Krauthammer, both Pulitzer Prize–winning columnists; *Fortune* magazine senior editor Nina Easton; Emmy Award–winning veteran reporters Brit Hume and Chris Wallace; two CNN veterans in Ed Henry, former White House Correspondents Association Board President, and Emmy Award–winner John Roberts; and straight arrow reporters Carl Cameron and Shepard Smith, who are respected by not only conservatives, but open-minded liberals, if not the Obama administration. And of course there are many others, but the point is that Fox has an array of respected professional journalists that would be the pride of any network. But the illiberal left cannot tolerate dissent, and so treats Fox News as a pariah.

THE LEFT'S WAR ON FOX WOMEN

One of the worst aspects of the illiberal left is its heinous sexism against women with whom they disagree.

Megyn Kelly, a former lawyer, is a serious and highly successful television journalist. When her contract was up for renewal in 2013, the *New York Times* reported that both CNN and NBC wanted to hire her away from Fox,[45] a strange thing to desire if Fox News is not a "legitimate" news outlet.

But to the illiberal left, Megyn Kelly is not a reporter or a commentator or a woman to be respected for her achievements. She is a Fox "babe" to be characterized by her looks. The Huffington Post linked to a *New York Times* story about Kelly adding the headline, "Megyn Kelly, 'Attractive-Looking Blond' Anchorwoman, Leads the Pack at Fox News,"[46] twisting a flattering quote from the story to make it seem as if the only positive attribute she possessed were her looks. Over at the feminist website Jezebel, where they are all about being "pro-woman," one writer said she liked Kelly the way she did "Ursula from the Little Mermaid," adding that she "sort of" loved her despite Kelly being "largely a horrible, terrible person with many horrible, stupid thoughts and opinions." This was the same "feminist" site that had previously described the prime-time host and former corporate litigator as a "Fox Newsbot."[47]

It is also a website that the illiberal left considers a "legitimate" news source, as there were no complaints when MSNBC hired former Salon. com columnist Irin Carmon, who also happened to be a former blogger for Jezebel,[48] to be a national reporter to cover politics and women's issues. The outspoken liberal feminist and supporter of Democrats has a fellowship at Yale University on Reproductive Justice. (Imagine if Fox News hired a conservative "pro-life" blogger and gave her the title of national reporter and had her covering women's issues.) The website Capital New York ran a January 2015 profile on Carmon, in which they asked her, "Was it a tough adjustment going from opinionated blogging with a strong voice to reporting for cable news?" Carmon explained that, "Well, we get to do some opinionating and strong voice-ing on the air around here...but I've always seen myself as a reporter first...."[49] At Fox News there is a sharp distinction between commentators and opinion hosts and reporters. In the media corners of the illiberal left, not so much. Carmon explained that, "there's so much more space now for reporting with a passionate point of view, which is where I see my own work, than there was even a few years ago when I was starting out."

If Carmon is an example of a woman the illiberal left considers a legitimate journalist, Megyn Kelly is someone the illiberal left tries to delegitimize through the oldest sexist trick in the book—objectifying her as a woman. In 2010, the *New Republic*'s Jonathan Chait posted a screenshot of Kelly seemingly in mid-sentence under the headline, "The Quintessential Fox News Image." He wrote: "Everything you need to know about Fox News is captured in this screenshot: the American flags, the fear-mongering image in the upper-right corner, the blond anchor with a facial expression that somehow combines sneering with absolute terror."[50] Kelly wasn't sneering or looking frightened, though she is blonde and is on Fox which to the illiberal left means she's a nameless "blond anchor" and candidate for being objectified and dehumanized.

Liberal journalist Lee Siegel[51] wrote for *Men's Journal* explaining to liberal men what they were missing about "the blondes of Fox News." He explained how fun it was to watch them, as "Fox women are studies in passive-aggressive revolt against their ideological masters." These "masters" are white men who the "Fox women" secretly believe are "fools." His article was headlined, "The Right, Hot, and Bothered Blondes of Fox News: One man's guilty obsession with Megyn Kelly and the blondes of Fox News." He explained his liberal brethren needed to appreciate that, "Most blonde anchors on Fox are dyed blondes," and a woman who dyes her hair blonde has "on some level, subordinated her will to male desire." But there's more. The Fox News blonde "is also dangerous. She has another identity concealed by the one she submissively shares with you. Lurking within every Fox blonde is a CNN brunette." He closed with, "Fox blondes hold out the promise of rational intelligence and sexual gratification—two precious and tragically incompatible human qualities. Of all the shameless lies Fox tells, that beautiful illusion may be the most potent."

VH1.com ran a July feature, "Meet the Blondes of Fox News" featuring a picture of Megyn Kelly, Dana Perino, and Elisabeth Hasselbeck along with a photo gallery of a few of Fox's female journalists. "If you thought Fox News Channel was just a boys club, think again," VH1 exclaimed. (Who ever thought that?) They went on to explain that yes, Fox hires women, "but they're not necessarily adding sensibility to Fox News' reporting. We're all for strong women in the newsroom, but we're not sure if Fox

News' blondes fit that bill." In particular, they explained that "Fox News' blonde bombshells" such as Megyn Kelly "can't be taken seriously" and included Greta Van Susteren, who holds a law degree from Georgetown and whose show *On the Record* has been top in its time slot for more than a decade, and Laura Ingraham, who holds a law degree from the University of Virginia, in their roundup of dumb blondes.

Allure, a women's beauty magazine, ran a poem by one of their editors, David DeNicolo, under the headline "Fox News Anchors: Hot or Not? With its bevy of babes, the network should be called the Foxy News Channel." DeNicolo rhymed about the legs and hair and "gleaming smiles" of Fox News anchors and then, "Sure, Rachel Maddow has the smarts, But can she work her giggly parts?"

Jonathan Chait at *New York* magazine wrote: "If you have never seen Fox News before, here is a four-minute clip that captures the essence of the network so perfectly that you need never watch anything on it again. It's all here. At the center, you have an old conservative white guy who is enraged about a fact that exists only in his addled brain. At his side, there's a blonde sidekick who nods along with him but doesn't get in the way."[52] The alleged cipher and "blonde sidekick" was Monica Crowley, a conservative radio host who holds a Ph.D. from Columbia University in international affairs.

So pervasive is the smear that all the female commentators and anchors on Fox are dumb blonde chicks that it was actually fact-checked by PolitiFact. That's not a joke. They analyzed the female hosts' and anchors' hair color and found the assertion "mostly false,"[53] because Fox had its fair share of black-haired and brunette women.

What might have been more elevating was recognizing the achievements of Fox News' female anchors, reporters, and commentators. Mentioning for instance that Gretchen Carlson is an Emmy Award–winning reporter who used to work for CBS, or that Kimberly Guilfoyle of *The Five* is a former assistant district attorney, or that Jeanine Pirro is a former judge and district attorney. But acknowledging the talent and achievements of the people who work at Fox News contradicts the illiberal left's propaganda that Fox News is somehow illegitimate. It is only "illegitimate" because the illiberal left wants to silence dissent and seeks to do so not through besting its opponents in argument and debate but through the lowest form of scurrilous sexism or simple refusal to tolerate other points of view.

THE WAR ON FOX INTENSIFIES

By 2011, Media Matters was dedicating almost its entire $10 million annual budget to the destruction of Fox News. *Politico*'s Ben Smith reported, "The liberal group Media Matters has quietly transformed itself in preparation for what its founder, David Brock, described in an interview as an all-out campaign of 'guerrilla warfare and sabotage' aimed at the Fox News Channel."[54]

While Media Matters pretended to *Politico* that the organization had "transformed" itself into a vehicle to shut down Fox News; in fact its purpose had long been to harass anyone who deviates from leftist dogma and, in particular, delegitimize Fox. It says something that Media Matters felt comfortable being so transparent about its purpose, which involved "sabotaging" a news organization. More noteworthy is how little interest there was in this "transformation." It's hard to imagine such a collective yawn if a conservative organization was annually spending $10 million of some of the Republican Party's highest profile donors' money to destroy a media outlet, especially if the president of the United States (let's just say President George W. Bush, for example) was joining in the fun.

Media Matters outlined its McCarthyite campaign in a 2010 memo to liberal donors which was provided to *Politico*. In it, Media Matters complained of the "pervasive unwillingness among members of the media to officially kick Fox News to the curb of the press club" and outlined how they planned to change that through targeting elite media figures and turning them against Fox. They shared a plan to set up a legal fund to sue (harass) conservatives for any "slanderous" comments they make about progressives on air. They outlined how they had plans to assemble opposition research on Fox News employees. Incredibly, this "progressive organization" identified one of the best journalists around, Jake Tapper, as a problem because he questioned the White House about calling Fox News "illegitimate." Media Matters, like the Obama administration, not only thought Fox News was illegitimate: they would only be satisfied when the mainstream media as a whole adopted their viewpoint.

In their strategy memo, Media Matters complained about "an expansive view of legal precedent protecting the freedom of the press" and described the "progressive movement's own commitment to the First Amendment" as an impediment to be overcome or changed. Media Matters was "consider[ing] pushing prominent progressives to stop appearing on Fox News"—putting Media Matters in the rather odd position of claiming that Fox doesn't give sufficient airtime to "progressive" points of view while Media Matters itself plotted to keep "prominent progressives" off the channel. The memo stated that Media Matters was considering publishing the names of Democrats who appeared on the channel as a way to shame them. If that didn't work, presumably they could just shave their heads and march them down Constitution Avenue.

FOX NEWS DERANGEMENT SYNDROME

It is astonishing to me as a liberal not only how illiberal so many self-proclaimed liberals can be, but also how willingly they adopt tactics they claim to discern and detest in conservatives. In 2009, Jacob Weisberg, editor-in-chief of the Slate Group, was happy to amplify the Obama administration's anti-Fox message in *Newsweek*. In his column titled, "The O'Garbage Factor,"[55] Weisberg channeled Joseph McCarthy, calling Fox "un-American." He warned: "Respectable journalists—I'm talking to you, [NPR correspondent] Mara Liasson—should stop appearing on [Fox News] programs."[56] Weisberg's broadside against Fox sprinkled in a little of that infamous leftist sexism for good measure, dismissing the female anchors, guests, and journalists who appear on Fox News as that "familiar roster of platinum pundettes and anchor androids reciting...soundbites." Where are the "War on Women" warriors when you need them?

Howell Raines, the former executive editor of the *New York Times*, wrote a March 2010 op-ed for the *Washington Post* titled, "Why don't honest journalists take on Roger Ailes and Fox News?" Raines criticized Ailes, the president of Fox News, for his "clever use of the Fox News Channel and its cadre of raucous commentators [to overturn] standards of fairness and objectivity" in journalism. He complained that members of the journalism establishment were failing to speak out against Fox News, a sentiment the *Washington Post* promoted in the headline. "This is not a liberal-versus-conservative issue," Raines promised. "It is a matter of Fox turning reality on its head with, among other tactics, its endless repetition of its uber-lie: 'The American people do not want health-care reform.'"[57]

I vigorously supported Obamacare, but Raines's rant was jaw-dropping in its blinkered political arrogance—as if popular opposition to Obamacare, well testified to in all the polling data, was entirely the result of opinion-leaders at Fox News.[58] Moreover, isn't the job of the press to critically examine government programs, policies, and proposals? Or should the "objective" press simply cheer on Obamacare because it is "objectively" good for the country, as least if you hold liberal beliefs. The real "uber-lie" about Obamacare was nothing that came from the mouth of a Fox anchor, but President Obama's "If you like your health care plan you can keep it" mantra. PolitiFact named this its 2013 "Lie of the year."[59]

But the illiberal left, acting as chorus, couldn't stop singing from the anti-Fox hymnal. In March 2010, the Huffington Post's Washington bureau chief, Dan Froomkin, wrote a column headlined, "Why Journalists Shouldn't Be Defending Fox News" and argued—you guessed it—that "Fox News is not a legitimate news organization."[60] Salon.com ran a column proclaiming that Fox News is populated with, "charlatans, conspiracy theorists and...religious fanatics endangering democracy."[61] *Rolling Stone* contributing editor Tim Dickinson argued in a 2011 article[62] that Fox News was the "most profitable propaganda machine in history." The former *Mother Jones* editor complained that the existence of Fox News "enables the GOP to bypass skeptical reporters and wage an around-the-clock, partisan assault on public opinion." There again is that illiberal left hubris. If Fox has commentators who buck the leftist line, they are waging a "partisan assault on *public opinion*"—or at least the opinions of former editors of *Mother Jones* and the *New York Times*. Moreover, Dickinson's fantasy world where Republicans "bypass" the mainstream media doesn't exist. If Dickinson is so worried about public officials bypassing skeptical reporters, President Obama would be a better target for concern, as we will see in the next chapter.

Sometimes the anti-Fox derangement syndrome among leftists is almost beyond belief. Salon.com editor Joan Walsh tweeted in September 2014, "Imagine Fox covering slavery. It's not even hard: Promoting the 'job creators' and hyping any rumor of violence."[63] The illiberal left has to demonize its opponents; it won't engage them. And it can't even see its own double standards. Of course no one who works for Fox has ever defended slavery, but MSNBC, where Walsh is a political analyst, has more than once indulged its inner racist, including making fun of a Romney family-photo Christmas card with its inclusion of a black baby (an adopted Mitt Romney grandchild) and an MSNBC segment about Cinco de Mayo when an MSNBC personality danced around in a sombrero on air as he shook maracas and pretended to down a bottle of tequila. The president of the National Association of Hispanic Journalists called it "abominable."[64] It was meant as a joke, but not the sort of joke the illiberal left would ever tolerate in a conservative. Imagine if O'Reilly or Hannity had done that.

If you want to rail against cable news, or the state of media in general, by all means, be my guest. There is plenty to gripe about. But that's not what the illiberal left does. They troll for evidence to delegitimize Fox News and then weave a narrative to "prove" that Fox is terrible, when in fact it stands up pretty well against its rivals in terms of news reporting and credibility.

Even though a recent Pew study showed that CNN and the Fox News Channel provide a roughly 50/50 distribution between news and opinion compared to MSNBC's "full 85 percent opinion," MSNBC is the news network that former Obama flacks Robert Gibbs and David Axelrod joined as political analysts after leaving the Obama administration. What happened to all their fretting about "real news"? MSNBC's premier host, Rachel Maddow, asserted in January 2012, "There may be liberals on TV at MSNBC, but the network is not operating with a political objective." Contrast this with a November 2012 Pew Research study that reported that MSNBC's coverage of Mitt Romney during the final week of the 2012 campaign was 68 percent negative with no positive stories in the sample. Did you get that? MSNBC offered not a single positive story about Mitt Romney at the conclusion of the presidential campaign. Pew noted their coverage "was far more negative than the overall press, and even more negative than it had been during October 1 to 28 when 5 percent was positive and 57 percent was negative."

The sad fact is the illiberal left expect members of the media to support their ideological and partisan goals—or else. As reporter Sharyl Attkisson said in an interview after leaving CBS, "The troubling part is that some in the news media routinely allow themselves to be used as a tool in this propaganda effort. Instead of questioning authority, they question those who question authority. By way of example, my news reporting has an impeccable record for accuracy while the Obama administration's record for providing accurate facts is decidedly mixed. Yet some in the media question me with a skepticism and zeal that they would never think of applying to the wildly false and unfounded claims raised by 'the other side.'"[65]

Charles Krauthammer once noted that Fox News' success is due to its appeal to a niche market: *half the country.* And unlike much of the rest of the media, Fox distinguishes between opinion and straight news shows. The problem with the illiberal left is that it believes a "progressive" take on issues is an objective take, and cannot conceive that there are other legitimate points of view. As William F. Buckley Jr. once quipped, a liberal is someone who claims to be open to all points of view—and then is surprised and offended to find there are other points of view. I think liberals should be better than that and at least acknowledge their own biases. Veteran reporter and Fox News Senior Political Analyst Brit Hume likes to point out that everyone has a bias. He has told me many times, "The people who are dangerous are those who don't know it and fail to correct for it." Because so many in the media believe their liberal worldview is merely a reflection of settled truth, we end up with a leftist echo chamber, which helps nobody, including liberals.

THE PYRRHIC VICTORY

In late 2014, Media Matters Executive Vice President Angelo Carusone declared the war against Fox News over. He said, "And it's not just that it's over, but it was very successful. To a large extent, we won."[66] This was a strange claim considering that the Media Matters website continued to hyperventilate over all things Fox News. On January 5, 2015, as an example, the front page of the Media Matters website featured seventeen posts about Fox News including banner stories demonizing Fox News host Mike Huckabee, who had just announced he was leaving Fox News to explore a presidential run.

It is unclear exactly what Media Matters won. Despite its concerted attack, Fox News continued to dominate the ratings to the point of humiliating its competitors. A December 30, 2014, *Variety* headline declared, "Fox News Dominates Cable News Ratings in 2014; MSNBC Tumbles."[67] The article explained, "Fox News finished on top in both total viewers and the adults 25-54 news demo for a 13th straight year...." The cable network, "had the top five programs in cable news" and "in primetime for the year, Fox News ranked second in total viewers among all ad-supported basic cable networks," ahead of AMC and TNT and behind only ESPN. As for its competitors, "CNN posted its all-time low primetime average in total viewers as well as its lowest-ever total-day tune-in among adults 25-54. MSNBC hit a nine-year low in total viewers."[68]

Following the 2014 midterm elections, *Baltimore Sun* media critic David Zurawik wrote, "Any day now, I am expecting to turn on the tube and see an ad that says, 'More Americans get their TV news from Fox than anywhere else.'" He pointed out that, "Much of the media establishment seems bent on ignoring the incredible ratings success of Fox News…[that] show Fox News rising to a new and remarkable level of dominance…."

He proffered the evidence: "Fox News beat not just CNN and MSNBC, but also ABC, NBC and CBS on Nov. 4, the night of the mid-term elections. It did so in both total viewers and the key news demographic: viewers 25 to 54 years of age. Fox more than tripled the audiences of MSNBC and CNN in total viewers, while beating ABC, NBC and CBS by more than 3 million, 2 million and 1 million viewers respectively. On a watershed political night, more Americans tuned to Fox for information about the vote than anywhere else. I have been covering media long enough to remember when CBS, NBC or ABC was the big story on election night in the 1970s and '80s."[69]

Zurawik seemed to be on to something. A June 2014 Public Religion Research Institute (PRRI) survey done in partnership with the Brookings Institution found that Fox News was America's most trusted television news source.[70] MSNBC was dead last. In response to the question, "Which of the following television news sources do you trust the most to provide accurate information about politics and current events?" 25 percent of survey respondents answered Fox News. Broadcast news came in second at 23 percent, followed by CNN (17 percent), PBS (12 percent), and Jon Stewart's the *Daily Show* (8 percent). MSNBC trailed the fake news show with just 5 percent of respondents describing it as their most trusted news source.

In his *Baltimore Sun* piece, Zurawik urged the media establishment to stop ignoring Fox News' success and, "start seriously trying to figure out how and why it has come to pass that Bret Baier and Megyn Kelly matter more to Americans on election night than Brian Williams, Scott Pelley, George Stephanopoulos, Anderson Cooper or Wolf Blitzer—way more than the latter two."

When the Obama administration dismissed administration scandals as Fox News stories, the mainstream networks were inclined to stay away, while Fox led the charge to investigate what happened at Benghazi (where the administration initially trotted out a ludicrous story, blaming the death of the American ambassador to Libya as a violent reaction to an anti-Muslim YouTube video) and in the IRS targeting scandals and much else besides. A White House aide told me, while I was working on a column about Benghazi and citing a Fox story, "you know that can't be trusted because it's Fox News." That's the line the White House peddles to reporters all the time.

"I think one of the reasons for this latest evolution of ratings dominance might be that Fox was a far better watchdog on the Obama White House than any other TV news organization," theorized Zurawik in his *Baltimore Sun* column. "It took the heat and the blowback from an administration that showed an enmity for the press not seen on Pennsylvania Avenue since the dark days of Richard Nixon, but it stayed the course. And now with viewers seeing the contempt this administration had for them and the truth, they respect what Fox did the last six years." As for Fox critics who insist the only people who watch Fox are stupid partisans, he warned, "we shouldn't let our biases blind us to the serious media criticism [of other media outlets] that demands to be done."

Fox News has shown the virtues of resisting the intimidation and demonization by government officials, media elites, and even a self-described media watchdog group that can't tolerate dissent. It should be disconcerting for every true liberal that so many of their own media outlets have been content to be led and used by the Obama administration, and to use their power to try to silence others.

SEVEN

MUDDY MEDIA WATERS

[T]he only security of all, is in a free press. The force of public opinion cannot be resisted, when permitted freely to be expressed. The agitation it produces must be submitted to. It is necessary, to keep the waters pure.[1]

—THOMAS JEFFERSON, 1823

"**M**aking government accountable to the people isn't just a cause of this campaign—it's been a cause of my life for two decades," then-Senator Barack Obama said during his 2008 run for the White House.[2] On the campaign trail, Obama repeatedly denounced the Bush administration as "one of the most secretive administrations in our history" and vowed to be a different kind of president.[3] Shortly after his inauguration, the White House announced that, "President Obama has committed to making his administration the most open and transparent in history."[4]

Instead, Obama's White House has appalled reporters with its Nixon-like secrecy, lack of transparency, and hostility to being held accountable by the media. Veteran ABC News Reporter Ann Compton told me in January 2015 that the Obama administration has "flunked" the "test of transparency." She explained that to the Obama White House "transparency" seems to mean little more than an avalanche of administration "photographs and videos and blogs" posted online—in other words, government created "news" that is little better than propaganda. As Compton explained, reporters "are looking for transparency about how the president comes to...policy decisions." Instead transparency, to this White House, is simply another means to spin the media.

Compton has covered every president starting with Gerald R. Ford. The most open West Wing, in her experience, was Ronald Reagan's. Reporters had easy access to Reagan's top three advisors, Mike Deaver, Edwin Meese, and Jim Baker. She also thought the administrations of George H. W. Bush and Bill Clinton were often open with reporters. The George W. Bush administration, by comparison, tightly controlled its media message and limited the press corps' access. The Obama administration, however, took that several steps farther. "Obama is the first [president] to have his own videographer. His shop goes out aggressively with a message. Much more so than Bush," Compton noted. "But [when it comes to] the thought process, the consultations that go into making domestic policy, I felt I had better access with policy teams under Bush than under Obama. When it comes to what I thought mattered most...hearing what was happening with policy creation, I felt I had it in the [George W.] Bush years."

At the end of Obama's first term, presidential scholar Martha Joynt Kumar crunched the numbers.[5] She found that over four years, President Obama held a total of 79 press conferences. The "most transparent administration in history" was beat out by George W. Bush's 89, Bill Clinton's 133, and George H. W. Bush's 143 press conferences in their first terms. As for short question and answer sessions with reporters, it was even worse. President Obama opened himself up to such questioning only 107 times in four years, compared to George W. Bush's 354 and Clinton's 612.

Moreover, the president avoids serious journalists. In 2013, *Politico* noted that "The president has not granted an interview to print reporters at The New York Times, The Washington Post, The Wall Street Journal, POLITICO and others in years. These are the reporters who are often most likely to ask tough, unpredictable questions."[6] The president would rather appear on the *View*.

While the Obama administration's top strategy team held briefings every few weeks where a senior administration official would meet with selected reporters, the briefings soon became essentially useless because they were off the record and the officials spoke in generalities, leaving reporters feeling, as Ann Compton said, that "they had learned nothing." The briefers said "all the same things they said on the morning talk shows."

Politico further reported in "Obama: The Puppet Master," that, "President Barack Obama is a master at limiting, shaping and manipulating media coverage of himself and his White House." Calling it a "dangerous development," veteran reporters Mike Allen and Jim VandeHei noted that, "the balance of power between the White House and press has tipped unmistakably toward the government." One troubling development that differed from past White Houses was "extensive government creation of content (photos of the president, videos of White House officials, blog posts written by Obama aides), which can then be instantly released to the masses through social media. They often include footage unavailable to the press." Brooks Kraft, a contributing photographer to *Time* magazine added, "White House handout photos used to be reserved for historically important events—9/11, or deliberations about war. This White House regularly releases [day-in-the-life] images of the president...a nice picture of the president looking pensive...from events that could have been covered by the press pool."[7]

By the end of 2013, dozens of America's leading news organizations had become so frustrated they signed a letter hand-delivered to then-Press Secretary Jay Carney to complain about "limits on press access" so pervasive as to "raise constitutional concerns." The letter, signed by outlets such as ABC, CBS, NBC, Bloomberg, CNN, Fox News, Reuters, and thirty others, said in part, "Journalists are routinely being denied the right to photograph or videotape the president while he is performing his official duties. As surely as if they were placing a hand over a journalist's camera lens, officials in this administration are blocking the public from having an independent view of important functions of the Executive Branch of government.... You are, in effect, replacing independent photojournalism with visual press releases."[8]

Put another way: the Obama administration is staffed with masters of creating government propaganda and making sure there is nothing to compete with it. When Obama nominated Elena Kagan for the Supreme Court, she gave one interview—to the Orwellian-sounding "White House TV." Guess who produces that? Obama aides.[9] When questioned about reporters' lack of access to the president, Jen Psaki, the Obama campaign's traveling press secretary, told *Politico*'s Allen and VandeHei: "The goal is not to satisfy the requester, but doing what is necessary to get into people's homes and communicate your agenda to the American people."

Bill Clinton's former White House press secretary, Mike McCurry, told me in a 2015 interview, "What has defined so much of Obama strategy is to self publish, to create content to deliver to people they are trying to reach. It is aimed at a base they are trying keep strong, not the middle."

While the administration disdains on-the-record interviews with actual journalists, Obama regularly grants them to people like Stephen Colbert, Jay Leno, Jimmy Fallon, Steve Harvey, and even an online satirical interview with goofball Zach Galifianakis and meet-ups with such YouTube video blog sensations as comic GloZell Green (3.4 million YouTube subscribers), movie and music commentator Hank Green (2 million subscribers), and makeup and home decorating advice teen Bethany Mota (8 million subscribers). There is nothing wrong with the president trying to reach different audiences. But no one should confuse chats with these entertainers as being held accountable by the Fourth Estate.

In early 2013, Paul Farhi of the *Washington Post* decided to investigate just whom the White House deemed deserving of an interview with the president of the United States. Wrote Farhi: "*Entertainment Tonight* scored [an interview with the president] last year. *The New York Times* did not. *The View* has gotten several. *The Washington Post* hasn't had one in years.

Albuquerque radio station KOB-FM's *Morning Mayhem* crew interviewed [President Obama] in August. The last time the *Wall Street Journal* did so was in 2009."[10]

Farhi concluded: "Obama may be the least newspaper-friendly president in a generation." Jackie Calmes, a White House reporter for the *New York Times* told Farhi, "It used to be taken as a matter of course that the major newspapers would get an annual interview. Now I take it for granted that it's not going to happen." How can there be transparency and accountability if the president refuses to speak to the country's most influential dailies?

While the White House prefers to line up the president with fanzines and their equivalent, when the doors finally do open to serious journalists, the Press Office selects reporters who, though not fanzine fawners, are prepared to play them on TV. In January 2013, *60 Minutes* embarrassed itself in service of the White House propaganda machine, running a fluff piece featuring outgoing Secretary of State Hillary Clinton and the president that mined such fascinating and critically important topics as how the two get along. The facilitator of this love fest was Steve Kroft who informed Piers Morgan in an interview that President Obama liked to do *60 Minutes* because "I think he knows that we're not going to play gotcha with him, that we're not going to go out of our way to make him look bad or stupid and we'll let him answer the questions."[11] *60 Minutes* was once famous for asking hard questions. Now, at least if you're President Obama, an interview with *60 Minutes* looks more like a campaign promo.

National Journal Reporter Ron Fournier, a former Associated Press Washington bureau chief, told me that President Obama "is an incredibly thin-skinned man. He likes the idea of transparency, but not if it makes him look bad." And as a result, the Obama administration is the most hostile to journalists and transparency that he's seen.

He continued, "[Obama] is so sure that he knows what is right for the country that anything that makes him look bad is therefore evil. So a whistleblower is 'anti-Obama' and 'anti-American' because he is taking down President Obama who [sees himself as the] epitome of America. He is incredibly self-righteous. [President Obama] is ultimately responsible for the White House being un-transparent and combative with the media and attacking the whistleblowers...."

In July 2014, the Society of Professional Journalists sent President Obama a letter[12] complaining about his White House's lack of transparency. In extraordinarily blunt language, the Society wrote, "You recently expressed concern that frustration in the country is breeding cynicism about democratic government. You need look no further than your own administration for a major source of that frustration—politically driven suppression of news and information about federal agencies. We call on you to take a stand to stop the spin and let the sunshine in."

The letter blasted the president for "the stifling of free expression [that] is happening despite your pledge on your first day in office to bring 'a new era of openness' to federal government." It cited a recent survey that found, "40 percent of public affairs officers [in the federal government] admitted they blocked certain reporters because they did not like what they wrote."

The Obama administration has even taken to censoring White House "pool reports," from the rotating "pool" of reporters covering the president's daily activities. Though the White House Press Office distributes the pool report to news outlets, federal agencies, and others, it has always been understood that the Press Office did not determine the content of the pool reports. No longer. On a number of occasions over the last six years, reporters have been told to change the reports or the White House would not distribute them.

In one illustrative incident, then-Deputy White House Press Secretary Josh Earnest nixed a passage by a *Washington Post* reporter that "contained a comment juxtaposing a speech Obama had given two days earlier lauding freedom of the press with the administration's decision to limit access to presidential photo ops on the trip."[13]

Just how unprecedented and egregious is this kind of governmental interference with the media? *National Journal*'s Tom DeFrank told the

Washington Post's Paul Farhi that in his decades covering the White House he was only asked to alter a pool report one time. It was during the Ford administration and he refused. He said, "My view is the White House has no right to touch a pool report. It's none of their business. If they want to challenge something by putting out a statement of their own, that's their right. It's also their prerogative to jawbone a reporter, which often happens. But they have no right to alter a pool report unilaterally."

SPYING ON REPORTERS

More serious were cases of the Obama administration using the power of the federal government to harass reporters.

In 2010, the Justice Department obtained search warrants, authorized by Attorney General Eric Holder, and secretly seized phone records and e-mails of Fox News reporter James Rosen,[14] including a phone number belonging to his parents.[15] The Justice Department argued that Rosen was a co-conspirator with a contractor who had allegedly leaked information for reports Rosen filed on North Korea.[16] The investigation coincided with the White House's increasingly vitriolic attacks on Fox News as not a real news network.[17] Attorneys for Rosen's source argued that the government had shrugged off author Bob Woodward's use of much more sensitive unauthorized revelations from high level administration sources in his 2010 book *Obama's Wars*; and former Undersecretary of State John Bolton termed the material in Rosen's reports "neither particularly sensitive nor all that surprising."[18]

In testimony before Congress in 2013, after the probe became public, Holder denied that the Justice Department had been preparing to prosecute Rosen and refused to acknowledge that he had crossed a line in authorizing the investigation.[19] Indeed, he called spying on a reporter "appropriate." It was not until October 2014—a year after the Obama administration came under blistering criticism for its chilling overreach[20]—that, after announcing his retirement, Holder conceded that "I could have been a little more careful looking at the language that was contained in the filing that we made with the court—that he [Rosen] was labeled as a co-conspirator."[21] That's quite an understatement.

But the Rosen investigation turned out to be just one of a number in which the administration targeted reporters. In a brazen move by the Justice Department, federal investigators secretly seized phone logs of Associated Press editors and reporters following the AP's publication of stories about Yemen-based terrorism in May 2012. This seizure included logs for numerous office lines, the AP main line in the House of Representatives, and journalists' home phones and cell phones.[22] The Justice Department had seized phone records from individual journalists before, but the scale of the seizures—covering a period of two months from lines accessed by more than one hundred reporters—was unprecedented.[23] The Department of Justice's disregard for their own legal process guidelines when seeking such information about members of the press—only as a last resort, only with the express authorization of the attorney general, and only when the need for information outweighs "the public's interest in the free dissemination of ideas and information"[24]—resulted in a full scale backlash from the national media. Caroline Little, CEO of the Newspaper Association of America, said the Justice Department's action was a "shock" and violated "the critical freedom of the press protected by the US Constitution and the Bill of Rights."[25] AP president and CEO Gary Pruitt was understandably outraged, saying, "There can be no possible justification for such an overbroad collection of the telephone communications of The Associated Press and its reporters. These records potentially reveal communications with confidential sources across all of the newsgathering activities undertaken by the AP during a two-month period, provide a road map to AP's newsgathering operations and disclose information about AP's activities and operations that the government has no conceivable right to know."[26] But this was unfortunately par for the course with the Obama administration. As the *New York Times* noted, under the Obama administration, the "Justice Department has brought more charges in leak cases than were brought in all previous administrations combined."[27]

New York Times investigative reporter James Risen, a two-time Pulitzer Prize winner who was one of those hounded by the administration, said, "I don't think any of this would be happening under the Obama administration if Obama didn't want to do it. I think Obama hates the press. I think he doesn't like the press and he hates leaks."[28]

WAR ON WHISTLEBLOWERS

In the 2008 Obama/Biden campaign manifesto "Document for Change" the Democratic candidates promised to protect whistleblowers. The document celebrated government employees who were willing to speak out about fraud, waste, and abuse in government and promised to empower them to be "watchdogs of wrongdoing and partners in performance" by strengthening whistleblower protection laws if elected. "Such acts of courage and patriotism, which can sometimes save lives and often save taxpayer dollars, should be encouraged rather than stifled.... Obama will ensure that federal agencies expedite the process for reviewing whistleblower claims and whistleblowers have full access to courts and due process," the document said.[29]

Five years later, a 2013 report issued by the Committee to Protect Journalists (CPJ) documented the administration's hostility to whistleblowers. The report's author, former *Washington Post* Executive Editor Leonard Downie Jr. wrote, "The [Obama] administration's war on leaks and other efforts to control information are the most aggressive I've seen since the Nixon administration, when I was one of the editors involved in the *Washington Post*'s investigation of Watergate. The 30 experienced Washington journalists at a variety of news organizations whom I interviewed for this report could not remember any precedent."[30]

Former *New York Times* Executive Editor Jill Abramson agreed, saying, in a 2014 interview, "The Obama years are a benchmark for a new level of secrecy and control. It's created quite a challenging atmosphere for the *New York Times*, and for some of the best reporters in my newsroom who cover national security issues in Washington."[31]

"There's no question that sources are looking over their shoulders," said Michael Oreskes, senior managing editor of the Associated Press. "Sources are more jittery and more standoffish, not just in national security reporting. A lot of skittishness is at the more routine level. The Obama administration has been extremely controlling and extremely resistant to journalistic intervention. There's a mind-set and approach that holds journalists at a greater distance."[32]

As a result, journalists must work doubly hard to collect sensitive information while protecting their sources. First Amendment Attorney Carey Shenkman observed that as a result of the Obama administration's behavior, journalists are now avoiding digital communication, such as telephone calls and e-mails with sources, and are relying on personal meetings or in some cases using encrypted communications.[33] Leonard Downie Jr., former executive editor of the *Washington Post*, confirms that "a few news organizations have even set up separate computer networks and safe rooms for journalists trained in encryption and other ways to thwart surveillance."[34] News organizations being forced to institute measures to hide their reporting processes from spying government eyes is something one would expect in China or Iran, not the United States. Instead of guarding the rights of a free press, the Obama administration has treated the press as if they were hostile agents of a foreign power.

Downie's sweeping study for the Committee to Protect Journalists concluded that as a result of the administration's investigations and prosecution of leakers, government officials are increasingly afraid to talk to the press.[35] Before the report was released, Downie wrote in the *Washington Post* that the administration "has disregarded the First Amendment and intimidated a growing number of government sources of information—most of which would not be classified—that is vital for journalists to hold leaders accountable."[36]

The *Guardian's* Glenn Greenwald summed things up in a 2012 column noting that when it comes to transparency and protecting whistleblowers, "[Obama's] administration exploits secrecy laws to punish those who expose high-level wrongdoing while leaking at will for political gain. More remarkable is that a Democratic presidential candidate [Obama, running for reelection] is sticking his chest out and proudly touting that he has tried to imprison more whistleblowers *on espionage charges* than all previous presidents in history *combined*.... what Obama is doing with the power he has been vested is the exact opposite of what [he and the Democratic Party] claimed they believed four years ago."[37]

PURGING THE MEDIA OF DISSENTERS

The vast majority of people who work in the mainstream media are left of center. That's been true for decades, and some prominent liberal journalists have openly confessed it. Daniel Okrent, for one, conceded in July 2004, when he was an editor at the *New York Times*, that on "social issues: gay rights, gun control, abortion and environmental regulation... if you think the *Times* plays it down the middle on any of them, you've been reading the paper with your eyes closed."[38] Similarly at the *Washington Post* in 2005, one of the paper's editors, Marie Arana, wrote "The elephant in the newsroom is our narrowness. Too often, we wear liberalism on our sleeve and are intolerant of other lifestyles and opinions.... We're not very subtle about it at this paper: If you work here, you must be one of us. You must be liberal, progressive, a Democrat." She added, "I've been in communal gatherings in the *Post*, watching election returns, and have been flabbergasted to see my colleagues cheer unabashedly for the Democrats."[39]

Longtime *Washington Post* political reporter Thomas Edsall wrote in the *Columbia Journalism Review* in 2009: "The mainstream press is liberal... [and journalists] tend to favor abortion rights, women's rights, civil rights, and gay rights.... If reporters were the only ones allowed to vote,

Walter Mondale, Michael Dukakis, Al Gore, and John Kerry would have won the White House by landslide margins."[40]

What was true then is true now. *Politico*'s Jim VandeHei, for instance, said in March 2012 that, "I've worked at the *Wall Street Journal*, the *Washington Post*, and worked here at *Politico*," he said. "If I had to guess, if you put all of the reporters that I've ever worked with on truth serum, most of them vote Democratic."[41]

Obviously, mainstream reporters can be liberals or Democrats and still provide fair reporting so long as they are willing to check their bias at the door. Unfortunately, they seem to be blinded by their biases too often, and because so few people who don't share their worldview exist in the newsrooms, there is nobody to push back against their biases. How was it, for instance, that the mainstream media managed to ignore the trial of abortion doctor Kermit Gosnell, a grisly but hugely important story? *Slate*'s Dave Weigel explained in an April 2013 column that this journalistic lapse was the result of unified cultural and ideological views amongst a media that skewed left. "Let's just state the obvious: National political reporters are, by and large, socially liberal," he wrote. "We are more likely to know a gay couple than to know someone who owns an 'assault weapon.' We are, generally, pro-choice. Twice, in D.C., I've caused a friend to literally leave a conversation and freeze me out for a day or so because I suggested that the Stupak Amendment and the Hyde Amendment [barring federal taxpayer dollars from funding abortions] made sense. There *is* a bubble. Horror stories of abortionists are less likely to permeate that bubble than, say, a story about a right-wing pundit attacking an abortionist who then claims to have gotten death threats."[42]

What is even more concerning than news judgments skewed by political bias is the effort by the illiberal left to politically cleanse the already largely liberal media of all dissent. How much control over the media do they need exactly? This is an effort in which the Obama administration participated with its war on Fox News. But the silencing campaign is not limited to the leading cable news network in the country. It's been extended to startup websites, even one led by a liberal.

In 2014, Media Matters spearheaded a campaign to pressure liberal columnist and editor of the new Vox.com website Ezra Klein into firing journalist Brandon Ambrosino. Ambrosino's sin? Though gay he did not hold the "correct" positions on homosexuality, including his suggestion that gay rights activists should be more tolerant of the opposition, and find "a way to condemn evil without condemning the evildoer" like Martin Luther King Jr. "We no longer prize intellectual conversation, preferring instead to dismiss our opponents in 140-character feats of rhetoric," Ambrosino noted. "We routinely scour the private lives and social media accounts of our political opponents in the hopes of demonizing them as archaic, unthinking, and bigoted."[43]

As he asked gay activists to be more tolerant of opposing points of view, he was lambasted by the illiberal left for preaching this tolerance. Media Matters blasted out the headline, "Meet Brandon Ambrosino, Homophobes' Favorite Gay Writer and *Vox's* Newest Hire" and called him "a gay writer [conservatives] can hide behind to shield themselves from accusations of bigotry."[44] The *American Prospect* called Ambrosino's hire "clickbait contrarianism at its worst."[45] *Slate's* Mark Joseph Stern called the hire "unbelievably terrible," dismissing Ambrosino's beliefs as "reckless, retrograde, and vapid . . . [and] an embarrassment to us all."[46]

Ambrosino wasn't hired to cover lesbian, gay, bisexual, or transgender (LGBT) issues. The illiberal lefties wanted him fired for believing in tolerance and expressing a willingness to listen to opposing points of view. It didn't matter that he wasn't going to write about LGBT issues. He needed to be ostracized for his prior heresies. Klein kept Ambrosino on but appeased his attackers with a promise to keep an eye on the heretic, "Brandon isn't our LGBT correspondent," explained Klein. "He is a young writer who we think has talent who's going to receive a lot of editing and a lot of guidance."[47]

Another issue that brings out the ire of the illiberal left is climate change. In 2014 a group named Forecast the Facts called on the *Washington Post* to stop publishing anyone who questioned climate change. In support of their case they included a petition with over one hundred thousand signatures. The petition singled out "prominent climate change deniers George Will, Charles Krauthammer, and the *Volokh Conspiracy* blog." They praised the *Los Angeles Times* policy of refusing "to publish letters to the editor that deny climate change." They complained about a letter to the editor that asserted, "Ask 100 scientists to quantify the human effect on 'climate change' and you'll get 100 answers." The problem according to Forecast's budding Robespierres? "This is not science; this is opinion," they wrote. Yes, and letters to the editor are published in the "opinion" section.[48] Forecast the Facts itself isn't a board of scientists—even if it were, they shouldn't be allowed to shut down debate—but, is in its own words, "a grassroots human rights organization"[49] that holds the fundamental human rights of freedom of expression and thought in contempt.

I asked Sharyl Attkisson, an investigative reporter who spent more than twenty years at CBS before leaving the network, if she thought any one group in particular was leading the illiberal left's inquisition of dissident journalists. She pointed to Media Matters, which "has played a significant role in creating a toxic media climate for mainstream journalists trying to do their job fairly and honestly." Media Matters, she said, "prints sometimes almost verbatim from the Obama administration…and the quasi-press will report it as if Media Matters was a neutral news organization…and then it gets picked up, and the social media campaign starts, and I think it has outgunned news organizations."

Attkisson noted, "We are just trying to do our jobs and then we are met with campaigns that are well financed and we are outmatched. We don't have the resources to be a counterpart. It's easier in the minds of some bosses to not have the headache." During her last two years at CBS, after she was put in the Obama doghouse for her investigative reporting, she said CBS "didn't want me to do investigative stories on anything. They assigned me to cover Benghazi, because they saw a good story. But then it elevates and the pushback comes. They wanted me to cover Fast and Furious, but then after a couple of weeks the pushback came. They did accept my story on Republican freshmen fundraising hypocrisy [which won an Emmy]. They liked that story."

Attkisson believes that the quashing of stories that upset liberals is not a result of bias among the liberal network brass or staff. While such bias exists, she says the larger problem is that the controversy of social media campaigns intimidates news organizations like CBS.

I asked her if CBS felt similar pressure from conservatives. She replied that the social media "pushback was fairly isolated" to groups supporting the Obama administration "and even though I did stories that targeted GOP interests... [that] didn't get pushback at all."

Perhaps the most brazen example of the illiberal left's attempts to shut down debate has been the assault on one of the nation's most articulate and respected columnists, George Will.

In his June 6, 2014, *Washington Post* column, Will wrote:

> [A]cademia's progressivism has rendered it intellectually defenseless now that progressivism's achievement, the regulatory state, has decided it is academia's turn to be broken to government's saddle.... [The Education Department] mandates adoption of a minimal "preponderance of the evidence" standard when adjudicating sexual assault charges between males and the female "survivors"—note the language of prejudgment. Combine this with capacious definitions of sexual assault... [and] the doctrine that the consent of a female who has been drinking might not protect a male from being found guilty of rape. Then comes costly litigation against institutions that have denied due process to males they accuse of what society considers serious felonies.... What government is inflicting on colleges and universities, and what they are

inflicting on themselves, diminishes their autonomy, resources, prestige and comity. Which serves them right. They have asked for this by asking for progressivism.[50]

Agree or disagree, Will was making a serious point about critical developments in American higher education. You would never have known it from the reactions of the new inquisitors.

As assembled by National Review Online's Andrew Johnson:

> *Jezebel*'s Erin Gloria Ryan civilly characterized Will's piece as "Ladies Love Being Rape Victims, Says Asshole," and offered "a sincere and heartfelt *F[***] you, George Will.*" Meanwhile, at *The New Yorker*, Amy Davidson called Will's take "confused and contemptuous." Others said Will is not concerned about the issue of sexual assault. While Will clearly states that rape must be addressed and taken seriously and only criticized the current approach, *Salon*'s Katie McDonough stated that Will "does not think that sexual assault on campus is a big deal." Others joined... her in that sentiment, and launched the #SurvivorPrivilege hashtag. Meanwhile, Georgetown professor and fill-in MSNBC host Michael Eric Dyson took it one step further: As the *Washington Free Beacon* noted, Dyson said women were "re-raped" and "re-traumatized again verbally and rhetorically" by the publication of Will's column.[51]

Eager to get in on the act, Democratic U.S. Senators Tammy Baldwin, Richard Blumenthal, Robert Casey, and Dianne Feinstein wrote a harshly worded letter to Will, charging that "Your thesis and statistics fly in the face of everything we know about this issue."[52] But as Michael Miner of the *Chicago Reader* subsequently pointed out, the senators did not take the time to rebut Will's statistics.[53] In his own response to the letter (which was published on June 13, 2014, in the *Washington Post*), Will said the statistics he used "come from the Obama administration, and from simple arithmetic involving publicly available reports on campus sexual assaults." Will went on: "I think I take sexual assault much more seriously than you do. Which is why I worry about definitions of that category of crime that might by their breadth, tend to trivialize it."[54]

Meanwhile, even less concerned with actually engaging in reason and evidence than the senators, UltraViolet—described on its heavily trafficked website as "a powerful and rapidly growing community of people of all walks of life...mobilized to fight sexism and expand women's rights"— called for its followers to "Tell the *Washington Post*: Fire George Will."[55] Not to be outdone, the National Organization for Women echoed on its site: "*The Washington Post* needs to dump George Will now!"[56] Both provided space electronically to sign online petitions.

The anti-Will campaign scored some hits. Within days, the *St. Louis Post-Dispatch* dropped Will from its editorial lineup. Editorial page editor Tony Messenger claimed that the switch had been under consideration for some time, but he noted that Will's column "made the decision easier." He went on to call the column "offensive and inaccurate" and apologized for publishing it.[57]

Some editors had the courage to take on the illiberal left. Most prominent was *Washington Post* Editorial Page Editor Fred Hiatt, who responded directly to the criticisms. "George Will's column," he wrote, "was well within bounds of legitimate debate." He continued: "I welcomed his contribution, as I welcome the discussion it sparked and the responses, some of which we will be publishing on our pages and website. This is what a good opinion site should do. Rather than urge me to silence a viewpoint they disagree with, I would urge others to join the debate, and to do so without mischaracterizing the original column."[58]

It's sad that it has to be explained to liberals that engaging with ideas or opinions they don't like is a critical and expected part of life in the public square. But this is where we are with the illiberal left. Their intolerance is so unbound that the overwhelming dominance of lefty and pro-Democratic viewpoints in the media doesn't sate them. When it comes to views that dissent from their worldview, only one result is acceptable: total silence.

EIGHT

ILLIBERAL FEMINIST THOUGHT POLICE

The thought police would get him just the same. He had committed—would still have committed, even if he had never set pen to paper—the essential crime that contained all others in itself. Thoughtcrime, they called it. Thoughtcrime was not a thing that could be concealed forever. You might dodge successfully for a while, even for years, but sooner or later they were bound to get you.

—GEORGE ORWELL, *1984*

On June 30, 2014, in a closely watched case called *Burwell v. Hobby Lobby Stores, Inc.*, the United States Supreme Court ruled that regulations developed by the Department of Health and Human Services requiring employers to provide free birth control under the provisions of Obamacare violated the Religious Freedom Restoration Act.

That 1993 statute, which passed Congress on a nearly unanimous vote and was signed into law by President Clinton, was prompted by concerns that the heavy hand of government was intruding on Native American religious practices. But religious conservatives, namely the owners of the Hobby Lobby craft store chain, argued that it also should protect them from HHS regulations requiring employers to provide health insurance that covered a wide array of birth control procedures, including some it deemed in violation of their faith. Hobby Lobby covered sixteen of the twenty FDA-approved contraceptives mandated by HHS regulations, but opposed four that might take effect after the fertilization of an embryo.

Those included two forms of the "morning-after pill" (Ella and Plan B) and two types of intrauterine devices (hormonal and copper).[1] Plan B may be purchased over the counter at drug stores without a prescription.[2] On a 5 to 4 vote, the court agreed with Hobby Lobby, unleashing the fury of Democratic Party leaders and their illiberal allies.

"We are a corporate theocracy now," proclaimed a Salon.com headline. In an MSNBC interview, Democratic National Committee Chairwoman Representative Debbie Wasserman Schultz said the ruling would prevent women "from being able to join the middle class." To prominent atheist activist Ronald A. Lindsay, the moral of the story was that the Supreme Court has too many Catholics.

Among feminists of the illiberal left, however, the Hobby Lobby decision was attacked as illegitimate for a simpler reason: the five justices in the majority were male, while three of the Democrat-appointed dissenters were women.

"The men who wrote this decision on behalf of the Supreme Court have entered into a war on women," National Organization for Women (NOW) president Terry O'Neill[3] said on MSNBC. "They have become a blatantly politically activist anti-woman political organization."

This quickly became a Democratic Party talking point. "It's time that five men on the Supreme Court stop deciding what happens to women," tweeted then–Senate Majority Leader Harry Reid.[4] Reid also vowed in a press conference that Democrats would do something about the Hobby Lobby decision to "ensure that women's lives are not determined by virtue of five white men." He didn't say what he had in mind (or acknowledge the fact that Justice Clarence Thomas is actually black).

Democratic House leader Nancy Pelosi chimed in with a rhetorical barrage that displayed a lack of even a basic knowledge of what the case was about. "Really, we should be afraid of this court," Pelosi said. "The five guys who start determining what contraceptions are legal. Let's not even go there."[5] (Actually, the court hadn't gone there: the question wasn't what methods of birth control are legal, but what employers should be forced to pay for.) But the identity politics attack was, by then, in full swing. As Ruth Marcus wrote in the *Washington Post*: "Of course, a uterus is not a prerequisite for understanding the importance of access to birth control. See, e.g., Justice Stephen G. Breyer, who voted...to uphold the contraceptive mandate. But let's be clear: It helps."[6]

Not only is this line of argumentation ad hominem—all seven of the justices who wrote *Roe v. Wade* were men—but in the case of the Hobby Lobby decision, it's transparently inaccurate.

Millions of women in this country supported Hobby Lobby, many out of religious convictions, and some on libertarian grounds. A 2012 Gallup poll[7] on the Affordable Care Act contraception mandate found that 82 percent of Republican women and 48 percent of independent women supported religious leaders over the Obama administration regarding whether religious-based employers should have to provide contraception coverage for employees as part of their health plans.

Friend-of-the-court briefs submitted to the high court bore the signatures of female lawyers, legislators, theologians, and private citizens. The Becket Fund, which brought the suit on Hobby Lobby's behalf, had a legal team that was half female.[8] The team included six women; seven if you added Kristina Arriaga, the Becket Fund's executive director. Arriaga is a dynamic Cuban-American woman heading up a major legal organization that has had enormous success winning religious liberty cases.[9] Yet no mainstream media outlet profiled her in light of her organization's success in winning this case. They were too busy painting the court's ruling as a misogynistic assault on American women.

The same media that ignored Arriaga and the six women of the Becket Fund legal team treated a law student named Sandra Fluke as the second coming of Martin Luther King Jr. for her free contraception crusade. Texas State Senator Wendy Davis was similarly lionized as a crusader for women's rights for a filibuster opposing abortion clinic regulations and limits on late-term abortion. This happened despite the fact that a majority of American women opposed Davis's position on late-term abortion. Gallup polling on abortion shows Americans consistently oppose late-term abortion.[10] A *Washington Post*/ABC survey showed that 56 percent of Americans surveyed prefer to place limits on abortion after the first twenty weeks rather than after twenty-four weeks, as current law allows. When just women were asked, the figure jumped to 60 percent. Such measures are popular among every age range and income bracket. Even Democrats supported the measure 51 to 33 percent, though not voters who identified as "liberal."[11]

The list of those filing legal briefs in support of Hobby Lobby was comprised of 131 individual women signers and six women's groups: the Susan B. Anthony List, the Charlotte Lozier Institute, Concerned Women for America, Women Speak for Themselves, the Independent Women's Forum, and the Beverly LaHaye Institute.[12] The individual female signers included nine sitting U.S. senators and congresswomen, twenty-two state representatives, ten theologians, four international law and religion scholars, more than eighty members of the Breast Cancer Prevention Institute, and a number of law professors, including Helen Alvaré of the George Mason University School of Law and Mary Ann Glendon, the Learned Hand Professor of Law at Harvard Law School.[13]

The illiberal feminists nonetheless described the Hobby Lobby decision as an all-out assault on women. Jill Filipovic of *Cosmopolitan* tweeted that it meant that, "misogyny is acceptable if it's a sincerely-held religious belief."[14] When Ray Rice was caught on video knocking out his fiancée, a Salon.com writer tweeted,[15] "If Ray Rice continues to treat women like that, he'll end up running the Hobby Lobby."[16]

National Organization for Women's Terry O'Neill[17] explained on MSNBC that Hobby Lobby was guilty of "gender bigotry" and no matter how sincerely held Hobby Lobby's belief was, "There are some beliefs that are so heinous a government should not respect them no way, no how." She went on to compare not forcing Hobby Lobby to pay for emergency contraception to apartheid in South Africa, slavery, Jim Crow, and segregation.[18]

Not to be outdone, illiberal male feminists turned out in full force to explain how Hobby Lobby was a woman-hating oppressor and the men on the Supreme Court were waging a "War on Women." At Salon.com, Paul Rosenberg claimed that Hobby Lobby's refusal to pay for drugs they believed ended a human life put them in a position to "tyrannize" other people. "The tyrant's freedom," he asserted, "is everyone else's slavery."[19] MSNBC host Ed Schultz[20] proclaimed that the Hobby Lobby decision was "a real wake-up call to every woman in America that the Supreme Court is at war with women." Jimmy Williams,[21] another MSNBC personality, tweeted, "Five men just told women all across America that their employers decide anything they want about their bodies."[22] At the Huffington Post,[23] Lincoln Mitchell asserted that the Court's decision will "endanger the health and lives of many American women."

At *Slate*, Mark Joseph Stern played the minority card. Claiming that Hobby Lobby was opposed "to women controlling their own bodies," he said their stance—and the Supreme Court's decision—revealed "a deep mistrust of minorities' power to define their own destinies."[24]

ILLIBERAL FEMINISTS AGAINST FREE SPEECH

All this name-calling, deceptiveness, and misstating of what the court actually held in the Hobby Lobby case is no accident. It's part of a larger effort to demonize and delegitimize anyone who doesn't agree with the illiberal left's absolutist position on the issue of abortion. The goal is to shut down a debate they fear they are losing on the merits.

When men disagree with illiberal feminists, a favored silencing tactic is to accuse them of "mansplaining." The term grew out of a fairly brilliant 2008 essay by feminist writer Rebecca Solnit, who described the exquisitely annoying feeling of having a certain type of man condescendingly lecture a woman on a topic about which he knows very little—in this case Solnit's own book. This is certainly a phenomenon I and millions of other women have experienced, and it can be maddening. But the illiberal feminists have forged the notion of "mansplaining" into a weapon to silence any man who expresses an opinion at odds with feminist orthodoxy.

How it works is relatively simple. A "pro-life" man who talks about abortion with a "pro-choice" woman is "mansplaining." (But a "pro-choice" man agreeing with a "pro-choice" woman is not.) The *Atlantic* accused Texas Governor Rick Perry of "classic mansplaining" after he criticized Wendy Davis's thirteen-hour filibuster to prevent a vote on a bill that would have placed restrictions on abortion. His offending comment? He noted, "It's just unfortunate that she hasn't learned from her own example that every life must be given a chance to realize its full potential and that every life matters."[25] Perry was referencing the fact that Davis had experienced an unplanned pregnancy while a teenager, which resulted in the birth of her first daughter.

Marin Cogan at *GQ* accused Mitt Romney of trying to "mansplain [his] way to the White House" during his 2012 presidential run.[26] The examples she raised—his complaints about bureaucratic red tape or criticism about how security was being handled at the London Olympics—were standard political fare recast as "mansplaining." *New York* magazine accused Republican Senator Ted Cruz of "mansplaining" to Democratic Senator Dianne Feinstein when he made a conservative point about the Second Amendment during a hearing.[27] Salon.com accused Republican Senator Ron Johnson of Wisconsin of "mansplaining" to incoming Democratic Senator Tammy Baldwin of Wisconsin when he told a local paper, "Hopefully I can sit down and lay out for her my best understanding of the federal budget because they're simply the facts," he told the *Chippewa Herald*. "Hopefully she'll agree with what the facts are and work toward common sense solutions."[28]

Illiberal feminists turn simple ideological disagreements, whether about the federal budget or the Second Amendment or anything else, into excuses to engage in character assassination, dismissing their opponents as sexists. Conservatives are their favorite targets, but any dissident can land in their crosshairs.

In their ideological zeal, the feminists of the illiberal left don't seem to realize how they've given feminism a bad name. According to a 2013 Huffington Post/YouGov poll only 23 percent of American women said they would identify as a "feminist," despite the fact that majorities of male and female respondents said "men and women should be social, political, and economic equals."[29] Even among Democrats, the "feminist" label is in low repute: only 32 percent applied the term to themselves.

Still, illiberal feminists wield a perverse power among academics and media pundits who take for granted the feminists' outrageous claim that female dissidents from the illiberal left *aren't actually women.*

Feminist writer Naomi Wolf once described the foreign-policy analysis of Jeane Kirkpatrick as being "uninflected by the experiences of the female body." Feminist icon Gloria Steinem called former U.S. Senator Kay Bailey Hutchison a "female impersonator."[30] Patricia Ireland, former president of the National Organization for Women, once instructed Democrats to vote only for "authentic" (translation: pro–abortion rights) female political candidates. During the 2010 midterm election season, Democratic Congresswoman Janis Baird Sontany of Tennessee said of her GOP colleagues, "You have to lift their skirts to find out if they are women. You sure can't find out by how they vote."[31] In August 2010, liberal talk show host Stephanie Miller laughed uproariously when a female guest on her show said that if she ever met conservative columnist Michelle Malkin, "I would kick [her] right in the nuts," and warned, "Wear a cup, lady."[32] Ann Coulter is routinely referred to as "Mann Coulter" on liberal blogs.[33]

Dehumanizing slurs have routinely been used against Sarah Palin. In 2011, Gloria Steinem snarked that, "Sarah Palin and Michele Bachmann...are on my list of 'the women only a man could love.'"[34] Her comment echoed the illiberal feminist attacks during the 2008 election, when Palin was derided by the Huffington Post as "Bush in lipstick."[35] Wendy Doniger blogged at the *Washington Post* that Palin's "greatest hypocrisy is in her pretense that she is a woman."[36] Cintra Wilson wrote during the tsunami of anti-Palin hysteria in 2008, "Sarah Palin may be a lady, but she ain't no woman."[37] Get it? "Real women" are pro-abortion Democrats. And conservative women? Well, while reigning as the uber-liberal at Current TV, Keith Olbermann said on his show that conservative columnist S. E. Cupp should herself have been aborted.[38]

ILLIBERAL SEXISM

In 2012, when I criticized liberal men for their sexist attacks against conservative women in a Daily Beast column, Keith Olbermann went nuts.[39] He proclaimed on his show that people should ignore me because I was a "house tamed liberal at Fox News," comparing me to slaves forced to conform to the will of their masters.[40] He took to Twitter to continue his attacks, and his followers jumped in, saying I was a "wind-up toy," a "bobblehead," and "just another brainless plastic doll Fox puts on camera to appease the horned up 60-year-old white dudes at home."[41] Olbermann never tried to refute anything I wrote; in fact, by his behavior he only added to my column's many examples of liberal men making vicious sexist statements.

Character assassination was the method of discourse favored by Republican Senator Joseph McCarthy; and it was a tenet of the liberal creed to resist such tactics. But Olbermann and his ilk are happy to use delegitimizing and demonizing tactics in an effort to further their ideological causes.

Strangely, while illiberal feminists treat conservative women as men in drag, men who identify as women are treated as women. At Mount Holyoke College in 2015, a student theatre group canceled its scheduled performance of *The Vagina Monologues* because it was too "reductionist and exclusive." Who did this feminist masterpiece exclude? According to an e-mail sent to explain the decision, "At its core, the show offers an extremely narrow perspective on what it means to be a woman.... Gender is a wide and varied experience, one that cannot simply be reduced to biological or anatomical distinctions." The play's author, Eve Ensler, defended her work, saying in an interview that it wasn't meant to speak for all women and that "Women with and without vaginas need a voice."

When illiberal feminists aren't delegitimizing female dissenters from their worldview as fake women, they are portraying them in such a hyper-sexualized way that they are reduced to nonhuman objects. Avoiding classic sexist stereotypes would seem to be the minimum expected of avowed feminists. *Psychology Today*[42] reported in 2010 on multiple studies that found that "focusing on a woman's appearance (fully dressed) is enough for...men and women...to dehumanize a woman.... [P]eople assign female targets less 'human nature traits' when focus is on their appearance." The human traits that these men and women were seen as lacking include the ability to think, express emotions, or even feel pain.[43] They noted that a key study on the issue found that when "women were dressed sexually.... people implicitly associated them more with animals."

Illiberal feminists don't need *Psychology Today* to tell them that treating women as sex objects is dehumanizing. Feminist scholars have been arguing this for decades.

Yet, in her 2011 *Elle* piece titled "The Best and the Rightest,"[44] writer Nina Burleigh described conservative women who were on the rise as, "right-wing girl Millennials" who were following "in the high heels of the former governor of Alaska." One woman, she wrote, moved "from chair to podium with the lithe, twitchy ease of a big cat, hazel-eyed and trailing a honey-colored mane, all 20 tawny years of her packed into a skintight electric blue stretch-satin cocktail dress." Another woman was described as, "A curvaceous, dark-haired 25-year-old... [with] a diamond-studded cross dangling above very visible cleavage."[45]

When Senator Joni Ernst—a GOP rising star—delivered the State of the Union response in January 2015, MSNBC host Ronan Farrow tweeted, "Joni Ernst delivering response in the style of an in-flight safety video." And again, pretending to quote her: "'We'll also cut wasteful spending and balance the budget' [pantomimes latching shut safety belt]."[46] This attempt to dismiss her as a serious person echoed comments made by then-Senator Tom Harkin who was campaigning for Ernst's opponent in her 2014 race to fill Harkin's seat. "In this Senate race, I've been watching some of these ads," Harkin said. "And there's sort of this sense that, 'Well, I hear so much about Joni Ernst. She is really attractive, and she sounds nice.'... Well, I got to thinking about that," he said. "I don't care if she's as good looking as Taylor Swift or as nice as Mr. Rogers, but if she votes like [Minnesota Congresswoman] Michele Bachmann, she's wrong for the state of Iowa."[47] Pretty Republican women are apparently interchangeable, but it's worth noting that Joni Ernst is, among other things, a lieutenant colonel in the Iowa National Guard, a veteran of Operation Iraqi Freedom, and had served in the Iowa State Senate. She is, in other words, more than just a pretty face, and certainly entitled to political opinions that differ from Tom Harkin's.

In a 2008 Salon.com piece, Cintra Wilson referred to Sarah Palin as a "Christian Stepford wife in a 'sexy librarian' costume" and the GOP's "hardcore pornographic centerfold spread."[48] *Daily Kos*, a leading liberal blog, ran a mock *Playboy* cover featuring the forty-four-year-old then-governor of Alaska. The Huffington Post ran a photo montage of Palin—only the second woman to join a presidential ticket—headlined "Former Beauty Queen, Future VP?"[49] MSNBC ran a November 2009 segment showing photo-shopped pictures of Palin wearing an American flag bikini and holding a rifle; and one of her wearing a tight black miniskirt. When they flashed on the screen, the host noted, "She's hot." MSNBC apologized later for not alerting viewers that the pictures were photo-shopped, but offered no apology for the sexist segment.[50]

In a Salon.com column headlined "Forget the tea party—what about the crumpets?" Gene Lyons wrote that, "The most entertaining aspect of the 2010 election season has been the rise of the right-wing cuties—political celebrities whose main qualification is looking terrific on television. From where I sit, in a comfortable chair in front of the tube, the GOP Cupcake Factor has enlivened an otherwise dreary campaign season."[51] Liberal British comedian Russell Brand explained that the only reason Sarah Palin has any appeal is, "People want to f-ck her."[52] During the 2008 campaign, Paul Hackett, a high-profile but unsuccessful former

Democratic congressional candidate in Ohio, suggested that Democrats run against the McCain/Palin ticket by pointing out that Palin "accidentally got pregnant at age 43 and the tax payers of Alaska have to pay for the care of her disabled child." "War on Women," anyone? And so much for being "pro-choice."

In April 2014 actress Kirsten Dunst, who describes herself as a feminist, told the UK edition of *Harper's Bazaar*, "I feel like the feminine has been a little undervalued."

"We all have to get our own jobs and make our own money, but staying at home, nurturing, being the mother, cooking—it's a valuable thing my mom created," she added. She also praised men: "Sometimes, you need your knight in shining armor," she said. "I'm sorry. You need a man to be a man and a woman to be a woman. That's why relationships work."

The illiberal feminists were enraged. Jezebel ran a story saying that Dunst, an "actress and blonde who looks good in clothes," is "not paid to write gender theory so it shouldn't surprise anyone that she's kind of dumb about it."[53] On Twitter, a few illiberal feminists wrote that, "She should just keep quiet. I wasn't aware Kirsten Dunst could be more unlikable" and suggested Dunst be added to "the list of famous women who should never be allowed to talk near young girls. Ever."[54] Since Dunst didn't say the right thing, she was labeled a sex object with no brains and essentially told to keep her pretty little mouth shut.

In her *Elle* hit piece on young conservative women, Nina Burleigh added insult to infantilizing. Not content with labeling the half dozen conservative women as "girls," she dubbed them "Baby Palins."[55] Karin Agness, one of the women featured in the article, pointed out in a piece for *National Review* that "Rather than try to understand how some women could be conservative and the arguments we have against feminism, it is often much easier to explain us all away as 'Baby Palins.' The Palin brand has been so damaged by the media that the 'Baby Palin' label serves the purpose of quickly stereotyping and delegitimizing us at the same time."[56]

In May 2010, Palin rocked the feminist establishment when she asserted in a speech to the Susan B. Anthony List that there is an "emerging, conservative, feminist identity."[57] She dubbed this "Western Feminism."[58] Illiberal feminists circled the wagons to begin the process of delegitimizing her. Gloria Steinem declared to Katie Couric that Palin was not a feminist because "you can't be a feminist who says that other women can't [have an abortion] and criminalizes abortion."[59]

Never mind that many of the Suffragettes, the first American feminists, were anti-abortion, or that feminism is supposed to be about women making "choices" which should include the choice to decide their own beliefs. Feminist writer Amanda Marcotte asserted: "You look at someone like Sarah Palin trying to wear... [the feminist] mantle, and you see the flaw in trying to be a so-called conservative feminist, which is that you're not very pro-women."[60] Jessica Valenti, founder of *Feministing*, blasted "the fake feminism of Sarah Palin" in the *Washington Post*, and argued, "Given that so-called conservative feminists don't support women's rights, how can they paint their movement as pro-woman? Why are they not being laughed out of the room?"[61]

The demonizing continued unabated. Steinem told *New York* magazine that conservative women leaders like Bachmann and Palin are "there to oppose the women's movement. That's their job.... it's inevitable.... there have always been women like this."[62] Note the distinction Steinem is making with "women like this." Conservative women don't just have differing opinions, they are double agents pretending to care about women while their real plan is to destroy women's rights. This echoed something Steinem said to me when I told her I was writing a profile of Bachmann for *Elle* magazine: "Who are the people who are putting these women—Palin and Bachmann—up to running?" Steinem asked. Then she answered her question: "It's men who want them to run."[63]

There really is no winning with the illiberal feminists. They become enraged when the "wrong" people call themselves feminist, but then turn contemptuous when a woman says she isn't. In Nina Burleigh's *Elle* profile of conservative women, she blasted her subjects for saying they were not feminists. She wrote, "Behold the new face of conservative womanhood. Young women [who] are the unintended, some might say ungrateful, daughters of feminism...." Perplexed as to why these under-thirty-five women "who pride themselves on being totally modern" might not identify with a movement that treats conservative women like garbage, she landed on a theory. It was "politics and ambition" that drove them to say they weren't feminists because, "Feminist bashing remains the surest way to earn cred in the conservative movement, and 'feminist' is an easy, all-purpose insult...."

When actress Kaley Cuoco-Sweeting (Penny on the *Big Bang Theory*) told *Redbook* magazine that she didn't consider herself a feminist, the illiberal left turned on her, calling her a "talentless bitch"[64] and telling her "Being a feminist is about wanting equality. If you don't believe in equality, you're a shit human."[65] It became such a controversy that the actress prostrated herself before the illiberal mob, which was duly reported in the Associated Press under the headline, "Kaley Cuoco-Sweeting apologizes for comments on feminism."[66]

For Ann Romney it was a Mother's Day 2012 op-ed for *USA Today* that celebrated motherhood. She closed her piece with this: "Women wear many hats in their lives. Daughter, sister, student, breadwinner. But no matter where we are or what we're doing, one hat that moms never take off is the crown of motherhood. There is no crown more glorious."[67] Dissing the column on MSNBC,[68] *Newsweek*/Daily Beast columnist Michelle Goldberg called Romney "insufferable" as other "pro-women" panelists giggled as she said the phrase "crown of motherhood" reminded her of Hitler and Stalin. This saccharine op-ed written for Mother's Day was, claimed Goldberg, just like when authoritarian societies gave awards to women who had big families. In a column responding to people upset with her comparison of Ann Romney to two of the worst mass murderers in history, Goldberg doubled down on the demonization, writing, "bombastic odes to traditional maternity have a sinister ring, especially when they come from people who want to curtail women's rights."[69]

THE WRONG KIND OF "PRO-CHOICE" DEMOCRATIC FEMINIST

In 2014, the Pennsylvania chapter of the National Organization for Women (NOW), and allegedly pro-women Planned Parenthood backed the male primary opponent of State Representative Margo Davidson—the first Democrat, woman, and African American to represent her district—because Davidson supported proposals that would regulate abortion clinics. She did so based on the grand jury report on the gruesome abortion/infanticide mill run by Kermit Gosnell. Davidson was one of more than forty Democrats who voted for the bill, yet none of the others found themselves on the receiving end of the illiberal feminist demonization campaign.[70]

Why was she treated differently? Davidson told me in a December 2014 interview, "I was singled out because I was so vocal and I did not back down on my views. Nor did I back down that I was pro-choice but I thought that was a reasonable accommodation to keep women safe. They hate it when I say this, but when a woman loses her life, she loses all her choices." Davidson knew this all too well: her young cousin, Semika Shaw, was one of the women who died from being in Gosnell's clinic. Davidson told me that after Planned Parenthood started targeting her, her campaign manager talked to them and said, "You and Margo are aligned on a lot more issues than not. Can't you make a consideration for the fact that her cousin died?" They said no.

The Pennsylvania State National Organization for Women took the lead in demonizing Davidson, the only female candidate in her Democratic primary. In a robocall in support of her Democratic primary opponent Billy Smith, Caryn Hunt, president of the Pennsylvania State NOW, told voters that Davidson's "votes are dangerous to women,"[71] when in fact her support for regulating abortion clinics was *explicitly to protect women.* Davidson told me in an interview how Planned Parenthood sent out mailers suggesting she didn't support screenings for cervical and breast cancers, even though they knew she did. "I was surprised and disappointed by their behavior," she said. "I thought it was a smack in the face to the people they say they represent: women." In the end, the illiberal feminists' attempts to punish her for speaking out on an issue failed. Davidson narrowly won her primary[72] and in the fall won reelection to her third term.[73]

Davidson learned the lesson that supporting even commonsense regulations spurred by the abuse and deaths of countless women is something the illiberal left considers extremist behavior. Imagine how the illiberal left views people who aren't "pro–abortion rights." Abortion opponents are routinely described as "extremists" and "anti-women's health."[74] Planned Parenthood inevitably invokes the label "anti-choice extremists"[75] to describe the roughly half of America that opposes abortion.[76] They've even used that label to describe people who support parental consent for minors seeking an abortion,[77] making most Americans "extremists." (A 2011 Gallup poll put support for parental consent laws at 71 percent.)[78] The National Organization for Women calls the U.S. Conference of Catholic Bishops, representing the largest religious denomination in the United States, "anti-abortion radicals."[79] NARAL Pro-Choice America was inventive, blasting Ohio Governor John Kasich not for something he did, but for something he didn't do: failing to use his line item veto to remove "anti-woman, anti-choice provisions from the budget" and thus of supporting "extremist policies."[80] Kansas Governor Sam Brownback is married and has three daughters (among five children), but NARAL Pro-Choice America said his signing of a bill regulating abortion "indicates his disdain for women."[81] Maybe it does the reverse.

Illiberal feminists can't seem to fathom that some people actually believe that an unborn human matters or that abortion is harmful to women. Sometimes the mask comes off and what we see is that illiberal feminism is often driven by a base hatred of Christianity. Amanda Marcotte, a feminist who writes for *Slate* and the *Guardian*, once posted this "joke" on her blog:

> **Q**: What if Mary had taken Plan B after the Lord filled her with his hot, white, sticky Holy Spirit?

A: You'd have to justify your misogyny with another ancient mythology.[82]

At other times abortion opponents are dismissed as stupid and prim-itive. Accepting an award for her support of abortion rights at Planned Parenthood's 2014 annual gala, Nancy Pelosi bashed abortion opponents as close-minded and "dumb."[83] When Republicans proposed a law grant-ing doctors and nurses a conscience exemption from having to perform abortions, Pelosi called it "savage." Although the effort received support from some Democrats, she said, "When the Republicans vote for this bill today, they will be voting to say that women can die on the floor and health-care providers do not have to intervene...."[84]

As we've seen, even being a Democrat is no protection. When Demo-cratic Congressman Bart Stupak proposed an amendment to prevent federal funds from being used for abortion under Obamacare, Democratic Congresswoman Nita Lowey characterized the amendment as being driven by "anti-choice extremists."[85] At Salon.com, Katie McDonough "explained" what "'pro-life' efforts actually do: threaten, intimidate and squash wom-en's constitutional rights."[86]

And that's not the end of it. A Planned Parenthood newsletter reported on a keynote speech by feminist journalist Michelle Goldberg: "Goldberg explained how fundamentalist forces everywhere use an anti-choice agenda as a key leverage point in their fight to keep women under the oppression of 'traditional' gender roles."[87]

Such conspiracy theories are rife among illiberal feminists. "While the rote use of the word 'life' as a code word to describe a series of anti-woman and anti-sex beliefs is probably going nowhere, there does seem to be a bit more willingness among anti-choicers lately to admit that what really offends them is that women are having sex without their permission,"[88] explained Amanda Marcotte in one of her intolerant diatribes.

"[A]nti-choicers will claim to mainstream media that they're only in this for the fetuses," she explained in an earlier screed, "but when they are speaking to each other, they're very clear that this is about repressing sex and putting women back into the kitchen."[89] How Marcotte knows what "anti-choicers" say to each other in private is a mystery.

In a Daily Beast piece titled, "Paul Ryan's Extreme Abortion Views," Michelle Goldberg asserted that people who oppose abortion rights have a "disregard for the exigencies of women's lives...."[90] Goldberg included in that camp Michele Bachmann, whose views, she said, were virtually identical to Ryan's. But it would also cover any woman who voted for Paul Ryan or is anti-abortion.

The feminist group Emily's List also takes it upon itself to decide what women are allowed to think. In 2015, after Republican Senator Joni Ernst delivered the GOP's rebuttal to President Obama's State of the Union address, Emily's List issued a press release,[91] which asserted that "Choosing Joni Ernst to give the State of the Union response is a transparent attempt to appeal to women without having to offer any policies that appeal to women. What they don't seem to realize is that Ernst being a woman politician does not make her a pro-woman politician." Ernst was dismissed as "window-dressing." What would make her "pro-woman"? Being a "pro-choice" Democrat.

INTOLERABLE MEN AND OTHER OPPONENTS

Intolerance is a weapon hard to control once it's unleashed. Michelle Goldberg found this out when her own tactics were used against her. Writing in the *Nation*, Goldberg took issue with the "growing left-wing tendency toward censoriousness and hair-trigger offense." For this apostasy she was rebuked in Salon.com by left-wing Rutgers professor Brittney Cooper. "The demand to be reasonable," Cooper wrote without any sense of irony, "is a disingenuous demand."

Likewise, when Jonathan Chait reported on this exchange in a *New York* magazine piece about the authoritarian impulses of the practitioners of political correctness, he was—you guessed it—attacked not for his ideas, but for being a white male. Sometimes not even that sin is required. In 2013, feminist Hanna Rosin, a senior editor at the *Atlantic* and founder of *Slate*'s feminist *Double X* blog, penned an article for *Slate* announcing that "the patriarchy is dead."[92] Rather than popping some champagne, many illiberal feminists were enraged because of their investment in the story line that they experience unrelenting oppression at the hands of white men. *New Republic* editor Nora Caplan-Bricker accused Rosin of "mansplaining" because she was allegedly telling women what they must think.[93] But that's not what Rosin was doing. She was expressing her opinion on an issue on which she had done plenty of research. Unfortunately for her, it makes no difference. She reached the "wrong" conclusion which made her a tool of the patriarchy according to Caplan-Bricker and "a terrible human being" according to another aggrieved feminist who vandalized Rosin's Wikipedia page in the wake of her heretical claim.[94]

Rosin's article stemmed from her book *The End of Men*, which proclaimed a bittersweet victory for women's liberation. Women, she argued, are better adapted to modern society than men, women have exceeded men in terms of power dynamics, and areas of dissatisfaction for American women are likely the result of their own choices rather than caused by the patriarchy. Rosin expected men to be offended by her book, but instead the outrage came from feminists. The *New Republic* charged Rosin with assisting the patriarchy[95] and Jezebel mocked her in a piece titled, "Patriarchy Is Dead if You're a Rich White Lady."[96] A *New York* magazine writer took the smear a step further and thought it fair to suggest Rosin was dismissing the tragedy of women who are raped and murdered.[97]

Rosin experienced the cold reality of what silencing feels like. She didn't like it. "Her response since then has been to avoid committing a provocation, especially on Twitter," Jonathan Chait explained in *New York* magazine. "If you tweet something straightforwardly feminist, you immediately get a wave of love and favorites, but if you tweet something in a cranky feminist mode then the opposite happens," Rosin told Chait. "'The price is too high; you feel like there might be banishment waiting for you.'

Social media, where swarms of jeering critics can materialize in an instant, paradoxically creates this feeling of isolation. 'You do immediately get the sense that it's one against millions, even though it's not.' Subjects of these massed attacks often describe an impulse to withdraw," Chait wrote.[98] That's the whole point. The silencing campaign is enormously effective.

In November 2010, the women's magazine *More* hosted a panel to discuss feminism. Jessica Valenti, "a gutsy young third wave feminist,"[99] according to the *New York Times*, canceled her appearance on the panel because it included Allison Kasic, a conservative from the Independent Women's Forum.[100] On her blog, Valenti explained she dropped out because she didn't want to "validate" the idea that conservatives could be feminists.[101]

"When I agree to be on a panel I'm accepting the terms of a debate," she wrote. "And it's not a debatable point whether people whose policies actively harm women are feminists. I don't want to validate that this is a question open for reasonable conversation." Reasonable conversations aren't something illiberal feminists do.

A scheduled 2014 Oxford University debate was canceled following illiberal feminist outrage that two men would be allowed to debate the topic of whether "abortion culture" was harmful to society. The event hosted by Oxford Students for Life was to feature Tim Stanley, a historian who writes for the *Daily Telegraph* and Brendan O'Neill, editor of *Spiked* and a columnist for the *Australian*. Stanley was to argue that abortion was harmful to society; O'Neill, who considers himself a left-leaning libertarian, would oppose that notion. O'Neill has written, "The right to choose frees a woman from official prying into the decisions she makes about her body and her life; it increases her humanity, it makes her a fuller, more independent human being."

The delegitimizing started with a bang. A group called "Oxrev fems" set up a webpage called, "What the f-ck is 'Abortion Culture'?"[102]

Protesters were urged to attend the event with some "non-destructive but oh so disruptive instruments to help demonstrate to the anti-choicers what we think of their 'debate.'" Around three hundred people signed up to protest an event that was expecting around sixty attendees.[103] Oxford University's Student Union Women's Campaign put out a statement saying, we "condemn OSFL for holding this debate.... By only giving a platform to these men, OSFL are participating in a culture where reproductive rights are limited and policed by people who will never experience needing an abortion."[104]

Ultimately, they won. The venue, Christ Church, informed Students for Life they would have to find another venue for their event, which they were not able to do on such short notice.[105] Oxford undergraduate Niamh McIntyre, gloated in an *Independent* piece headlined, "I helped shut down an abortion debate between two men because my uterus isn't up for their discussion." She argued that, "Feminists are all too used to encountering...[the] indignant assertion that 'Free speech is a vital principle of a democratic society.'"[106] She argued that the "pro-life" groups could find another platform to express their views, so there was no infringement on free speech. But she added, "The idea that in a free society absolutely everything should be open to debate has a detrimental effect on marginalised groups."[107]

O'Neill wrote in response, "Orwell must be kicking himself in his coffin for not thinking of putting such doublespeaking words in the mouths of his tyrannical characters in *1984*. Just as they insisted that 'war is peace,' so today's Big Sisters on campus claim 'censorship is freedom.'"[108]

Slate's Will Saletan, a liberal and pro–abortion rights supporter, has experienced the same kind of demonizing from illiberal feminists. His heresies include writing articles exposing lax oversight at abortion clinics and suggesting that abortion might not be the most ideal outcome for a pregnant woman. For writing articles like this, Saletan has been described[109] as "anti-choice"[110] and "misogynist."[111]

"The mere fact you are a male instantly disqualifies you," Saletan told me in an interview. "If a man disagrees with them, they ascribe it to the fact he is a man and doesn't understand the woman's perspective. They complain about sexism rightly and then apply it by instantly dismissing men." He notes, "Some of these people weren't even born yet when I was carrying signs for the Equal Rights Amendment on the Louisiana border. It's laughable that they think they represent feminism and I don't."

For liberals, free speech is a fundamental value. Debate is a good thing. So is tolerance of differing viewpoints. But the illiberal feminists and the illiberal left reject the ideas of free speech and tolerance. They believe that views that don't align with their ideology should be silenced.

So rabid is this intolerance that they find the very existence of opposing groups an offense. On college and university campuses, the illiberal left work to ban group groups they dislike or vandalize displays. In 2013 at DePaul University,[112] thirteen students admitted to vandalizing a "pro-life" display erected by the DePaul chapter of Young Americans for Freedom (YAF) to commemorate the fortieth anniversary of the Supreme Court's *Roe v. Wade* decision. The offending display consisted of roughly five hundred pink and blue flags planted in the ground of the campus quad. This so angered some pro–abortion rights students that they tore the flags from the ground and threw them in trash cans. At Dartmouth College, a student ran his car over a display of American flags representing aborted pregnancies. At Northern Kentucky University, a professor encouraged the destruction of a "pro-life" display, saying "any violence perpetrated against that silly display was minor compared to how I felt when I saw it."[113]

Johns Hopkins University freshman Andrew Guernsey was exposed to this hostility when he sought to establish a "pro-life" campus group in 2013. Voice for Life would provide "sidewalk counseling" at abortion clinics and hand out "pro-life" literature on campus. The Student Government Association (SGA) promptly denied the request and compared Voice for Life to white supremacists.[114] The SGA claimed that sidewalk counseling would violate undergraduate anti-harassment policies, even if it were off university property. An SGA member told a reporter that anti-abortion rights demonstrations made her feel "personally violated, targeted and attacked at a place where we previously felt safe and free to live our lives."

Another SGA leader told a reporter that, "We have the right to protect our students from things that are uncomfortable.... Why should people have to defend their beliefs on their way to class?"[115]

There was no evidence that anyone would ever be asked to "defend their beliefs" any more than an anti-abortion rights student might have to "defend their beliefs" by passing a pro–abortion rights demonstration. Students shouldn't be "protected"—to use the SGA leaders' term—from beliefs that upset them. A true liberal would say that it is by debating our beliefs that we come together to reason and seek the truth. Isn't that what universities are supposed to be about?

A *Baltimore Sun* article quoted a female student complaining that with Voice for Life, "group members would be approaching students and talking to them about how abortion is immoral. That's an impingement on someone's personal beliefs."[116] Here, at one of the nation's most elite universities, a student truly believes that another person expressing a viewpoint with which another person disagrees is impinging on someone's personal beliefs. Actually, it's called "dialogue" or "free speech" or "debate."

It's worth noting that while university administrators and student government groups appear to embrace the pro–abortion rights agenda, the same shouldn't be assumed for all college students. A 2011 Thomson Reuters poll for NPR found that among Americans under thirty-five, 65.5 percent believed "having an abortion is wrong," the highest percent of any age group (it was 57 percent for those between thirty-five and sixty-four, and 60.9 percent for those older than sixty-four).[117] The left-leaning Public Religion Research Institute (PRRI) reported in 2011 that "Millennials are conflicted about the morality of abortion," with 50 percent saying they don't think having an abortion is morally acceptable.[118] Ultimately, how Millennials feel about abortion should not dictate whether a "pro-life" group should gain university status. At a minimum though, it shows that groups like Voice for Life do not represent a fringe view, except to the illiberal left.

If the illiberal feminists were truly confident in their views, they would welcome disagreement and dissent. It's interesting to note that anti-abortion student groups on college campuses aren't afraid of debate. They are willing to face hostility to express their point of view. It is the illiberal left and the illiberal feminists who fear debate, who seek "protection" from opposing points of view, and who want to simply ban ideas they don't like.

Freedom of speech is supposed to be protected by the Johns Hopkins student government constitution. But another one of the reasons the Student Government Association denied Voice for Life's request for university status was because Voice for Life's website linked to the Center for Bio-Ethical Reform's website, which was judged "offensive" for showing pictures of bloody fetuses.[119] The complaint was not that the group linked to pictures that were falsified or untrue. Just that they offended the sensibilities of the liberals on campus who claim to love scientific facts, except in situations where it might make them feel bad. Voice for Life's Andrew Guernsey said the obvious: the student government is "ultimately intolerant of pro-life views being expressed on campus. They want to censor the message…."[120]

Guernsey was under no illusions that his plans for a "pro-life" group on campus would be popular, but he was surprised that the members of the student government did not "separate their personal views from being able to tolerate differences of opinion on campus."[121]

Eventually, the group was able to appeal to the Student Government Association Judiciary, which overturned[122] the SGA's decision to deny recognition. Finally, Voice for Life was allowed on campus after having to fight tooth and nail for the basic rights and recognition that liberal students take for granted.[123]

ILLIBERAL FEMINISTS AGAINST HUMOR

It should not be a surprise at this point to learn that illiberal feminists also suffer from a humor deficit. In late 2014, when the European Space

Agency landed the *Philae* spacecraft on a comet, scientists and engineers involved in the mission participated in a live-stream of the event. One of the scientists, Dr. Matt Taylor, wore a wild shirt with cartoonish pinups on it. The feminist blogosphere, which apparently had nothing better to do, exploded with outrage. The *Guardian*'s[124] Alice Bell complained that the European Space Agency "can't see misogyny under their noses" and called the shirt "sexist." The *Atlantic*'s Rose Eveleth tweeted, "No no women are toooootally welcome in our community, just ask the dude in this shirt."[125] A headline at the *Verge* blared, "I don't care if you landed a spacecraft on a comet, your shirt is sexist and ostracizing."[126] One of the writers alleged, "This is the sort of casual misogyny that stops women from entering certain scientific fields" and noted the ESA hadn't apologized.[127]

At *xoJane*, a writer accused the astrophysicist of "casual sexism" and claimed his "unbelievably sexist" shirt helped create an "environment where a lot of women might feel uncomfortable."[128] She fretted that the shirt "with naked women"—though none were naked—explained the shortage of women in the Science, Technology, and Math (STEM) fields. "We ask why more women don't want to become astrophysicists, or mathematicians, or bench researchers, and, well, this is one example of why," she proclaimed.[129]

Really? It's hard to believe that a crazy variation of a loud, Hawaiian shirt could be so powerful. One might more plausibly say that feminists obsessed with a sexist shirt, rather than with the science of the story, are a bigger problem. Or maybe, just maybe, the unequal distribution of women in different fields has something to do with many women's choices to be mothers and spend more time with their families.

It turned out that a female friend had made Taylor the shirt for his birthday.[130] It was something of a joke. But the facts be damned, the illiberal mob got what they wanted. On a live-stream two days later Taylor apologized with a sob, saying, "I made a big mistake, and I offended many people, and I'm very sorry about this." Syndicated columnist Jonah Goldberg called it "very North Korean." The *Daily Telegraph* blared the headline: "Matt Taylor's Sexist Shirt and the Day Political Correctness Officially Went Mad."[131]

A British scientist had his shirt. A student at the University of Alaska-Fairbanks had her April Fools' Day joke, a faux story about the university's plan to build "a new building in the shape of a vagina." The story ran with a picture of oversized legs protruding from a building.[132]

Sine Anahita, a sociology associate professor and the coordinator of the school's women and gender studies program, was not amused. She filed a sexual harassment complaint with the university's Diversity and Equal Opportunity office, accusing the paper of creating a "hostile environment"[133] that contributed to "rape culture."[134] She invented the term "sexual slander" and lobbed it against the paper for attributing a fake quote to a professor at the university. Anahita deemed the picture, taken from a PG-13 movie, *Patch Adams*, "patently offensive."

The perpetrator of this alleged misogynistic travesty was a female African American student named Lakeidra Chavis, editor-in-chief of the student newspaper. She told me she thought the piece was "funny" and was intended "to poke fun at the political culture" at a university where the majority of the students are women. Chavis, who describes herself as a feminist, was shocked by the illiberal feminist reaction to her satire. She was accused of sexual harassment for writing the piece and at one point the campus police visited the newspaper as part of an official university investigation.[135]

The university dropped its case against the student newspaper when lawyers from the Foundation for Individual Rights in Education (FIRE) sent a letter warning the public university that it could be sued for violating the First Amendment.

ILLIBERAL FEMINISTS AGAINST SCIENCE

In February 2011, Dr. Lazar Greenfield—an emeritus professor of surgery at the University of Michigan School of Medicine and president-elect of the American College of Surgeons—reported in *Surgery News* on the discovery of mood-enhancing effects of semen. Research from the Archives of Sexual Behavior discovered that female college students practicing unprotected sex were less likely to suffer from depression than those whose partners used condoms. The kicker of the seventy-eight-year-old Greenfield's article was clearly meant to be clever. "So there's a deeper bond between men and women than St. Valentine would have suspected, and now we know there's a better gift for that day than chocolates."

Perhaps his kicker fell short. That's hardly a reason to fire someone. Yet even though Greenfield apologized to the Women in Surgery Committee and the Association of Women Surgeons, five women surgeons[136] on the governing board of the American College of Surgeons (ACS) issued a letter demanding Greenfield step down as president-elect. The then-ACS president tried to argue that, "If someone is truly apologetic, we have to consider that," but it didn't matter.

The illiberal feminist mob wanted a scalp and they got one. Greenfield—the author of one of the major textbooks of surgery—was forced to step down as editor of *Surgery News* and as president-elect of the ACS. In an interview, Greenfield explained what should have been obvious to anyone reading the article: "The editorial was a review of what I thought was some fascinating new findings related to semen, and the way in which nature is trying to promote a stronger bond between men and women. It impressed me. It seemed as though it was a gift from nature. And so that was the reason for my lighthearted comments."

Indeed, it is fascinating research. But thanks to the feminist jihad against this man, the entire February issue of *Surgery News* was removed from the website in the hopes that this medical information would disappear forever. The study Greenfield referred to in his article was done by a group of evolutionary psychologists at SUNY-Albany. Remarking on the controversy that met Greenfield's article, one of the researchers, Gordon Gallup, told the *Guardian*, "I think it's a tragic overreaction. The point at which we begin to let political agenda dictate what science is all about is the point when science ceases to be a viable enterprise."[137]

A *New York Times* wellness blog noted that "Many surgeons chose not to comment on the matter, for fear of professional repercussions, but one said, 'It's frankly been heartbreaking for all of us.'"[138] The few who did speak out were ignored. Dr. Diane M. Simeone, professor of surgery at the University of Michigan, told the *New York Times* that while gender bias exists in surgery, she never saw it expressed by Dr. Greenfield. She described him as "always…completely above board and a role model for supporting women in surgery."[139] Dr. Mary T. Hawn described him as "always…above reproach." She should know. Before becoming an associate professor of surgery at the University of Alabama School of Medicine in Birmingham, Hawn worked as a medical student, surgeon-in-training, and faculty member under Dr. Greenfield. She said that "he went out of his way to recruit women on the trainee and faculty level."[140]

After his resignation, Dr. Barbara Lee Bass, chairwoman of surgery at the Methodist Hospital in Houston, told the *New York Times* she was glad he resigned, despite his positive track record, saying "some things you can't recover from if you're in a leadership role." That's true. It's just that nobody thought that the "things you can't recover from" would include citing a peer reviewed scientific study. Three of the researchers who produced the study—Drs. Steven M. Platek, Rebecca L. Burch, and Gordon G. Gallup Jr.—issued a statement that concluded: "How can someone be asked to resign for citing a peer-reviewed paper? Dr. Greenfield was forced to resign based on politics, not evidence. His resignation is more a reflection of the feminist and anti-scientific attitudes of some self-righteous and indignant members of the American College of Surgeons. Science is based on evidence, not politics. In science knowing is always preferable to not knowing."[141]

Illiberal feminists love to crow about how they are the intellectual members of society; the only ones who rely on science, not faith for their worldview. They invoke their worship of "facts" and "science" usually in furtherance of whatever silencing campaign they are on that particular day. But what to do when science says that women benefit mentally and emotionally from male sperm? This doesn't fit with feminist dogma—after all, "A woman needs a man like a fish needs a bicycle," according to the slogan popularized by feminist icon Gloria Steinem. The idea that there might be some symbiotic relationship between men and women is offensive to this notion. The only option here is to silence the person sharing medical research that undermines feminist ideology. The fact that it might be interesting to the majority of the population that is heterosexual is irrelevant. Big Sister will decide what information you need to know.

ILLIBERAL FEMINIST STATISTICS

Illiberal feminists are as committed to silencing research they don't like as they are to promoting phony facts and statistics that support their ideological goals. If one questions these statistics, then a campaign of delegitimization begins.

As we will see in the following chapter, they have intimidated and shamed anyone who doubts their questionable rape statistics. But this shading of the facts goes beyond one issue. Domestic abuse is a serious enough issue without its prevalence needing to be inflated. In 2009, Attorney General Eric Holder claimed that intimate partner homicide was the leading cause of death for African American women aged fifteen to forty-five. *Washington Post* "Fact Checker" Glenn Kessler investigated this claim and found the statistic was made up. Charting a lengthy and complex genesis over more than eleven years, Kessler traces the statistic back to 2003 studies in the *American Journal of Public Health*[142] and the Justice Department's *National Institute of Justice Journal,*[143] which themselves erroneously cite a 1998 Bureau of Justice Statistics survey that says nothing of the sort.[144] Confusing though this years-long factual mutation may be, the truth is simple—the number is entirely fabricated.[145] The Department of Justice admitted they learned the fact was wrong after Christina Hoff Sommers (widely considered a feminist antichrist by the illiberal left for her frequent debunking of their pet theories) pointed it out in *USA Today*[146] but did not correct their website until the *Washington Post* raised the issue in 2013.[147]

Another favorite "liberal fact" is that American women earn 77 cents for each dollar[148] a man earns. The White House often cites this "fact" even though they know it's been thoroughly discredited. A number of publications—including *Forbes*,[149] the *Washington Post*,[150] and the *Wall Street Journal*[151]—have outlined how the calculations are based on the difference between median earnings for men and women, and do not compare men and women with the same jobs in the same industries.[152] The statistics also fail to take into consideration the fact that women tend to work fewer hours in a year, and often leave the workforce upon having children. A study done for the Department of Labor in 2009 suggested that the gap "may be almost entirely the result of individual choices being made by both male and female workers."[153]

Liberal journalist Hanna Rosin blasted the statistic at *Slate* in 2014. She asked, "How many times have you heard that 'women are paid 77 cents on the dollar[154] for doing the same work as men'? Barack Obama said it during his last campaign. Women's groups say it every April 9, which is Equal Pay Day...I've heard the line enough times that I feel the need to set the record straight: It's not true."[155] The data, she wrote, show that women earn 91 percent of what men do.

This does not mean that there isn't a debate to be had on these issues. There are plenty of women who could share horror stories about experiencing wage discrimination or domestic abuse. The problem is the willful deception in presenting thoroughly debunked statistics as gospel. Even worse is trying to silence people who question the statistics. One *Forbes* writer, for example, was accused of "victim-blaming"[156] for discussing how differing life decisions between the sexes might affect the pay gap.

Best of all, though, is the Center for American Progress, which dismisses facts altogether, calling the "77 cents" figure a "colloquialism—shorthand for expressing a complex economic truth."[157]

It's not true but it represents truth. Got that? And don't you dare question it.

NINE

FEMINISTS AGAINST FACTS, FAIRNESS, AND THE RULE OF LAW

"No, no!" said the Queen. "Sentence first—verdict afterwards."

—ALICE'S ADVENTURES IN WONDERLAND

A Chicago-area seventh-grader returned home from school in the spring of 2014 upset about an announcement made by her middle school's principal that day. Students had been informed of a revised dress code policy. Yoga pants were no longer allowed, the girl recounted, as they were too "distracting" to boys. The girl's parents—both educators, she at Columbia College and he at New Trier High School—wrote to the principal to express their outrage and urged the school to consider how a yoga pants ban "contribute[d] to rape culture." Blaming girls for distracting teenage boys—an allegation the school later vigorously denied—was a "message... squarely on a continuum that blames girls and women for assault by men."

Eliana Dockterman declared in *Time* that the school's argument that the pants created a distraction "is not that distant from the arguments made by those who accuse rape victims of asking to be assaulted by dressing a certain way."[1] The feminist website Jezebel asked why "the solution is to make girls cover up instead of…teaching boys to not be gross sexist pigs?"[2] A feminist writer tweeted, "#RapeCultureIsWhen we tell 13-year-old girls they can't wear leggings because it's 'distracting' to the boys."[3] School administrators say they never claimed that the form-fitting pants were distracting to boys, though they no doubt are.[4] Saying so does not promote rape culture or "blame" girls for anything, because boys noticing girls' bodies is not an offense unless it is done in a harassing or intimidating way, which was never alleged. It turns out all the principal asked was that the teen girls wear a shirt or skirt over their bum-hugging yoga pants.[5] A parent reported that the principal told her the school was merely "trying to figure out a way to tamp down the sexualization of middle-school girls," which seems like something feminists might support if they weren't so busy promoting the idea of a "rape culture."[6]

Rape is a heinous crime. Feminists invoking the term "rape culture" to condemn actions they perceive as a slight is a stark misuse of the word. In *Transforming a Rape Culture*, Emilie Buchwald defines rape culture as "a complex set of beliefs that encourage male sexual aggression and supports violence against women." She wrote, "A rape culture condones physical and emotional terrorism against women as the norm.… In a rape culture both men and women assume that sexual violence is a fact of life, inevitable."[7] Does this sound like the United States of America to anyone? How many people who live in this country today actually condone "physical and emotional terrorism" against women?

Yet illiberal feminists hurl the horrific accusation of being a "rape apologist" or supporting "rape culture" with abandon to demonize anyone who has offended them or won't affirm their ideological or partisan worldview.

Even trying to prevent rape can be labeled part of "rape culture." Students at Arizona State University who had organized an anti-rape rally were accused of "perpetuat[ing] sexism and rape culture"[8] by campus newspaper columnist Kaelyn Polick-Kirkpatrick. The groups—Man Up ASU and WOW Factor!—were created, according to their mission statement, "to build a culture of respect between men and women at ASU." All Polick-Kirkpatrick could see was a stew of toxic misogyny. As she wrote in the school's paper, the name "Man Up" was offensive because "the phrase ... is one of the most common, and most misogynistic, expressions of patriarchy." The problem with "Wow Factor" was that it stood for "Women of Worth," sending a message that if a woman didn't belong to their group, she had no worth, Polick-Kirkpatrick said. The columnist was also upset that a video for the 2013 rally featured someone applauding the fact that, "300 men have pledged to respect women on campus." She wrote, "Are we really *rewarding* men for respecting women? Shouldn't that be a given? And why should women have the responsibility of ensuring they obtain the respect of men? Together, Man Up and WOW Factor! are handing out gold stars to mildly decent human beings who probably don't even realize the organizations they are a part of are full of sexism and misogyny. Ignorance must be bliss."

In 2014, four male college students invented a nail polish that would detect if a date rape drug—known as a "roofie"—had been slipped into a woman's drink. They explained it was meant to "empower women to protect themselves from this heinous and quietly pervasive crime" of rape. Women wearing the polish could test their beverages by dunking a finger and seeing if the polish reacted. Liberal blog *ThinkProgress* published a story that explained the nail polish "actually reinforces a pervasive rape culture in our society" by putting the onus on women to take steps to protect themselves.[9] Rebecca Nagle of FORCE: Upsetting Rape Culture complained, "I don't want to f--king test my drink when I'm at the bar. That's not the world I want to live in."[10] Alexandra Brodsky, a law student at Yale University and a founding co-director of Know Your IX (a "student-driven campaign to end campus sexual violence"), said that the nail polish could end up "fueling victim blaming." Truly, no good deed goes unpunished.

Roofie-detecting nail polish, middle-school dress codes, and anti-rape rallies are all proof of "rape culture" but when an actual rape culture was uncovered in Rotherham, England, in 2014 the illiberal feminists mostly yawned. Authorities discovered that between 1997 and 2013, some 1,400 girls had been raped, abused, and trafficked in the northern English town. "Some children were doused in gasoline and threatened with being set on fire if they reported their abusers," the *New York Times* reported, "and others were forced to watch rapes and threatened with the same fate. In more than a third of the cases, the victims appear to have been known to child protection agencies, but the police and local government officials failed to act."[11] The reason officials turned a blind eye? They did not want to be called racists. The girls who were systematically raped were underprivileged white girls and the perpetrators were mostly Pakistani-British men.

Against this real rape culture, the illiberal feminists were mostly silent. Salon.com ran one story on the issue: a brief Associated Press report about how Muslims were outraged by the Rotherham report. Jezebel and *Feministing*—two prominent illiberal feminist websites—each provided one post. Perhaps they didn't know what to do with a real "rape culture" because it doesn't fit into their parochial, imagined dystopia of America, a land where privileged white boys, the junior patriarchy, relentlessly assault female college students.[12]

ILLIBERAL FEMINIST "FACTS"

Illiberal feminists have injected a variety of sketchy statistics into the mainstream media's bloodstream. The most potent is that women on American campuses are living amidst a "rape epidemic" that their uniformly liberal college administrators have chosen to ignore (for what reason is unclear). Illiberal feminists frequently claim one in five women will be a victim of a sexual assault by the time they graduate from college. So, college campuses are "havens for rape and sexual assault," where "women are at a higher risk of sexual assault"[13] as New York Democratic Senator Kirsten Gillibrand has said. The data allegedly proving this comes from the "Campus Sexual Assault Study,"[14] a survey of two public universities done over the period of January 2005 to December 2007.[15] The narrow web survey was not meant to be proffered as a national statistic, yet politicians and activists have attacked and maligned those who dare to question it.

Indeed, the one-in-five statistic has repeatedly been shown[16] to be inaccurate.[17] If it were true it "would mean," as Emily Yoffe pointed out in *Slate*, "that young American college women are raped at a rate similar to women in Congo, where rape has been used as a weapon of war."[18] Even Christopher Krebs, who led the Campus Sexual Assault Study, has said, "The one-in-five statistic is not anything we trotted out as a national statistic. But it has certainly been used in that way."[19]

Still, to publicly question any of the illiberal feminist rape statistics is to be demonized as a defender of rape. In June 2014, Pulitzer Prize–winning columnist George Will was widely excoriated, as we saw, for asserting in his *Washington Post* column that on college campuses victimhood has become a "coveted status." He called the "rape culture" mantra into question and specifically expressed skepticism about the "one-in-five" statistic.[20] At no point did he argue that rapes did not occur on campus or that a woman who had been raped played any role in her attack. No matter: the illiberal feminists wanted his head.

National Organization for Women President Terry O'Neill said in an interview that "*The Washington Post* needs to take a break from [Will's] column, they need to dump him." She added menacingly, "We want him to back off…and we want the *The Washington Post* to stop carrying his column."[21] Another women's group, UltraViolet, started a petition to pressure the *Post* into firing Will. MoveOn.org started another petition with almost identical language that garnered 45,000 signatures.[22] The group wrote, "By publishing George Will's piece, *The Washington Post* is amplifying some of the most insidious lies that perpetuate rape culture. It's not just wrong—it's dangerous. Tell *The Washington Post*: 'Rape is real. No one *wants* to be a victim. Fire George Will."[23] Four Democratic U.S. Senators—

Senators Tammy Baldwin, Richard Blumenthal, Robert Casey, and Dianne Feinstein—accused the iconic conservative columnist of "contribut[ing] to the exact culture that discourages reporting and forces victims into hiding and away from much-needed services" in a harshly worded letter.[24] Naturally, the senators did not take the time to refute any of Will's statistics or arguments, or have any good answer to Will's subsequent point that by broadening the definition of rape one risks trivializing it.[25]

HAZY STATISTICS AND ALCOHOL

As if the one-in-five statistic isn't bad enough, some feminist groups claim that one-in-four women will be raped by the time they graduate from college. Yoffe debunked that statistic as well.[26] This one comes from a Justice Department study "The Sexual Victimization of College Women."[27] Yoffe explained that the actual study "found a completed rape rate among its respondents of 1.7 percent." From this six-month sample, the researchers extrapolated that 20–25 percent of female college students "might" be raped. To get from 1.7 percent to up to 25 percent, they included the 1.1 percent of women who reported "attempted rape" and then engaged in conjecture[28] that should not be part of serious statistical research.

Yoffe noted that in a footnote in the study[29] "the authors acknowledge that asserting that one-quarter of college students 'might' be raped is not based on actual evidence." "These projections are suggestive," the note says. "To assess accurately the victimization risk for women throughout a college career, longitudinal research following a cohort of female students across time is needed."

Following her article, Yoffe was attacked on Twitter as a "longtime rape apologist," and MRA (Men's Rights Activist). She was accused of "perpetuating rape culture" while one user asked if her son was "a serial rapist or something."[30] Alexandra Brodsky, the founding co-director of Know Your Title IX, wrote at *Feministing* that Yoffe was a "rape denialist"[31] and tweeted, "There is a special place in hell for women who are Emily Yoffe."[32]

Yoffe has been attacked by illiberal feminists before for suggesting that female college students should be warned about the dangers of drinking too much, because of the connection between alcohol consumption and sexual assault, as confirmed by a study the *Slate* columnist wrote about in late 2013. The study found that on campus, "Most sexual assaults occurred after women voluntarily consumed alcohol, whereas few occurred after women had been given a drug without their knowledge or consent."[33] Yoffe noted that "Frequently both the man and the woman have been drinking."

Yoffe stated, "Let's be totally clear: Perpetrators are the ones responsible for committing their crimes, and they should be brought to justice. But we are failing to let women know that when they render themselves defenseless, terrible things can be done to them." She argued in favor of educating female students about the peril in which they place themselves when their judgment is impaired by alcohol over-consumption.

Guardian columnist Jessica Valenti—founder of *Feministing* and named one of "the left's most influential journalists"[34] by the Daily Beast—tweeted, "[I] hope Emily Yoffe can sleep well tonight knowing she made the world a little bit safer for rapists" to which "sexpert" Logan Levkoff replied "I can see her telling women to bind their breasts because they may be too 'appealing' for certain men, too."[35] *Feministing* called her article "a rape denialism manifesto." The UK's *Daily Mail* claimed Yoffe was telling women, "Don't drink if you don't want to get raped." One feminist blogger characterized Yoffe's article as rape "victim blaming."[36] The *Yes Means Yes* blog called it "rape apologism" that urged women to "negotiat[e] with terrorists." Salon.com's Katie McDonough accused her of "blaming assault on women's drinking."[37]

In a response to the deliberately misleading characterizations of her article, Yoffe quoted University of Virginia Law Professor Anne Coughlin—a feminist—who shared an e-mail she had sent to a student upset by

Yoffe's column. "Heavy consumption of alcohol and rape go hand-in-hand," wrote Coughlin. "The correlation is staggering, much too significant to ignore. [O]ver the years, I have had students tell me that feminists were doing them a disservice by not raising these questions." So Coughlin came to believe that it was her job to provide practical advice that included warning female students about the connection between over-consumption of alcohol and rape.[38] However obvious and factually based this connection is, it is not a message that the illiberal feminists want women to hear, which is why they demonized Yoffe in an attempt to delegitimize her.

ILLIBERAL FEMINISM'S CONTEMPT FOR TRUTH

No story better illustrates illiberal feminists' contempt for truth than their reaction to the unraveling of the now infamous 2014 *Rolling Stone* piece about an alleged gang rape of a University of Virginia student by a group of fraternity brothers. The horrifying story of a woman, "Jackie," suffering a terrifying and brutal gang rape at a fraternity house drew plenty of national attention and outrage. It also attracted skepticism. Syndicated conservative columnist Jonah Goldberg questioned the UVA story[39] and was deemed a rape apologist immediately. The *Los Angeles Times*—which runs Goldberg's column—sent out a tweet that read "[Jonah Goldberg's] column questioning UVA story is the kind of berating that prevents rape victims from coming forward" and linked to a piece trashing both him and his column. When another male journalist questioned the veracity of the story, he was immediately attacked by Jezebel, which ran a story titled, "'Is the UVA Rape Story a Gigantic Hoax?' Asks Idiot."[40]

It seems the "idiot" was on to something. *Rolling Stone* was ultimately forced to retract significant portions of the story. As the story began to unravel, *Slate*'s Amanda Marcotte went on a Twitter tirade, calling people who discredited the false story "rape apologists."[41] At Salon.com, Katie McDonough wrote, "Because so many of these protests about ethics and transparency are just the latest cover for the same tired bullshit: derailing public conversations about rape so that we will talk about virtually anything else."[42] For illiberal feminists, the truth is secondary and journalists who seek it are clearly up to no good.

When the article first appeared, Bonnie Gordon, an associate professor of music at UVA, with a special interest in "gender and music," took to *Slate* to argue that nobody should be surprised by the story because, "UVA has a rape culture problem...." Look no further, she said, than the fact that, "our sacred founder, Thomas Jefferson, had sex with a 14-year-old enslaved girl. (That's not consensual.)" More than two hundred years ago. And an allegation that has never been proven.[43] She also pointed to a mural in the University's main auditorium that "depicts...a male faculty member standing on a porch and tossing a mostly naked student her bra as his beleaguered wife comes up the stairs."[44] While that certainly sounds inappropriate for a campus, it has nothing to do with rape.

It turned out that there was plenty to be surprised about in the *Rolling Stone* article. *Rolling Stone*, in an apology, explained there were serious discrepancies in Jackie's account:

> The fraternity has issued a formal statement denying the assault and asserting that there was no "date function or formal event" on the night in question. Jackie herself is now unsure if the man she says lured her into the room where the rape occurred, identified in the story as "Drew," was a Phi Psi brother. According to the *Washington Post*, "Drew" actually belongs to a different fraternity and when contacted by the paper, he denied knowing Jackie. Jackie told *Rolling Stone* that after she was assaulted, she ran into "Drew" at a UVA pool where they both worked as lifeguards. In its statement, Phi Psi says none of its members worked at the pool in the fall of 2012. A friend of Jackie's (who we were told would not speak to *Rolling Stone*) told the *Washington Post* that he found Jackie that night a mile from the school's fraternities. She did not appear to be "physically injured

at the time" but was shaken. She told him that she had been forced to have oral sex with a group of men at a fraternity party, but he does not remember her identifying a specific house. Other friends of Jackie's told the *Washington Post* that they now have doubts about her narrative....

After *Rolling Stone* apologized for the story,[45] Jessica Valenti wrote in the *Guardian* that she still chose to believe Jackie. "I lose nothing by doing so, even if I'm later proven wrong," wrote Valenti. "[A]t least I will still be able to sleep at night for having stood by a young woman who may have been through an awful trauma."[46] What about the "trauma" inflicted on the fraternity that was humiliated and actually punished by the university for an incident that it now appears never took place? From bricks thrown through windows to death threats and vandalized property, the fraternity suffered profoundly. The *Cavalier Daily* reports that members slept in the same room, afraid to be near doors and windows.[47] And the ramifications extended beyond Phi Kappa Psi. After the story broke, UVA president Theresa Sullivan suspended all fraternity social events without any due process, a move condemned by both professors and students alike.[48] Valenti also complained that people were rushing to "indict" Jackie, as if expecting a journalist to investigate claims of gang rape is an attack upon the person making the claim.

Facts and fairness don't move illiberal feminists. Everything is viewed through a preordained narrative—in this case, that frat boys are presumed rapists—and nothing will shake their resolve in believing that to be true. There is no reason to investigate or practice responsible journalism. If a woman says it happened, then write it, print it, and everyone else shut up.

The Poynter Institute awarded *Rolling Stone* its "Error of the Year" award for the story. The journalism institute noted that the UVA story, "should go down as one of the most cautionary tales of confirmation bias in journalism." They recounted how in an interview the writer, "described how she scoured the country for just the right rape story to be the focus of her article. Once she found it, the bias was set to believe it to be true, and to report it in a way the reinforced that."[49] They blasted the magazine and its reporter for cherry-picking the story and failing to verify it. Poynter characterized the magazine's attempts to downplay their journalistic malfeasance as "shameful."[50]

Yet illiberal feminists continued to defend the story. "We should believe, as a matter of default, what an accuser says," liberal commentator Zerlina Maxwell wrote in the *Washington Post*.[51] "Ultimately, the costs of wrongly disbelieving a survivor far outweigh the costs of calling someone a rapist." According to Maxwell, "The accused would have a rough period. He might be suspended from his job; friends might de-friend him on Facebook." Really? Is that all? If falsely accusing someone of being a rapist isn't that serious, then how serious is rape itself? Maxwell's dismissal of the real damage that flows from a false rape accusation is detached from reality. In one case at Harvard, a male grad student was accused of sexual assault and then barred from continuing his studies. The student was later acquitted in court on all six counts of rape and assault, after his accuser was found to be fabricating parts of her story. Even after the acquittal, however, Harvard refused to readmit the student or, as the Foundation for Individual Rights in Education reported, "drop its own charges against him."[52]

When three Duke lacrosse players were accused of gang-raping an exotic dancer at their fraternity house in 2006, the illiberal left convicted them in the court of public opinion. Following their indictment, the students were banned from Duke's campus by the college president. Even after they were exonerated of the charges, the accused found their lives substantially altered. One of the accused players, David Evans, had his job offer with J.P. Morgan Chase rescinded following his 2006 indictment.[53] The other two accused students ended up transferring to other universities.

Even members of the lacrosse team who weren't accused of being involved in the incident saw their lives turned upside down. Their season was canceled; their coach forced to resign. One lacrosse player, who sent an e-mail the day of the alleged incident referencing the film *American Psycho*, was subsequently vilified in the press. According to a 2014 *Vanity Fair* article, he has had trouble finding gainful employment ever since.[54] A complaint brought[55] by nearly forty members of the Duke lacrosse team against the university outlined what life was like for them after three of their teammates were accused of rape: "For 13 months in 2006-2007 these students were reviled almost daily in the local and national media as a depraved gang of privileged, white hooligans who had hired a black exotic dancer to perform at a team party, had brutally gang raped and sodomized her in a crowded bathroom, and had joined together in a 'wall of silence' to hide the truth of their heinous crimes. But it was a vile and shameful lie, and it caused the plaintiffs tremendous suffering and grievous, lasting injuries."[56]

Zerlina Maxwell isn't interested in such things. She says, "The cost of disbelieving women [who make false accusations]...signals that women don't matter and that they are disposable...." No, it signals that we believe that people are innocent until proven guilty, that an accusation is not the end of the conversation, but the beginning. It signals that we are not an authoritarian society that punishes people without due process. Any person with a son, brother, nephew, husband, or a passing interest in the humanity of men in society should be deeply alarmed by the callous dismissal of the basic rights of men to be presumed innocent.

During the Duke lacrosse rape case, feminist writer Amanda Marcotte called people defending the accused "rape-loving scum" and characterized legitimate questions about the case as akin to saying, "Can't a few white boys sexually assault a black woman anymore without people getting all wound up about it? So unfair."[57] She accused columnists David Brooks and Kathleen Parker of writing "rape apologies"[58] when they raised issues about the case. A mob of Duke students banged pots and pans outside the house of Provost Peter Lange, who eventually came out to engage them. As the students harassed him, he repeatedly urged respect for due process, saying, "We don't know the facts of what happened in the house." "Bullshit!" a protestor cried out immediately in response.[59]

In *New York* magazine, Kurt Anderson[60] blasted the *New York Times'* biased coverage for abetting the rhetorical lynch mob and quoted one *Times* reporter saying "I've never felt so ill" as he did about the paper's slanted treatment of the story. The story was just too perfect to resist, let alone investigate fairly: white, privileged men were abusing a black single mother. So facts be damned and saddle up the bias nag, we're riding herd! Anderson recounted how one Duke associate professor, Wahneema Lubiano gleefully blogged[61] about how the lacrosse players "are almost perfect offenders." Why? Because they are "the exemplars of the upper end of the class hierarchy...and the dominant social group on campus." So, "regardless of the 'truth'.... Whatever happens with the court case, what people are asking is that something changes."

A Duke University Women's Studies and English professor named Karla F. C. Holloway was a primary persecutor of the accused students. Holloway, who also is a professor at Duke Law School, penned an article for the 2006 summer edition of a Barnard College *Scholar & Feminist Online* webjournal,[62] in which she demonized the lacrosse players as privileged white men who deserved a presumption of guilt. She accused the players of engaging in the "debasement of other human beings" and alleged that their "presumption of privilege that their elite sports' performance had earned seemed their entitlement... to behaving badly and without concern for consequence." She wrote, "In nearly every social context that emerged following the team's crude conduct, innocence and guilt have been assessed through a metric of race and gender. White innocence means black guilt. Men's innocence means women's guilt." Holloway is still employed by Duke University.[63]

In a letter to Duke University, Houston Baker, a professor now at Vanderbilt, was quick to demonize and convict the lacrosse players. Their actions were the natural conclusion of Duke's culture of "white, male, athletic violence." He accused the University of the "blind-eyeing of male athletes, veritably given license to rape, maraud, deploy hate speech, and feel proud of themselves in the bargain."[64] He wasn't the only one. After

the case first broke in 2006, Wendy Murphy, a lawyer and adjunct professor at the New England School of Law, went on a tear against the players
in various interviews, arguing, "To suggest [the indicted players] were well
behaved: Hitler never beat his wife either. So what?"[65] She speculated about
the accused players, "I bet one or more of the players was, you know,
molested or something as a child."[66] And then this: "I never, ever met a
false rape claim, by the way. My own statistics speak to the truth."[67]

But there was no truth in the accusations. Eventually all charges were
dropped[68] against the students and the district attorney who brought the
case was fired and disbarred for his actions. Few, if any, apologies were
forthcoming from the members of the illiberal mob who harassed and
slandered anyone who refused to leap to a presumption of guilt against the
players. After North Carolina Attorney General Roy Cooper declared the
three accused students "innocent," Dr. Julianne Malveaux—incoming
president of Bennett College, an all-women's school—told National Public Radio that the students were hooligans and "bad apples" and "don't
deserve an apology."[69]

Arguing to condemn accused men despite the lack of evidence is not
a new phenomenon. Al Sharpton, a card carrying member in good standing of the illiberal left, employed these methods when he represented a
fifteen-year-old African American girl named Tawana Brawley who had
allegedly suffered a brutal rape at the hands of racists in 1987. "We have
the facts and the evidence that an assistant district attorney and a state
trooper did this," Sharpton alleged at a press conference. The *New York
Times*[70] reported that Sharpton called Governor Mario M. Cuomo a racist
and warned that powerful state officials were complicit. When asked
whether Ms. Brawley would speak with the state attorney general, Robert
Abrams, Mr. Sharpton said that would be like "asking someone in a con-
centration camp to talk to Hitler." A grand jury later determined the entire
story was made up.[71] When asked by the *New York Times* in 2014 about the
destructive hoax, Sharpton said, "Whatever happened . . . you're dealing
with a minor who was missing four days. So it's clear that something wrong

happened."[72] No apology. No contrition. For the illiberal left, facts don't matter, only ideology does, and vilifying your opponents.

PRESUMED GUILTY

The Obama administration has used the illiberal feminists' bad statistics and presumption of guilt to justify requiring universities to adjudicate rape accusations, something that should be left to law enforcement and the courts. In April 2011, the Department of Education's Office for Civil Rights (OCR) issued a "Dear Colleague" letter reminding colleges and universities throughout the country of their obligation to comply with the requirements of Title IX in order to receive federal funding. Specifically, the letter informed schools of their duty to investigate and adjudicate claims of sexual harassment and assault, no matter the status of a police investigation.[73] This requirement is not in the text of Title IX itself, but rather stems from piecemeal statutory amendments and administrative interpretations.[74]

Thanks to this policy, schools risk losing government funding unless they agree to handle rape allegations according to a system that provides little due process for the accused. The letter informed colleges and universities of OCR's expectation that they use the "preponderance of the evidence" standard in these investigations—the lowest standard used by a court of law (usually in civil cases), and far from the "beyond a reasonable doubt" standard that would be used in a typical rape investigation. Using the preponderance of evidence standard, the school is told to determine whether it is "more likely than not that sexual harassment or violence occurred."[75] Pursuant to that standard, the letter reminds colleges that "[c]onduct may constitute unlawful sexual harassment under Title IX even if the police do not have sufficient evidence of a criminal violation."[76]

The letter also placed harsh limitations on the accused's right of cross-examination, stating that, "OCR strongly discourages schools from allowing the parties personally to question or cross-examine each other during the hearing. Allowing an alleged perpetrator to question an alleged victim directly may be traumatic or intimidating, thereby possibly escalating or perpetuating a hostile environment."[77]

Even some Title IX advocates have expressed concern over the possibility of wrongful convictions under the new standards. In an April 2014 newsletter, Brett A. Sokolow, executive director for the Association of Title IX Administrators, wrote that he had seen at least five recent drunken hookup cases in which he felt the accused was wrongfully convicted.[78] Harvard civil rights law professor Elizabeth Bartholet has called the government's position "madness."[79] The *New Republic*'s Judith Shulevitz blasted the campus "shadow judicial system"[80] and explained that "the government, via Title IX, is effectively acting on the notion popularized in the 1970s and '80s by [radical feminists] Andrea Dworkin and Catharine MacKinnon that male domination is so pervasive that women need special protection from the rigors of the law."

After Harvard University announced a new sexual harassment policy in compliance with the 2011 letter, twenty-eight members of the Harvard Law School faculty issued a statement expressing strong opposition. The group said the new regulations "lack the most basic elements of fairness and due process, are overwhelmingly stacked against the accused, and are in no way required by Title IX law or regulation."[81] Specifically, the professors highlighted the lack of notice and discovery (the right to know what the accusations are and the evidence and testimony of the accuser), as well as the inability of accused students to obtain counsel and cross-examine their accusers as guaranteed by an adversarial judicial system. The letter further decries "[t]he lodging of the functions of investigation, prosecution, fact-finding, and appellate review in one office, and the fact that that office is itself a Title IX compliance office rather than an entity that could be considered structurally impartial."[82] Harvard Law Professor Jennie Suk—one of the signatories—noted in the *New Yorker*, that there is a "growing rape exceptionalism, which allows fears of inflicting or re-inflicting trauma to justify foregoing usual procedures and practices of truth-seeking."[83]

Yale Law Professor Jed Rubenfeld penned a *New York Times* op-ed arguing for a new approach[84] to the issue of campus rape. "Mistaken findings of guilt are a real possibility because the federal government is forcing schools to use a lowered evidentiary standard—the 'more likely than not' standard, which is much less exacting than criminal law's 'proof beyond a reasonable doubt' requirement—at their rape trials," he wrote. Rubenfeld blasted the dangerous definition many universities were using for the word "rape" in telling their students "that intercourse with someone 'under the influence' of alcohol is always rape." He pointed to a posting on a Hampshire, Mount Holyoke, and Smith website: "Agreement given while under the influence of alcohol or other drugs is not considered consent" and "if you have not consented to sexual intercourse, it is rape." In other words: if you have sex after drinking alcohol, you have been raped.

This kind of lunacy has become the unquestioned dogma of illiberal feminists and their enablers in university and governmental institutions. Rubenfeld reported that a Duke University dean who was asked what to do if both parties are under the influence answered, "Assuming it is a male and female, it is the responsibility in the case of the male to gain consent."[85] How Victorian. So, a drunk woman can't consent to sex, but a drunk man can. Rubenfeld wrote, "This answer shows more ideology than logic. In fact, sex with someone under the influence is not automatically rape. That misleading statement misrepresents both the law and universities' official policies. The general rule is that sex with someone incapacitated by alcohol or other drugs is rape. There is—or at least used to be—a big difference. Incapacitation typically means you no longer know what's happening around you or can't manage basic physical activity like walking or standing."

Jessica Valenti called Rubenfeld's op-ed a "rape apology."[86] She wrote in the *Guardian*, "The worst offense is Rubenfeld's apparent belief that there is a debate' to be had—as if there are two equal sides, both with reasonable and legitimate points. There are not." That's the illiberal left position in a nutshell. "On the one side, there are the 20 percent of college

women who can expect to be victimized by rapists and would-be rapists,"
wrote Valenti. "On the other side is a bunch of adult men (and a few
women) worrying themselves to death that a few college-aged men might
have to find a new college to attend." Anti-rape activist Alexandra Brodsky
defended the "preponderance of evidence" standard and dismissed the
potential harm to male college students "Getting kicked out of school
sucks, but it's not the same as imprisonment," she wrote.[87]

Remember, the same illiberal feminists who think it is no big deal to
kick an innocent man out of college, trash his reputation, and harm his
future job prospects on the basis of false accusations are also likely to think
that if a woman has to walk past an anti-abortion demonstration on campus she has suffered grievous harm.

Abusing official power through kangaroo court campus rape "trials"
was a precursor to another illiberal feminist pet cause: "affirmative consent" laws. California Governor Jerry Brown signed a bill in 2014[88] that
required "affirmative consent" for all sexual interactions on California
state campuses. For people who are forever proclaiming that they want
government out of their bedrooms, it's odd that illiberal feminists supported a law that put the State of California in the middle of every physically romantic interaction on California campuses.

As first written, the bill, SB 967, required the governing boards of
community and state colleges as well as California State University to
adopt an affirmative consent standard. This version required that consent
be sought at every stage of an encounter—one question for touching,
another for kissing, and so on. It required that consent be "expressed
either by words or clear, unambiguous actions" though "relying solely on
nonverbal communication can lead to misunderstanding." Consent had
to be "present throughout sexual activity"; if "confusion" over consent
arises, "it is essential that the participants stop the activity until the confusion can be clearly resolved." The accused may not invoke confusion
over consent as a defense if he or she "did not take reasonable steps, in the
circumstances known to the accused at the time, to ascertain that the

complainant was consenting." The version that passed was less specific and cut the line about "misunderstanding," but the spirit remained the same.[89]

Shikha Dalmia blasted the law in a Reason.com column[90] titled "California's Sexual Consent Law Will Ruin Good Sex for Women." The subtitle was "And it won't stop rape." Dalmia, who describes herself as an agnostic and progressive libertarian, argued that the majority of campus assaults were not "the result of miscommunication." She noted, "Most assaulters know exactly what they are doing. The vast majority of campus rapes are committed by a small minority of repeat offenders who give not a damn about what the woman wants." She also argued that, "[W]hether due to nurture or nature, there is usually a difference in tempo between men and women, with women generally requiring more 'convincing.' And someone who requires convincing is not yet in a position to offer 'affirmative' much less 'enthusiastic' consent. That doesn't mean that the final experience is unsatisfying—but it does mean that initially one has to be coaxed out of one's comfort zone. Affirmative consent would criminalize that." In other words, seduction itself is now a crime.

Perhaps it's not a perfect analysis, but rather than debating Dalmia's argument, you can guess exactly how the illiberal feminists reacted. Kalli Joy Gray of the liberal blog *Wonkette* called Dalmia "some dumb lady" who is "too dumb to be having sex in the first place. Please stop."[91] Erin Gloria Ryan of Jezebel wrote an article headlined, "Consent laws are ruining sex, says writer who probably has awful sex" and accused Dalmia of defending rapists.[92] Jill Filipovic, the political editor of *Cosmopolitan*, tweeted that Dalmia's column proved she was "bad at sex."[93]

It's strange isn't it, that illiberal feminists seem obsessed with sexual "freedom," while at the same time wanting to have every aspect of it regulated by the government, practically requiring a court order. It's odd that they "slut-shame" and "sex-shame" their female opponents in ways that they would condemn in a man, or any ideological opponent. Illiberal feminists seem at war with nature, with the facts, and with truth. Most of all, they are at war with the freedom of speech and of legal due process that allows us to find the truth.

EPILOGUE

As I was finishing this book, I attended a dinner party where three of the guests had firsthand experience with the illiberal left's silencing campaign. A retired Stanford professor and a current Harvard Law School student, both evangelical Christians and conservatives, described being intimidated into silence on their respective campuses. Like the "closeted conservatives" New York University Professor Jonathan Haidt discovered in his research, they felt forced to hide their religious and political beliefs lest they be discriminated against or ostracized. A third dinner guest—a former professor at a Washington, D.C., area university— was passed over for a position because she was suspected (correctly) of being conservative. This is in writing.

A few days later, I participated in an Oxford-style debate[1] hosted by Intelligence Squared in Washington, D.C. FIRE's president Greg Lukianoff and I argued in favor of the motion, "Liberals are stifling intellectual diversity on campuses." Arguing against was George Mason University professor Jeremy Meyer and Angus Johnston, an historian of student activism.

Greg and I won the debate. But such victories are bittersweet. There is little pleasure in making a persuasive case that people on the left side of the political spectrum are intimidating and demonizing others into silence.

Just as disheartening was realizing how great a chasm of disagreement exists on this topic. Meyer cited research from a 2008 book he co-authored—*Closed Minds*[2]—which found that even though liberals outnumber conservatives within faculty ranks, 85 percent of conservatives surveyed argued that ideology played no role in tenure in their departments.

Personally, I have not encountered a single conservative academic who believes there is no ideological bias at the college or university at which they are or were employed. Instead, I'm inundated with chilling stories from fair-minded and brilliant academics who would like to just do their research and teach their students without the thought police on their tails. Moreover, the illiberal prejudices of predominantly liberal colleges and universities are too well documented to ignore.

Meyer argued that the reason liberals overwhelmingly outnumber conservatives in academia isn't because of anything liberals are doing; it's because conservatives only care about making money, are hostile to science, and embrace anti-intellectualism.[3]

Gee, why would any conservative be worried about discrimination in academia with attitudes like that?

As I listened to this kind of talk, it occurred to me that the only way any person could believe what Meyer was saying was if they had no meaningful relationships with conservatives. One visit to my church would dispel all three of his claims. A little research into evangelical ministries would lay to rest the idea that conservatives only care about making money. And perhaps he'd like to meet my aforementioned dinner party companions to discuss the anti-intellectualism charge.

It seemed even odder to hear Meyer's argument as I sat next to Greg, a liberal atheist who receives phone calls every week from people seeking legal representation to protect them from actions taken due to ideological or anti-religious bias in higher education. As Greg noted in his opening statement, there is this unfortunate truth: "If you're going to be censored on the modern college campus for your opinion, chances are you're going to be censored by the Left."

The Intelligence Squared debate was focused narrowly on higher education, but our opponents' arguments were familiar. I regularly hear them from journalists who insist that the lack of conservatives in the mainstream media has nothing to do with the behavior of the overwhelming number of liberals who populate that profession. They claim there is no bias in how they cover the news, even as they acknowledge there is a complete lack of ideological and political diversity in the newsroom. It's not uncommon to hear members of the media make assertions similar to Meyer's by stereotyping conservatives and evangelicals as greedy flat-earthers.

I've chronicled in this book the myriad ways such a hostile and baseless bias has seeped into our culture. We've seen an Internet executive forced from his job for a private donation to a same-sex marriage initiative and a fast-food employee verbally accosted for working at Chick-fil-A. By this time next year there will likely be another ream of examples of illiberal silencing. So, what can be done?

The first step toward change is to acknowledge the problem. I hope this book will serve as a starting place for such an acknowledgment among sincere liberals. While the illiberal left likely will not be swayed from their silencing campaign, the more open-minded liberals who provide aid and comfort to them might be.

David French, a free speech advocate who currently serves as senior counsel for the American Center for Law and Justice (ACLJ), shared a story with me recently that illustrates how this might work. French, a Harvard Law School graduate and evangelical Christian, was serving on the admissions committee of Cornell Law School when a student hailing from a religious college was put up for consideration. "I'll never forget watching the committee almost vote to reject an incredibly qualified candidate

because—and they put this in writing—they didn't want a 'Bible thump-
ing' student who might be a member of the 'God squad,'" French told me.
After French confronted the committee, noting that his own background
was similar to the applicant's, they appeared chagrined and ultimately
accepted the student.

But what if French hadn't been there? The student almost certainly
would have been rejected.

"That episode taught me a couple things," said French. "First, anti-
Christian discrimination can be reflexive; and second, a little bit of true
intellectual diversity can go a long way towards reversing its effects. Those
folks were my friends, yet their biases were deeply ingrained."

The moral of this story is simple: we should all make efforts to invite
people who hold different views into our worlds. Contrary to popular
thought, familiarity doesn't breed contempt. It breeds understanding and
tolerance. Now, go make some unlikely friends.

NOTES

INTRODUCTION

1. Gary A. Tobin and Aryeh K. Weinberg, "Profiles of the American University: Volume II: Religious Beliefs & Behavior of College Faculty," Institute for Jewish & Community Research, 2007, http://www.jewishresearch.org/PDFs2/ FacultyReligion07.pdf.
2. José L. Duarte et al., "Political Diversity Will Improve Social Psychological Science," *Behavioral and Brain Sciences* (Cambridge University Press, 2014), https://journals.cambridge.org/images/fileUpload/documents/Duarte-Haidt_ BBS-D-14-00108_preprint.pdf.

CHAPTER ONE: REPRESSIVE TOLERANCE

1. "Transcription of 'Challenging the Ideological Echo Chamber: Free Speech, Civil Discourse and the Liberal Arts,'" *Smith Sophian*, October 13, 2014, http://www. thesmithsophian.com/2014/10/13/transcription-of-challenging-the-ideological- echo-chamber-free-speech-civil-discourse-and-the-liberal-arts/.

2.   Ibid.

3.   Leah Willingham, "Smith College Community Reacts to Racially-Charged Remark by Alumna," *Mount Holyoke News*, October 22, 2014, http://mountholyokenews.org/2014/10/11/smith-college-community-reacts-to-racially-charged-remark-by-alumna/.

4.   "Transcription of 'Challenging the Ideological Echo Chamber.'"

5.   Willingham, "Smith College Community Reacts."

6.   Ibid.

7.   Jordan Houston, "5 Ways to Use White Privilege as an Ally," Huffington Post, October 15, 2014, updated December 15, 2014, http://www.huffingtonpost.com/jordan-houston/5-ways-to-use-white-privi_b_5991622.html.

8.   Fredrik deBoer, "Bingo Cards Go Both Ways," FredrikdeBoer.com, April 29, 2014, http://fredrikdeboer.com/2014/04/29/bingo-cards-go-both-ways/.

9.   "Tell the *Washington Post*: Don't Promote Climate Change Denial" petition, Forecast The Facts website, http://act.forecastthefacts.org/sign/tell_washpost_dontpublishlies/; "110K Call on the *Washington Post* to End Climate Change Denial in Its Editorial Page," Forecast The Facts website, February 20, 2014, http://forecastthefacts.org/press/releases/2014/2/20/110k-call-washington-post-end-climate-change-denia/.

10. Philip Caulfield, "Forbes Sacks Columnist over Piece Saying 'Drunk' Female Students Pose 'Gravest' Threat to Frats; Writer Responds, 'I Stand by Every Word,'" *New York Daily News*, September 24, 2014, http://www.nydailynews.com/news/national/forbes-columnist-sacked-piece-drunk-female-guests-grave-threat-frats-writer-responds-article-1.1951124; "Tell the *Washington Post*: Fire George Will" petition, UltraViolet, http://act.weareultraviolet.org/cms/sign/Fire_George_Will/; as seen on *On the Record with Greta Van Susteren*, "Student Says His Home Was Egged & He Was Fired for Conservative Column," Fox News, December 18, 2014, http://insider.foxnews.com/2014/12/18/student-says-his-home-was-egged-he-was-fired-conservative-column.

11. Mike Allen, "Fox 'Not Really News,' Says Axelrod," *Politico*, October 18, 2009, http://www.politico.com/news/stories/1009/28417.html#ixzz2IYVABVlp.

12. David Martosko, "Left-Wing Foundations Lavish Millions on Media Matters," Daily Caller, February 17, 2012, http://dailycaller.com/2012/02/17/left-wing-

foundations-lavish-millions-on-media-matters/; Media Matters for America (MMFA), DiscovertheNetworks.org, http://www.discoverthenetworks.org/printgroupProfile.asp?grpid=7150.

13. Ben Smith, "Media Matters' War against Fox," *Politico*, updated March 27, 2011, http://www.politico.com/news/stories/0311/51949.html.

14. "Media Matters 2012: A Three-Year Campaign," Media Matters for America, available on Scribd, 40, https://www.scribd.com/fullscreen/81500388?access_key=key-24nmzdhkwvvpj2lmcndy&allow_share=true&escape=false&view_mode=scroll; "Media Matters' 'War on Fox' Memo," Buzzfeed, February 13, 2012, http://www.buzzfeed.com/buzzfeedpolitics/media-matters-war-on-fox-memo#.neYAQ7NpG.

15. Ari Cohn, Foundation for Individual Rights in Education, February 24, 2015.

16. Greg Lukianoff, *Freedom from Speech* (New York: Encounter Books, 2014).

17. David Mark, "Contracting Out U.S. Security? And Will Branding Tea Party 'Racist' Work?," *Politico*, July 20, 2010, http://www.politico.com/arena/perm/Mary_Frances_Berry_91E3D9D5-C40D-440C-9D48-1C50CBC60C87.html.

18. "Maher vs. Muslim Journo on Berkeley Speech: 'Whoever Told You You Only Had to Hear What Didn't Upset You?'," RealClearPolitics, October 31, 2014, http://www.realclearpolitics.com/video/2014/10/31/maher_vs_muslim_guest_on_berkeley_speech_whoever_told_you_you_only_had_to_hear_what_didnt_upset_you.html.

19. Matt Wilstein, "Bill Maher Calls Out 'Bullshi*t' Petition ahead of Berkeley Speech," *Mediaite*, December 4, 2014, http://www.mediaite.com/online/bill-maher-calls-out-bullsht-petition-ahead-of-berkeley-speech/.

20. "Mozilla Leadership Changes," *Mozilla Blog*, March 24, 2014, https://blog.mozilla.org/blog/2014/03/24/mozilla-leadership-changes/.

21. Brendan Eich, "Community and Diversity," BrendanEich.com, April 5, 2012, https://brendaneich.com/2012/04/community-and-diversity/.

22. "Proposition 8: Who Gave in the Gay Marriage Battle?," *Los Angeles Times*, http://projects.latimes.com/prop8/donation/8930/.

23. Deborah Netburn, "Brendan Eich's Prop. 8 Contribution Gets Twittersphere Buzzing," *Los Angeles Times*, April 4, 2012, http://articles.latimes.com/2012/apr/04/business/la-fi-tn-brendan-eich-prop-8-contribution-20120404.

24.   "Inclusiveness at Mozilla," BrendanEich.com, March 26, 2014, https://brendaneich.com/2014/03/inclusiveness-at-mozilla/.

25.   Sunnivie Brydum, "Nearly 65K Demand Mozilla CEO Come Out for Marriage Equality," *Advocate*, March 31, 2014, http://www.advocate.com/business/technology/2014/03/31/nearly-65k-demand-mozilla-ceo-come-out-marriage-equality.

26.   "Brendan Eich Steps Down as Mozilla CEO," *Mozilla Blog*, April 3, 2014, https://blog.mozilla.org/blog/2014/04/03/brendan-eich-steps-down-as-mozilla-ceo/.

27.   Andrew Sullivan, "Here Comes the Groom," *New Republic*, August 28, 1989, http://www.newrepublic.com/article/79054/here-comes-the-groom.

28.   "Dissents of the Day," *TheDish*, April 4, 2014, http://dish.andrewsullivan.com/2014/04/04/dissents-of-the-day-63/.

29.   Charles Louis de Secondat, Baron de Montesquieu, *The Complete Works of M. de Montesquieu* (London: T. Evans, 1777), 4 vols., vol. 1., http://oll.libertyfund.org/titles/837.

30.   Alexis de Tocqueville, *Democracy in America.*

31.   Alex Doody, "Protests at Exeter over OSFL Abortion Panel Event," *Cherwell*, February 7, 2015, http://www.cherwell.org/news/topstories/2015/02/06/protests-at-exeter-over-osfl-abortion-panel-event.

32.   "Three Reasons to Affirm Free Speech—Keynote Address at FIRE's 15th Anniversary Dinner," FIRE, October 23, 2014, http://www.thefire.org/three-reasons-affirm-free-speech-keynote-address-fires-15th-anniversary-dinner/.

33.   Concurring opinion in *Whitney v. California*, 1927, text available at Legal Information Institute, https://www.law.cornell.edu/supremecourt/text/274/357.

34.   Geoffrey R. Stone, "Justice Brennan and the Freedom of Speech: A First Amendment Odyssey," *University of Pennsylvania Law Review*, http://scholarship.law.upenn.edu/cgi/viewcontent.cgi?article=3755&context=penn_law_review.

35.   *New York Times v. Sullivan*, 376 U.S. 254, 270 (1964).

36.   Marc Morano, "Update: Video: Robert F. Kennedy Jr. Wants to Jail His Political Opponents—Accuses Koch Brothers of 'Treason'—'They Ought to Be Serving Time for It,'" Climate Depot, September 21, 2014, see video, http://www.climatedepot.com/2014/09/21/robert-f-kennedy-jr-wants-to-jail-his-political-

opponents-accuses-koch-brothers-of-treason-they-ought-to-be-serving-time-for-it/.

37.   Stephen Brooks, *Understanding American Politics* (Toronto: University of Toronto Press, 2009), 287.

38.   "RFK Jr: Eternity in Jail for Coal CEO," *Green Hell Blog*, March 2, 2009, http://greenhellblog.com/2009/03/02/rfk-jr-eternity-in-jail-for-coal-ceo/.

39.   Floyd Abrams, speech provided to author.

40.   Steven H. Shiffrin, Cornell University Law School, http://www.lawschool.cornell.edu/faculty/bio.cfm?id=72.

41.   Steven H. Shiffrin, "The Dark Side of the First Amendment," *UCLA Law Review*, 61 UCLA L. Rev. 1480 (2014), http://www.uclalawreview.org/pdf/61-5-7.pdf.

42.   Eric Posner, "The World Doesn't Love the First Amendment," *Slate*, September 25, 2012, http://www.slate.com/articles/news_and_politics/jurisprudence/2012/09/the_vile_anti_muslim_video_and_the_first_amendment_does_the_u_s_overvalue_free_speech_.single.html.

43.   "State of the First Amendment: 2013," First Amendment Center, 2013, http://www.firstamendmentcenter.org/madison/wp-content/uploads/2013/07/SOFA-2013-final-report.pdf.

44.   Jonathan Haidt, "The Bright Future of Post-Partisan Social Psychology," Edge.org, February 11, 2011, https://edge.org/conversation/the-bright-future-of-post-partisan-social-psychology; John Tierney, "Social Scientist Sees Bias Within," *New York Times*, February 7, 2011, http://www.nytimes.com/2011/02/08/science/08tier.html?_r=0.

45.   "Three Reasons to Affirm Free Speech—Keynote Address at FIRE's 15th Anniversary Dinner."

CHAPTER TWO: DELEGITIMIZING DISSENT

1.   "Outstanding Coverage of a Breaking News Story in a Regularly Scheduled Newscast," in "NBC Nightly News with Brian Williams (1970–), Awards," IMDb, http://www.imdb.com/title/tt0231035/awards.

2.   Campbell Brown, "Teachers Unions Go to Bat for Sexual Predators," *Wall Street Journal*, July 29, 2012, http://www.wsj.com/articles/SB10000872396390443437504577547313612049308.

3.   Stephen Sawchuk, "A Twitter Debate on Teacher Sexual Misconduct," *Education Week*, August 2, 2014, http://blogs.edweek.org/edweek/teacherbeat/2012/08/a_twitter_debate_on_teacher_se.html.

4.   Stephanie Simon, "Obama Alums Join Anti-Teachers Union Case," *Politico*, June 24, 2014, http://www.politico.com/story/2014/06/robert-gibbs-ben-labolt-legal-fight-teachers-union-incite-agency-108243.html.

5.   Kirsten Powers, "Left-Wing Teacher Groups Launch Sexist Crusade," *USA Today*, August 19, 2014, http://www.usatoday.com/story/opinion/2014/08/19/powers-left-campbell-brown-school-choice-teacher-groups-sexist-crusade-column/14299039/.

6.   Paul Farhi, "Campbell Brown Goes after Teacher Tenure in Transition from Journalist to Advocate," *Washington Post*, July 14, 2014, http://www.washingtonpost.com/lifestyle/style/campbell-brown-goes-after-teacher-tenure-in-transition-from-journalist-to-advocate/2014/07/14/58fdb33e-0919-11e4-a0dd-f2b22a257353_story.html.

7.   Michelle Rhee, "My Break with the Democrats," Daily Beast, February 4, 2013, http://www.thedailybeast.com/articles/2013/02/04/michelle-rhee-my-break-with-the-democrats.html.

8.   Richard Whitmire, "What Is behind the Discrediting of Michelle Rhee?," *Education Week*, February 28, 2011, http://www.edweek.org/ew/articles/2011/03/02/22whitmire.h30.html.

9.   Ibid.

10.   Michele McNeil, "U.S. Dept. of Ed. Protesters Turn Fierce Rhetoric on 'Corporate' Reform," *Education Week*, April 4, 2013, http://blogs.edweek.org/edweek/campaign-k-12/2013/04/education_department_protesters_turn_fierce_rhetoric_on_corporate_reform.html.

11.   Jeff Bryant, "Michelle Rhee Misreads 'Shift among Democrats' on Education," Campaign for America's Future, October 12, 2012, http://ourfuture.org/20121012/michelle-rhee-misreads-shift-among-democrats-on-education.

12.   Jeff Bryant, "Education 'Reform's' New Ann Coulter: A Reeling Michelle Rhee Passes the Lead to Campbell Brown," Salon.com, July 23, 2014, http://www.salon.com/2014/07/23/education_reforms_new_ann_coulter_a_reeling_michelle_rhee_passes_the_lead_to_campbell_brown/.

13.   Alexander Russo, "Update: Union Defends Anti-Rhee Site/Attacks Rhee Secrecy," Scholastic's *This Week In Education*, August 29, 2011, http://scholasticadministrator.typepad.com/thisweekineducation/2011/08/confronted-with-information-published-in-politico-that-rheefirst-was-an-anonymous-attack-vehicle-secretly-created-inside-the.html#.VOafTilUXjQ.

14.   Jeremy Waldron, "Hate Speech and Free Speech, Part Two," *New York Times*, June 18, 2012, http://opinionator.blogs.nytimes.com/2012/06/18/hate-speech-and-free-speech-part-two/?_r=0.

15.   Andrew Kaczynski, "Democratic Congressman Makes Shocking Racial Comments about Republicans, Clarence Thomas, Mitch McConnell," Buzzfeed News, April 29, 2014, http://www.buzzfeed.com/andrewkaczynski/democratic-congressman-makes-shocking-racial-comments-about.

16.   Ron Christie, "Why Criticizing Obama Isn't Racist," Daily Beast, November 29, 2013, http://www.thedailybeast.com/articles/2013/11/29/criticizing-obama-isn-t-racist.html.

17.   Dexter Mullins, "Do Black People Really Know Their 'Uncle Tom'?," Grio, February 16, 2011, http://thegrio.com/2011/02/16/do-black-people-really-know-their-uncle-tom/; Adena Spingarn, "When 'Uncle Tom' Became an Insult," *Root*, May 17, 2010, http://www.theroot.com/articles/politics/2010/05/uncle_tom_from_compliment_to_insult.html.

18.   "Radio Host Calls Rice an 'Aunt Jemima,'" Fox News, November 19, 2004, http://www.foxnews.com/story/2004/11/19/radio-host-calls-rice-aunt-jemima/.

19.   See excerpt from Malcolm X, "The Race Problem," African Students Association and NAACP Campus Chapter, Michigan State University, January 23, 1963, available here: http://ccnmtl.columbia.edu/projects/mmt/mxp/speeches/mxa17.html.

20.   Raffi Williams, interview with author, January 16, 2015.

21.   "Steele Weighs in on the Oreo Incident," *Baltimore Sun*, November 15, 2005, http://articles.baltimoresun.com/2005-11-15/news/0511150358_1_oreo-cookies-ehrlich-steele; "Michael Steele Oreo Incident Eyewitness Report," Amy Ridenour, National Center Blog, National Center for Public Policy Research, November 23, 2005, http://www.nationalcenter.org/2005/11/michael-steele-oreo-incident.html.

22. "The Top 10 Sambos Living in America Today," ThyBlackMan, June 30, 2011, http://thyblackman.com/2011/06/30/the-top-10-sambos-living-in-america-today/.

23. Blogxilla GlobalGrindTV, "Samuel Jackson Talks Troubles of Playing a 'House Negro' In Django Unchained," YouTube, December 26, 2012, https://www.youtube.com/watch?v=tYkZe3yprKU; Jeff Poor, "Jason Whitlock Strikes again: Likens Thomas Sowell to 'House Negro' Film Character," Daily Caller, January 3, 2013, http://dailycaller.com/2013/01/03/jason-whitlock-likens-thomas-sowell-to-house-negro-film-character/.

24. "The Top 10 Sambos Living in America Today."

25. Ibid.

26. Ibid.

27. Pam Key, "MSNBC Guest: Jindal 'Trying to Scrub Some of the Brown Off His Skin," Breitbart, January 19, 2015, http://www.breitbart.com/video/2015/01/19/msnbc-guest-jindal-trying-to-scrub-some-of-the-brown-off-his-skin/.

28. Darron T. Smith, "She Looks Black, but Her Politics Are Red: What Mia Love's Victory Means for the Face of the GOP," Huffington Post, November 6, 2014, updated January 6, 2015, http://www.huffingtonpost.com/darron-t-smith-phd/mia-love_b_6116466.html.

29. Hamilton Nolan, "The Breathtaking Cynicism of the Mia Love Lovefest," *Gawker*, November 6, 2014, http://gawker.com/the-breathtaking-cynicism-of-the-mia-love-lovefest-1655416459.

30. Smith, "She Looks Black."

31. Erica Ritz, "RNC Star Mia Love's Wikipedia Reportedly Changed to 'Dirty, Worthless Wh*re' Who Is a 'House Ni**er,'" TheBlaze, August 29, 2012, http://www.theblaze.com/stories/2012/08/29/rnc-star-mia-loves-wikipedia-reportedly-changed-to-dirty-worthless-whre'-who-is-a-house-nier/.

32. "Sick: Wikipedia Entry Calls Mia Love 'Dirty, Worthless Whore' and 'House Nigger,'" Twitchy, August 29, 2012, http://twitchy.com/2012/08/29/sick-wikipedia-entry-calls-mia-love-dirty-worthless-whore-and-house-nigger/.

33. John Monk, "NC NAACP Chief Denounces Extremists of All Kinds, Including Conservatives," *State*, January 19, 2014, http://www.thestate.com/2014/01/19/3216854_in-fiery-pre-mlk-day-speech-nc.html?rh=1.

34. Jim Morrill, "Barber defends 'Dummy' remark," *Charlotte Observer,* January 23, 2014, available at NCSpin.com, http://www.ncspin.com/barber-defends-dummy-remark/.

35. Ben Terris, "The Undercover Senator: Tim Scott Goes Anecdote Shopping in South Carolina," *Washington Post,* May 7, 2014, http://www.washingtonpost.com/lifestyle/style/the-undercover-senator-sen-tim-scott-goes-anecdote-shopping-in-south-carolina/2014/05/06/98e534b0-cbb9-11e3-93eb-6c0037dde2ad_story.html.

36. Adolph L. Reed Jr., "The Puzzle of Black Republicans," *New York Times,* December 18, 2012, http://www.nytimes.com/2012/12/19/opinion/the-puzzle-of-black-republicans.html?_r=0.

37. Michelle Malkin, "Blocked by Alec Baldwin; Plus: Laughing at Liberal Hate," MichelleMalkin.com, September 23, 2011, http://michellemalkin.com/2011/09/23/blocke/.

38. Andrew Johnson, "Spanish-Language Paper Calls Gomez a LINO," National Review Online, June 4, 2013, http://www.nationalreview.com/corner/350132/spanish-language-paper-calls-gomez-lino-andrew-johnson.

39. Sean Sullivan, "New Mexico Dem Criticized for Saying Gov. Martinez 'Does Not Have a Latino Heart,'" *Washington Post,* September 10, 2014, http://www.washingtonpost.com/blogs/post-politics/wp/2014/09/10/new-mexico-dem-criticized-for-saying-gov-martinez-does-not-have-a-latino-heart/.

40. Z. Byron Wolf, "Harry Reid Doesn't Get Hispanic Republicans," ABC News, August 11, 2010, http://abcnews.go.com/blogs/politics/2010/08/harry-reid-doesnt-get-hispanic-republicans/.

41. Juan Williams, *Muzzled: The Assault on Honest Debate* (New York: Crown Publishing Group, 2012).

42. Michelle Malkin, "Conservative Women Finally React with Force to Attacks of Feminists," *Lubbock Avalanche-Journal,* April 13, 2012, http://lubbockonline.com/editorial-columnists/2012-04-14/malkin-conservative-women-finally-react-force-attacks-feminists#.VOqvEylUXjQ.

43. Naomi Wolf, "Are Opinions Male?" *New Republic,* November 29, 1993.

44. Derek Hunter, "Progressives Make Sexist Twitter Smears about Combat Veteran Joni Ernst," Daily Caller, January 20, 2015, http://dailycaller.com/2015/01/20/progressives-make-sexist-twitter-smears-about-combat-veteran-joni-ernst/.

45. Katie Glueck, "Tom Harkin: Joni Ernst as Pretty as Taylor Swift? So What?," Politico, updated November 3, 2014, http://www.politico.com/story/2014/11/2014-iowa-elections-tom-harkin-joni-ernst-taylor-swift-112433.html#ixzz3PgSeeW1.

46. Howard Kurtz, "A Blogger, a Baby, a Cry of Concern," Washington Post, September 2, 2008, http://www.washingtonpost.com/wp-dyn/content/article/2008/09/01/AR2008090102983_pf.html.

47. Paul Farhi, "Ed Schultz suspended from MSNBC after Calling Laura Ingraham a 'Right Wing Slut'," Washington Post, May 26, 2011, http://www.washingtonpost.com/lifestyle/style/ed-schultz-suspended-from-msnbc-after-calling-laura-ingraham-a-right-wing-slut/2011/05/26/AGOcV2BH_story.html.

48. Keith Olbermann, "On So Many Levels She's a Perfect Demonstration of the Necessity of the Work Planned Parenthood Does," Twitter, April 14, 2011, https://twitter.com/KeithOlbermann/status/58582265495683072.

49. Brad Wilmouth, "Olbermann: Without 'Fascistic Hatred,' Malkin Is Just a 'Mashed-Up Bag of Meat with Lipstick,'" MRC NewsBusters, October 13, 2009, http://newsbusters.org/blogs/brad-wilmouth/2009/10/13/olbermann-without-fascistic-hatred-malkin-just-mashed-bag-meat-lipsti#sthash.EORqTsri.dpuf.

50. "Maher Refuses to Apologize for Calling Palin C-Word," Fox News, no date, http://nation.foxnews.com/sarah-palin/2011/03/29/maher-refuses-apologize-calling-palin-c-word.

51. Kate Sheppard, "19 Percent of Congress Is Female. Why Not Half?," Mother Jones, November 20, 2012. http://www.motherjones.com/politics/2012/11/19-percent-congress-women-why-not-half.

52. See Kirsten Powers, "Rush Limbaugh Isn't the Only Media Misogynist," Daily Beast, March 4, 2012, http://www.thedailybeast.com/articles/2012/03/04/rush-limbaugh-s-apology-liberal-men-need-to-follow-suit.html.

53. Jane Fonda, Robin Morgan, and Gloria Steinem, "FCC Should Clear Limbaugh from Airwaves," CNN, March 12, 2012, http://www.cnn.com/2012/03/10/opinion/fonda-morgan-steinem-limbaugh/.

54. egalia, "Gloria Steinem on Bill Maher's Real Time Tonight," *Tennessee Guerilla Women*, March 4, 2011, http://guerillawomentn.blogspot.com/2011/03/gloria-steinem-on-bill-mahers-real-time.html; Alec Jacobs, "Ezzy Klein Goes to Hollywood," FishbowlDC at Adweek Network, March 4, 2011, http://www.adweek.com/fishbowldc/ezzy-klein-goes-to-hollywood/33696?red=dc.

55. "Jeffrey Meyer, Andrea Mitchell to GOP Strategist: You're Anti-Abortion, Not Pro-Life," MRC NewsBusters, January 9, 2013, http://newsbusters.org/blogs/jeffrey-meyer/2013/01/09/andrea-mitchell-gop-strategist-you-re-anti-abortion-not-pro-life.

56. Nina Burleigh, "The Best and the Rightest," *Elle*, August 12, 2011, http://www.elle.com/culture/career-politics/news/a12323/female-conservativism/.

57. "Carter again Cites Racism as Factor in Obama's Treatment," CNN, September 17, 2009, http://www.cnn.com/2009/POLITICS/09/15/carter.obama/index.html?eref=ib_us.

58. Alan Duke, "Redford: Women, Young People Must Save U.S. from Men 'Behaving Stupidly,'" CNN, October 16, 2013, http://www.cnn.com/2013/10/16/showbiz/robert-redford-all-is-lost/index.html.

59. Edward Walsh, "Panel Split Over 'Scumbag' Comment," *Washington Post*, April 22, 1998, http://www.washingtonpost.com/wp-srv/politics/special/clinton/stories/burton042298.htm.

60. Bob Nightengale, "40 Years Later, Hank Aaron's Grace a Beauty to Behold," *USA Today*, April 8, 2014, http://www.usatoday.com/story/sports/mlb/2014/04/07/hank-aaron-40th-anniversary-of-715-home-run-babe-ruth/7432225/?sf24769494=1.

61. Geoffrey Dickens, "The Top 20 Worst Chris Matthews Quotes Calling Obama Critics Racists," MRC NewsBusters, November 7, 2013, http://newsbusters.org/blogs/geoffrey-dickens/2013/11/07/top-20-worst-chris-matthews-quotes-calling-obama-critics-racist.

62. Chuck Todd and Carrie Dann, "Landrieu on Obama: South Not Always 'Friendliest Place for African-Americans," NBC News, October 30, 2014, http://www.nbcnews.com/politics/meet-the-voters/landrieu-obama-south-not-always-friendliest-place-african-americans-n237826.

63. Linda Feldmann, "Landrieu's Last Stand: Why Deep South White Democrats Are Vanishing," *Christian Science Monitor*, December 5, 2014, http://www.

csmonitor.com/USA/DC-Decoder/2014/1205/Landrieu-s-last-stand-why-Deep-South-white-Democrats-are-vanishing.

64. Melinda Deslatte and Bill Barrow, "Senate's Last Deep South Democrat Ousted in Runoff Election," PBS, December 7, 2014, http://www.pbs.org/newshour/rundown/senates-last-deep-south-democrat-ousted-runoff-election/.

65. Deirdre Walsh, "Last White Democrat from Deep South Loses Congressional Seat," CNN, updated November 5, 2014, http://www.cnn.com/2014/11/05/politics/last-southern-white-democrat-in-congress/.

66. Aaron Blake, "Louisiana Democratic Chair: Opposition to Obamacare Is about Race," *Washington Post*, May 29, 2013, http://www.washingtonpost.com/blogs/post-politics/wp/2013/05/29/louisiana-democratic-chair-opposition-to-obamacare-is-about-race/.

67. Andrew Kaczynski, "Democratic Congressman Makes Shocking Racial Comments about Republicans, Clarence Thomas, Mitch McConnell," Fox News, no date, http://nation.foxnews.com/2014/04/30/democratic-congressman-makes-shocking-racial-comments-about-republicans-clarence-thomas.

68. Burgess Everett, "Jay Rockefeller, Ron Johnson Duel over 'Race Card,'" *Politico*, updated May 23, 2014, http://www.politico.com/story/2014/05/jay-rockefeller-john-johnson-race-106983.html.

69. Kathryn A. Wolfe, "Jay Rockefeller: Some Obama Foes Think He's the 'Wrong Color,'" *Politico*, updated May 21, 2014, http://www.politico.com/story/2014/05/jay-rockefeller-barack-obama-106401.html.

70. Robert Scheer, "Racism and Cruelty: What's Behind the GOP's Healthcare Agenda?," *Nation*, October 8, 2013, http://www.thenation.com/article/176540/racism-and-cruelty-whats-behind-gops-healthcare-agenda#.

71. Sarah Kliff, "It's Official: The Feds Will Run Most Obamacare Exchanges," *Washington Post*, February 18, 2013, http://www.washingtonpost.com/blogs/wonkblog/wp/2013/02/18/its-official-the-feds-will-run-most-obamacare-exchanges/.

72. Robert Schlesinger, "DNC Chair: Romney Welfare Attacks Are Racist," *U.S. News & World Report*, August 30, 2012, http://www.usnews.com/opinion/blogs/robert-schlesinger/2012/08/30/dnc-chair-romney-welfare-attacks-are-racist.

73.   Al Sharpton, "Attorney General Eric Holder Has Been 'Stopped and Frisked,'" Huffington Post, August 20, 2012, http://www.huffingtonpost.com/rev-al-sharpton/eric-holder-contempt-fast-and-furious_b_1613079.html.

74.   Tom Kertscher, "In Context: Were Paul Ryan's Poverty Comments a 'Thinly Veiled Racial Attack'?," PolitiFact, March 14, 2014, http://www.politifact.com/wisconsin/article/2014/mar/14/context-paul-ryans-poverty-comments-racial-attack/.

75.   Paul Krugman, "That Old-Time Whistle," New York Times, March 16, 2014, http://www.nytimes.com/2014/03/17/opinion/krugman-that-old-time-whistle.html.

76.   Paul Krugman, "The Town Hall Mob," New York Times, August 6, 2009, http://www.nytimes.com/2009/08/07/opinion/07krugman.html.

77.   Noah Rothman, "Matthews on Tea Party Claiming Will of 'American People': 'Do They Still Count Blacks as 3/5ths?,'" Mediaite, October 17, 2013, http://www.mediaite.com/tv/matthews-on-tea-party-claiming-will-of-american-people-do-they-still-count-blacks-as-35ths/.

78.   Elias Isquith, "Charlie Rangel: Tea Party Is Made Up of 'Mean, Racist People' from Former 'Slave-Holding' States," Salon.com, March 19, 2014, http://www.salon.com/2014/03/19/charlie_rangel_tea_party_is_made_up_of_mean_racist_people_from_former_slave_holding_states/.

79.   "Olbermann: Racism Is in the Tea Party's Heart," RealClearPolitics, March 23, 2010, http://www.realclearpolitics.com/video/2010/03/23/olbermann_racism_is_in_the_tea_partys_heart.html.

80.   Ryan Grim and Luke Johnson, "Is the Tea Party Racist? Ask Some Actual, Out-of-the-Closet Racists," Huffington Post, updated November 5, 2013, http://www.huffingtonpost.com/2013/10/24/tea-party-racist_n_4158262.html.

81.   Colbert I. King, "The Tea Party Resurrects the Spirit of the Old Confederacy," Washington Post, October 4, 2013, http://www.washingtonpost.com/opinions/colbert-king-the-tea-party-resurrects-the-spirit-of-the-old-confederacy/2013/10/04/95b37f6e-2c7b-11e3-97a3-ff2758228523_story.html.

82.   Kenneth T. Walsh, "Obama Says Race a Key Component in Tea Party Protests," U.S. News & World Report, March 2, 2011, http://www.usnews.com/news/

articles/2011/03/02/obama-says-race-a-key-component-in-tea-party-protests?page=3.

83. Marjorie Kehe, "Kate Zernike on 'Boiling Mad: Inside Tea Party America,'" *Christian Science Monitor*, October 21, 2010, http://www.csmonitor.com/Books/chapter-and-verse/2010/1021/Kate-Zernike-on-Boiling-Mad-Inside-Tea-Party-America.

84. Jennifer Epstein, "Nancy Pelosi Calls GOP Budget 'a War on Women,'" *Politico*, April 8, 2011, http://www.politico.com/news/stories/0411/52793.html.

85. Amanda Marcotte, "Mad 21st Century Men," *American Prospect*, March 26, 2012.

86. Joan Walsh, "GOP's Economic War on Women about to Explode," Salon.com, September 25, 2013, http://www.salon.com/2013/09/25/gop's_economic_war_on_women_about_to_explode.

87. Kirsten Powers, "Bill O'Reilly Is Not Sexist," *USA Today*, September 9, 2014, http://www.usatoday.com/story/opinion/2014/09/09/kirsten-powers-bill-oreilly-is-no-sexist/15360175/.

88. Brad Wilmouth, "MSNBC Hits Limbaugh's 'Venom and Hate' and 'Anti-Women Crusader' Cuccinelli," Media Research Center, November 11, 2013, http://mrc.org/biasalerts/msnbc-hits-limbaughs-venom-and-hate-and-anti-women-crusader-cuccinelli.

89. Aaron Camp, "Ken Cuccinelli, of All People, Comes Out against Electoral College Rigging," *Daily Kos*, January 26, 2013, http://www.dailykos.com/story/2013/01/26/1182343/-Ken-Cuccinelli-of-all-people-comes-out-against-Electoral-College-rigging.

90. Exit Polls—Va. Governor, *New York Times*, 2013, http://www.nytimes.com/projects/elections/2013/general/virginia/exit-polls.html.

91. Michelle Goldberg, "Michelle Goldberg on the Ann Romney Hitler Tempest," Daily Beast, May 14, 2012, http://www.thedailybeast.com/articles/2012/05/14/michelle-goldberg-on-the-ann-romney-hitler-tempest.html.

92. Powers, "Bill O'Reilly Is Not Sexist."

93. Joe Strupp, "George Will Ohio Campus Appearance Sparks Protests over Rape Column," Media Matters for America, October 20, 2014, http://mediamatters.org/blog/2014/10/20/george-will-ohio-campus-appearance-sparks-prote/201233; Erin Gloria Ryan, "*Washington Post* Defends George Will's

Atrocious Rape Column," Jezebel, June 12, 2014, http://jezebel.com/washington-post-defends-george-wills-atrocious-rape-col-1590127910.

94.   Emily Yoffe, "College Women: Stop Getting Drunk," *Slate*, October 15, 2013, http://www.slate.com/articles/double_x/doublex/2013/10/sexual_assault_and_drinking_teach_women_the_connection.html.

95.   James Hamblin, "How Not to Talk about the Culture of Sexual Assault," *Atlantic*, March 29, 2014, http://www.theatlantic.com/health/archive/2014/03/how-not-to-talk-about-the-culture-of-sexual-assault/359845/; Lori Adelman, "Dear Prudence Columnist Publishes Rape Denialism Manifesto Advising Women to 'Stop Getting Drunk,'" *Feministing*, October 16, 2013, http://feministing.com/2013/10/16/emily-yoffe-aka-dear-prudence-publishes-rape-denialism-manifesto-tells-women-point-blank-to-stop-getting-drunk-to-avoid-rape/; Olivia Fleming, "'Don't Drink if You Don't Want to Get Raped': Female Advice Columnist Causes Backlash with Controversial Opinion on How to Prevent Sexual Assault," *Daily Mail*, October 17, 2013, http://www.dailymail.co.uk/femail/article-2465278/Dont-drink-dont-want-raped-Female-advice-columnist-causes-backlash-controversial-opinion-prevent-sexual-assault.html.

96.   Jed Rubenfeld, "Mishandling Rape," *New York Times*, November 15, 2014, http://www.nytimes.com/2014/11/16/opinion/sunday/mishandling-rape.html?_r=0.

97.   Robby Soave, "Liberal Feminists, Stop Smearing Critics as Rape Apologists," Reason.com, November 17, 2014, http://reason.com/blog/2014/11/17/liberal-feminists-stop-smearing-critics.

98.   Emily Yoffe, "Emily Yoffe Responds to Her Critics," *Slate*, October 18, 2013, http://www.slate.com/blogs/xx_factor/2013/10/18/rape_culture_and_binge_drinking_emily_yoffe_responds_to_her_critics.html.

99.   Ben Smith, "Media Matters' War against Fox," *Politico*, updated March 27, 2011, http://www.politico.com/news/stories/0311/51949.html.

100.   Lloyd Grove, "Was Reporter Sheryl Attkisson Too Right-Wing for CBS?," Daily Beast, October 29, 2014, http://www.thedailybeast.com/articles/2014/10/29/was-reporter-sharyl-attkisson-too-right-wing-for-cbs.html.

101.   Matt Gertz, "After Criticizing Journalists Who Are Too Close To Politicians, Sharyl Attkisson Parties With Darrell Issa," Media Matters for America, November 7, 2014 http://mediamatters.org/blog/2014/11/07/after-criticizing-

journalists-who-are-too-close/201495; Dylan Byers, "Sharyl Attkisson Resigns from CBS News," Politico, March 10, 2014, http://www.politico.com/blogs/media/2014/03/sharyl-attkisson-to-leave-cbs-news-184836.html.

102. "Was a Former CBS Correspondent Hacked by the Government?," MSNBC, November 7, 2014, http://www.msnbc.com/all-in/watch/chris-hayes-interviews-sharyl-attkisson-355291203735; Part 2: "The Cynic's Case against Sharyl Attkisson," MSNBC, November 7, 2014, http://www.msnbc.com/all-in/watch/the-cynics-case-against-sharyl-attkisson-355289667971 11-7-2014.

103. Matthew Yglesias, "Boyer Plate," *American Prospect*, November 17, 2003, http://prospect.org/article/boyer-plate.

104. Ibid.

105. "Who Is Fox News' Peter Boyer," Media Matters for America, January 24, 2014, http://mediamatters.org/blog/2014/01/24/who-is-fox-news-peter-boyer/197730.

106. "Biography: Peter Boyer—Correspondent," PBS, http://www.pbs.org/wgbh/pages/frontline/waco/peterboyer.html.

107. Ron Fournier, "On Deadline: Obama Walks Arrogance Line," Associated Press, March 17, 2008, available at DemocraticUnderground.com, http://www.democraticunderground.com/discuss/duboard.php?az=view_all&address=132x5123462.

108. Julia, "Late Night FDL: the Enemy of Your Enemy Might Not Be Your Friend," Firedoglake, March 28, 2008, http://firedoglake.com/2008/03/28/late-night-fdl-the-enemy-of-your-enemy-might-not-be-your-friend/.

109. Eric Boehlert, "The AP Has a Ron Fournier Problem," Media Matters for America, July 22, 2008, http://mediamatters.org/research/2008/07/22/the-ap-has-a-ron-fournier-problem/144113.

110. MrBurns17, "AP Conservative Shill Ron Fournier: Biden Pick Shows Lack of Confidence," *Daily Kos*, August 23, 2008, http://www.dailykos.com/story/2008/08/23/573459/-AP-Conservative-shill-Ron-Fournier-Biden-pick-shows-lack-of-confidence.

111. dday, "No Excuses: Ron Fournier Needs to Be Recused or Fired: Huge Update," *Daily Kos*, August 23, 2008, http://www.dailykos.com/story/2008/08/23/573650/-No-excuses-Ron-Fournier-needs-to-be-recused-or-fired-HUGE-UPDATE.

112. "AP: Stop the Anti-Democrat, Pro-McCain Bias," MoveOn.org, http://pol. moveon.org/call/?cp_id=797&tg=508.532.

113. Jane Hamsher, "Action: Tell AP to Remove Ron Fournier from the Presidential Beat," Firedoglake, August 23, 2008, http://firedoglake.com/2008/08/23/action-tell-ap-to-remove-ron-fournier-from-the-presidential-beat/.

114. "Remove Ron Fournier," Firedoglake, http://action.firedoglake.com/page/speakout/fournier.

115. Ron Fournier, "What if Obama Can't Lead?," *National Journal*, July 31, 2013, http://www.nationaljournal.com/politics/what-if-obama-can-t-lead-20130731.

116. Ron Fournier, "Why I'm Getting Sick of Defending Obamacare," *National Journal*, February 11, 2014, http://www.nationaljournal.com/white-house/why-i-m-getting-sick-of-defending-obamacare-20140211.

117. Tom Kludt, "Ron Fournier Is a Liberal Journalist, According to RNC Chairman," Talking Points Memo, February 12, 2014, http://talkingpointsmemo.com/livewire/ron-fournier-liberal-journalist-rnc-chairman-reince-priebus.

CHAPTER THREE: ILLIBERAL INTOLERANCE AND INTIMIDATION

1. "HRC Protests Chick-fil-A Food Truck," Human Rights Campaign, July 25, 2012, http://www.hrc.org/press-releases/entry/hrc-protests-chick-fil-a-food-truck; Cavan Sieczkowski, "Chick-Fil-A CEO Dan Cathy Speaks Out on Gay Marriage Controversy," Huffington Post, updated March 19, 2014, http://www.huffingtonpost.com/2014/03/17/chick-fil-a-dan-cathy-gay-marriage_n_4980682.html.

2. Lindsay Abrams, "Chick-fil-A: Antibiotic-Free, but Still Pretty Terrible," Salon.com, February 12, 2014, http://www.salon.com/2014/02/12/chick_fil_a_antibiotic_free_but_still_pretty_terrible/.

3. James King, "Chick-Fil-A Flap: Brooklyn Republican Invites Homophobic Chicken Peddler Dan Cathy to Open Restaurant," *Village Voice*, August 7, 2012, http://blogs.villagevoice.com/runninscared/2012/08/brooklyn_republ.php.

4. Erin Gloria Ryan, "Chick-fil-A's Delicious Chicken Sandwiches Are Deep Fried in Hate," Jezebel, July 18, 2012, http://jezebel.com/5927029/chick-fil-as-delicious-chicken-sandwiches-are-deep-fried-in-hate.

5.   Jesse Bering, "The Prideful, Arrogant President of Chick-fil-A," *Slate*, August 6, 2012, http://www.slate.com/articles/health_and_science/science/2012/08/chick_fil_a_controversy_why_dan_cathy_s_statements_are_dangerous_.html.

6.   Dana Musgrave, "Adam M. Smith's Harasses Rachael Chick-Fil-A's Hate Group," YouTube, August 3, 2012, https://www.youtube.com/watch?v=-Xdyzb6lBzI.

7.   Kim Bhasin, "Exec Who Got Fired for Bullying Chick-fil-A Worker Explains What Happened That Day," Business Insider, August 4, 2012, http://www.businessinsider.com/former-vante-cfo-adam-smith-apologizes-for-bullying-chick-fil-a-worker-2012-8#ixzz3SXlpWZtD.

8.   Perry Chiaramonte, "Arizona Chick-fil-A Worker Berated on Viral Video Wants to Meet with Bully," Fox News, August 7, 2012, http://www.foxnews.com/us/2012/08/07/arizona-chick-fil-worker-berated-on-viral-video-wants-to-meet-with-bully/.

9.   Lucas Grindley, "Chick-Fil-A Not Welcome in a Growing List of Places," *Advocate*, July 26, 2012, http://www.advocate.com/business/2012/07/26/chick-fil-not-welcome-growing-list-places.

10. Andrew Spencer, "Emory University Dumps Chik-fil-A," News WSB, March 12, 2013, http://www.wsbradio.com/news/news/emory-university-dumps-chick-fil-/nWpb7/.

11. "University Statement on Chick-fil-A," Emory University, August 2, 2012, http://news.emory.edu/stories/2012/08/upress_chickfila_statement/index.html.

12. Shane L. Windmeyer, "Colleges Rally to Kick Chick-fil-A Off Campus," *Advocate*, June 17, 2012, http://www.huffingtonpost.com/shane-l-windmeyer/chick-fil-a-colleges_b_1790565.html.

13. Ibid.

14. Michele Richinick, "Pope Francis Suggests Gay Marriage Threatens Traditional Families," MSNBC, January 16, 2015, http://www.msnbc.com/msnbc/pope-francis-suggests-gay-marriage-threatens-traditional-families.

15. Eliana Dockterman, "Boston Mayor Blocks Chick-Fil-A Franchise from City over Homophobic Attitudes," *Time*, July 23, 2012, http://newsfeed.time.com/2012/07/23/boston-mayor-blocks-chick-fil-a-franchise-from-city-over-homophobic-attitude/.

16. Hal Dardick, "Alderman to Chick-fil-A: No Deal," *Chicago Tribune*, July 25, 2012, http://www.chicagotribune.com/business/breaking/ct-met-chicago-chick-fil-a-20120725-story.html.

17. Tom Curry, "The 'Evolution' of Obama's Stance on Gay Marriage," NBC News, May 9, 2012, http://nbcpolitics.nbcnews.com/_news/2012/05/09/11623172-the-evolution-of-obamas-stance-on-gay-marriage?lite.

18. Dardick, "Alderman to Chick-fil-A: No deal."

19. Richard Lopez and Tiffany Hsu, "San Francisco Is Third City to Tell Chick-fil-A: Keep Out," *Los Angeles Times*, July 26, 2012, http://articles.latimes.com/2012/jul/26/business/la-fi-mo-san-franciso-mayor-to-chickfila-keep-out-20120726.

20. Mark Joseph Stern, "Yes, Opposing Gay Marriage Makes You a Homophobe," *Slate*, December 16, 2013, http://www.slate.com/blogs/outward/2013/12/16/gay_marriage_opponents_homophobic_does_opposing_gay_marriage_make_you_a.html.

21. John Shore, "Is Every Christian Who's against Gay Marriage Necessarily a Bigot?," Huffington Post, May 23, 2014, updated July 23, 2014, http://www.huffingtonpost.com/john-shore/is-every-christian-whos-against-gay-marriage-necessarily-a-bigot_b_5374429.html.

22. Zack Ford, "TIMELINE: Tracking Barack Obama's Position on Marriage Equality," *ThinkProgress*, June 22, 2011, http://thinkprogress.org/lgbt/2011/06/22/250931/timeline-barack-obama-marriage-equality/.

23. Paul Brandeis Raushenbush, "No Cardinal Dolan, the Catholic Church Wasn't 'Outmarketed' on Gay Marriage," Huffington Post, January 30, 2014. http://www.huffingtonpost.com/paul-raushenbush/cardinal-dolan-gay-marriage-_b_4364273.html.

24. Camille Beredjick, "Yes, Being against Marriage Equality Means You're against Gays," Patheos, January 12, 2014, http://www.patheos.com/blogs/friendlyatheist/2014/01/12/yes-being-against-marriage-equality-means-youre-against-gays/.

25. Gabriel Arana, "The Bigots Finally Go Down: How Anti-Gay Haters Officially Lost the Marriage Fight," Salon.com, October 8, 2014, http://www.salon.com/2014/10/08/the_bigots_have_finally_lost_how_anti_gay_haters_officially_got_beat_in_marriage_fight/.

26.   Zack Ford, "Why We Shouldn't Placate People with Anti-Gay Beliefs Just because They Don't Know Better," *ThinkProgress*, December 16, 2013, http://thinkprogress.org/lgbt/2013/12/16/3070891/anti-gay-bigotry/.

27.   Lindsay Beyerstein, "If You Oppose Equal Marriage, You Are a Bigot," Big Think, no date, http://bigthink.com/focal-point/if-you-oppose-equal-marriage-you-are-a-bigot.

28.   Carlos A. Ball, "Is It Possible to Be against Same-Sex Marriage without Being Homophobic?," Huffington Post, August 24, 2010, updated May 25, 2011, http://www.huffingtonpost.com/carlos-a-ball/is-it-possible-to-be-agai_b_692187.html; Noah Michelson, "Here's an Easy Test to Find Out if You're Anti-Gay (and Maybe Don't Even Know It," Huffington Post, December 16, 2013, updated February 15, 2014, http://www.huffingtonpost.com/noah-michelson/heres-an-easy-test-to-fin_b_4453662.html; Fred Sainz, Anti-Gay Lawyer Defending Virginia Marriage Ban Makes Homophobic Case against Equality," Human Rights Campaign, April 3, 2014, http://www.hrc.org/blog/entry/anti-gay-lawyer-defending-virginia-marriage-ban-makes-homophobic-case-again; Bigotry Watch, New Civil Rights Movement, http://www.thenewcivilrightsmovement.com/category/bigotry-watch; Kaili Joh Gray, "National Organization for Bigotry Wants You Schmucks to Be More Civil," *Daily Kos*, August 16, 2012, http://www.dailykos.com/story/2012/08/16/1120805/-National-Organization-for-Bigotry-wants-you-schmucks-to-be-more-civil.

29.   John McAdams, "Marquette Philosophy Instructor: 'Gay Rights' Can't Be Discussed in Class since Any Disagreement Would Offend Gay Students," *Marquette Warrior*, November 9, 2014, http://mu-warrior.blogspot.in/2014/11/marquette-philosophy-instructor-gay.html.

30.   Susan Kruth, "On Marquette Classroom Controversy, Rebuttal Ignores Facts," FIRE, November 18, 2014, http://www.thefire.org/marquette-classroom-controversy-rebuttal-ignores-facts/.

31.   McAdams, "Marquette Philosophy Instructor: 'Gay Rights' Can't Be Discussed in Class."

32.   Justin, "Philosophy Grad Student Target of Political Smear Campaign (Several Updates)," *Daily Nous*, November 18, 2014, http://dailynous.com/2014/11/18/philosophy-grad-student-target-of-political-smear-campaign/.

33. Colleen Flaherty, "Ethics Lesson," Inside Higher Ed, November 20, 2014, https://www.insidehighered.com/news/2014/11/20/marquette-u-grad-student-shes-being-targeted-after-ending-class-discussion-gay.

34. John Protevi, "Open Letter in Support of Cheryl Abbate," *John Protevi's Blog*, November 18, 2014, http://proteviblog.typepad.com/protevi/2014/11/open-letter-in-support-of-cheryl-abbate.html.

35. Flaherty, "Ethics Lesson."

36. Ibid.

37. Chuck Ross, "Marquette Prof Suspended for Criticizing Liberal Colleague Who Quashed Gay Rights Debate," Daily Caller, December 17, 2014, http://dailycaller.com/2014/12/17/marquette-prof-suspended-for-criticizing-liberal-colleague-who-squashed-gay-rights-debate/.

38. Susan, Kruth, "Marquette Harassment Training Forbids Certain Viewpoints," FIRE, October 1, 2014, http://www.thefire.org/marquette-harassment-training-forbids-certain-viewpoints/.

39. Ibid.

40. "Statutes on Faculty Appointment, Promotion and Tenure," "Chapter 306—Cause for Nonrenewal, Suspension, Termination," in Faculty Handbook Contents, Marquette University, http://www.marquette.edu/provost/306.shtml.

41. "UVA Scholar Responds to Student Attacks," NBC, updated May 30, 2014, http://www.nbc29.com/story/25539656/uva-scholar-responds-to-student-attacks.

42. Derek Quizon, "LGBT Activists Take U.Va. Professor to Task for Stance on Cases," *Richmond Times-Dispatch*, updated May 25, 2014, http://www.timesdispatch.com/news/latest-news-ap/lgbt-activists-take-u-va-professor-to-task-for-stance/article_fa5680ce-e36e-11e3-a4ed-0017a43b2370.html.

43. "The Purge Arrives at the University of Virginia: PC Thugs versus Douglas Laycock," ProfessorBainbridge.com, May 24, 2014, http://www.professorbainbridge.com/professorbainbridgecom/2014/05/the-purge-arrives-at-the-university-of-virginia-pc-thugs-versus-douglas-laycock.html.

44. Executive Order 11246—Equal Employment Opportunity, Office of Federal Contract Compliance Programs (OFCCP), Department of Labor, http://www.dol.gov/ofccp/regs/compliance/ca_11246.htm.

45.   Michelle Boorstein, "Faith Leaders: Exempt Religious Groups from Order Barring LGBT Bias in Hiring," *Washington Post*, July 2, 2014, http://www.washingtonpost.com/local/faith-leaders-exempt-religious-groups-from-order-barring-lgbt-bias-in-hiring/2014/07/02/d82e68da-01f1-11e4-b8ff-89afd3fad6bd_story.html; see also Kirsten Powers, "Religious Exemption Myths," *USA Today*, July 9, 2014, http://www.usatoday.com/story/opinion/2014/07/08/kirsten-powers-religious-exemption-myths-hobby-lobby-column/12385801/.

46.   "'The Rachel Maddow Show' for Wednesday, July 2nd, 2014," *Today*, updated July 3, 2014, http://www.today.com/id/55568725/ns/msnbc-rachel_maddow_show/t/rachel-maddow-show-wednesday-july-nd/#.VQNW8imq595.

47.   Zack Ford, "Anti-Gay Activist Implores Conservatives to Abandon 'Whiny' Religious Liberty Arguments," *ThinkProgress*, July 3, 2014, http://thinkprogress.org/lgbt/2014/07/03/3456355/religious-liberty-lgbt-employment/; Joan McCarter, "Here's That Hobby Lobby Slippery Slope in Action," *Daily Kos*, July 2, 2014, http://www.dailykos.com/story/2014/07/02/1311250/-Here-s-that-Hobby-Lobby-slippery-slope-in-nbsp-action#.

48.   Michael Terheyden, "Catholic Charities Forced to Shut Down Services around the Country," Catholic Online, June 7, 2011, http://www.catholic.org/news/national/story.php?id=41680.

49.   Scott Whitlock, "After His Islam Defense, Rosie O'Donnell Thrills: 'Ben Affleck for President!,'" MRC NewsBusters, October 6, 2014, http://newsbusters.org/blogs/scott-whitlock/2014/10/06/rosie-odonnell-bashed-radical-christianity-praises-affleck-islam.

50.   "'Hardball with Chris Matthews' for Monday, October 6th, 2014," NBC News, updated October 7, 2014, http://www.nbcnews.com/id/56191367/ns/msnbc-hardball_with_chris_matthews/t/hardball-chris-matthews-monday-october-th/#.VNkAYu85BD8.

51.   "PoliticsNation, Monday, October 6th, 2014," NBC News, updated October 7, 2014, http://www.nbcnews.com/id/56191279/ns/msnbc-politicsnation/t/politicsnation-monday-october-th/#.VNkBZ-85BD8.

52.   "Ben Affleck Calls Bill Maher's Views on Islam 'Racist' and 'Gross,'" MSNBC, October 7, 2014, http://www.msnbc.com/all-in/watch/affleck-decries-mahers-racist-views-on-islam-338613827548.

53.   "The Ed Show for Monday, October 6th, 2014, NBC News, updated October 6, 2014, http://www.nbcnews.com/id/56191358/ns/msnbc-the_ed_show/t/ed-show-monday-october-th/#.VQNaqymq595.

54.   Bill Maher Official Channel, "Bill Maher Trashes the Bible Noah Story and Psychotic Mass Murderer God," YouTube, March 18, 2014, https://www.youtube.com/watch?v=cyPy61xNBQY.

55.   Khwaja Ahmed, "Stop Bill Maher from Speaking at UC Berkeley's December Graduation," Change.org, https://www.change.org/p/university-of-california-berkeley-stop-bill-maher-from-speaking-at-uc-berkeley-s-december-graduation.

56.   "Campus Statement on Commencement Speaker," UC Berkeley, October 29, 2014, http://newscenter.berkeley.edu/2014/10/29/campus-statement-on-commencement-speaker/.

57.   Neely Tucker, "True Unbeliever," *Washington Post*, March 7, 2007, http://www.washingtonpost.com/wp-dyn/content/article/2007/03/06/AR2007030602145.html.

58.   Jessica Mack, "Ayaan Hirsi Ali: The (Feminist) Cheese Stands Alone," *Gender Across Borders*, June 16, 2010, http://www.genderacrossborders.com/2010/06/16/ayaan-hirsi-ali-the-feminist-cheese-stands-alone/.

59.   Ibid.

60.   Ashe Schow, "Ayaan Hirsi Ali Fights Radical Islam's Real War on Women," *Washington Examiner*, December 8, 2014, http://www.washingtonexaminer.com/article/2556984.

61.   Emma Brockes, "Ayaan Hirsi Ali: 'Why are Muslims So Hypersensitive?,'" *Guardian*, May 7, 2010, http://www.theguardian.com/world/2010/may/08/ayaan-hirsi-ali-interview.

62.   Emma Brockes, "Anne Rice: 'I Thought the Church Was Flat-Out Immoral. I Had to Leave,'" *Guardian*, October 24, 2010, http://www.theguardian.com/books/2010/oct/24/anne-rice-catholic-church-rejection-vampire.

63.   Christopher Hitchens, "Mommie Dearest," *Slate*, October 20, 2003, http://www.slate.com/articles/news_and_politics/fighting_words/2003/10/mommie_dearest.html.

64.   Ed Hornick, "Obama, McCain Talk Issues at Pastor's Forum," CNN, August 17, 2008, http://www.cnn.com/2008/POLITICS/08/16/warren.forum/.

65.   Charles Babington, "Christian Leaders Meet Privately with Obama," *USA Today*, June 11, 2008, http://usatoday30.usatoday.com/news/topstories/2008-06-11-9059223_x.htm.

66.   "Remarks by the President in Commencement Address at the University of Notre Dame," WhiteHouse.gov, May 17, 2009, http://www.whitehouse.gov/the_press_office/Remarks-by-the-President-at-Notre-Dame-Commencement.

67.   "White House Announces Troubling Faith-Based Order, ACLU Says Administration Is Heading into Uncharted Waters," American Civil Liberties Union, February 5, 2009, https://www.aclu.org/religion-belief/white-house-announces-troubling-faith-based-order-aclu-says-administration-heading-u.

68.   "Obama's Disappointing Directive: 'Faith-Based' Initiative Needs Overhaul," Americans United for Separation of Church and State, March 2009, https://www.au.org/church-state/march-2009-church-state/editorial/obamas-disappointing-directive.

69.   Susan Jacoby, "Keeping the Faith, Ignoring the History," *New York Times*, February 28, 2009, http://www.nytimes.com/2009/03/01/opinion/01jacoby.html?pagewanted=all.

70.   Lynn Sweet, "President-Elect Obama Defends Inviting Pastor Rick Warren to Speak at Inauguration," *Chicago Sun-Times*, December 18, 2008, http://blogs.suntimes.com/sweet/2008/12/presidentelect_obama_defends_i.html.

71.   Ibid.

72.   Josh Israel, "Inaugural Benediction to Be Delivered by Pastor Who Gave Vehemently Anti-Gay Sermon," *ThinkProgress*, January 9, 2013, http://thinkprogress.org/lgbt/2013/01/09/1422021/inaugural-benediction-to-be-delivered-by-anti-gay-pastor/.

73.   Natalie Jennings, "Louie Giglio Pulls Out of Inauguration over Anti-Gay Comments," *Washington Post*, January 10, 2013, http://www.washingtonpost.com/blogs/post-politics/wp/2013/01/10/louie-giglio-pulls-out-of-inaugural-over-anti-gay-comments/.

74.   "Pastor Nixed from Obama Inaugural over Anti-Gay Remarks," NBC News, January 10, 2013, http://usnews.nbcnews.com/_news/2013/01/10/16449097-pastor-nixed-from-obama-inaugural-over-anti-gay-remarks?lite.

CHAPTER FOUR: INTOLERANCE 101

1. University of California, Santa Barbara, Police Department Crime Report, March 4, 2014, http://media.independent.com/news/documents/2014/03/18/UCSB-Police-Report.pdf.

2. Ibid.

3. "Confrontation with UCSB Professor," including video of the incident, Survivors of the Abortion Holocaust, http://www.survivors.la/confrontation-with-ucsb-professor.

4. Ibid.

5. University of California, Santa Barbara, Police Department Crime Report, March 4, 2014, http://media.independent.com/news/documents/2014/03/18/UCSB-Police-Report.pdf.

6. Tyler Hayden, "UCSB Professor Sentenced to Probation, Community Service in Theft, Battery Case," *Santa Barbara Independent*, August 18, 2014, http://www.independent.com/news/2014/aug/18/ucsb-professor-sentenced-probation-community-servi/.

7. Tom Ciesielka, "Letters of Support for Mireille Miller-Young from Her Peers," Scribd, August 15, 2014, https://www.scribd.com/doc/236924952/Letters-of-support-for-Mireille-Miller-Young-from-her-peers.

8. Tom Ciesielka, "Catherine Short's Statement to Judge Hill in Regards to Mireille Miller-Young Assaulting Pro-Life Students," Scribd, August 15, 2014, https://www.scribd.com/doc/236925804/Catherine-Short-s-Statement-to-Judge-Hill-in-regards-to-Mireille-Miller-Young-Assaulting-Pro-Life-Students.

9. Alec Torres, "UCSB Smears Pro-Lifers After Professor's Attack on Pro-Life Student: Chancellor blames 'crusaders' for a porn teacher's violent assault on a minor," National Review Online, March 24, 2014, http://www.nationalreview.com/article/373957/ucsb-smears-pro-lifers-after-professors-attack-pro-life-student-alec-torres.

10. Lara Cooper, "UCSB Professor Sentenced to Probation, Anger Management in Abortion Confrontation," Noozhawk, August 15, 2014, http://www.noozhawk.com/article/ucsb_professor_sentenced_to_probation_anger_management.

11. Kathleen McCartney, "Follow-up to the Community Letter," Smith College, December 5, 2014, http://www.smith.edu/president/speeches-writings/grand-jury-decisions#followup.

12. Kathleen McCartney, "Messages in Response to Grand Jury Decisions," Smith College, December 5, 2014, http://www.smith.edu/president/speeches-writings/grand-jury-decisions.

13. Peter Bonilla, "At American University, Newspaper Theft Goes Unpunished, and Leaves Questions about Commitment to Free Speech," FIRE, August 6, 2010, http://thefire.org/article/12143.html.

14. "Sam Houston State University: Faulty Member Takes Box Cutter to Students' Free Speech Wall; Police Threaten Students with Misdemeanor," FIRE, http://thefire.org/case/873.

15. Wendy Kaminer, "The Heckler's Veto," *Atlantic*, March 31, 2010, http://www.theatlantic.com/national/archive/2010/03/the-hecklers-veto/38252/.

16. Anthea Butler, "Opposing View: Why 'Sam Bacile' Deserves Arrest," *USA Today*, September 13, 2012, http://www.usatoday.com/news/opinion/story/2012-09-12/Sam-Bacile-Anthea-Butler/57769732/1.

17. Wendy Kaminer, "The End of Free Speech at University of Colorado?," *Atlantic*, September 18, 2012, http://www.theatlantic.com/national/archive/2012/09/the-end-of-free-speech-at-university-of-colorado/262494/.

18. "Spotlight on Speech Codes 2015," FIRE, 2015, http://www.thefire.org/spotlight-speech-codes-2015/.

19. Ibid.

20. "New Report: 59% of Campuses Maintain Severe Speech Restrictions—But That's Actually an Improvement," FIRE, January 17, 2014, http://www.thefire.org/new-report-59-of-campuses-maintain-severe-speech-restrictions-but-thats-actually-an-improvement/; "Spotlight on Speech Codes 2015," FIRE, 2015.

21. Interview with Kirsten Powers, January 2015.

22. "Colorado College: Students Found Guilty for Satirical Flyer," FIRE, http://www.thefire.org/cases/colorado-college-students-found-guilty-for-satirical-flyer/.

23. F. Scott Fitzgerald, *This Side of Paradise*, Bartleby.com, http://www.bartleby.com/115/11.html.

24. "Brandeis University: Professor Found Guilty of Harassment for Protected Speech," FIRE, http://www.thefire.org/cases/brandeis-university-professor-found-guilty-of-harassment-for-protected-speech/.

25. Denise-Marie Ordway, "UCF Instructor Placed on Leave after 'Killing Spree' Comment," *Orlando Sentinel*, April 25, 2013, http://articles.orlandosentinel.com/2013-04-25/news/os-ucf-instructor-killing-spree-comment-20130425_1_killing-spree-ucf-spokesman-chad-binette-rosen-college.

26. "FIRE Letter to University of Central Florida," FIRE, April 26, 2013, http://www.thefire.org/fire-letter-to-university-of-central-florida/; "University of Central Florida Professor Reinstated after Suspension for In-Class Joke," FIRE, May 21, 2013, http://www.thefire.org/university-of-central-florida-professor-reinstated-after-suspension-for-in-class-joke/.

27. "Non-Discrimination and Anti-Harassment Policy and Complaint Procedures for Employees," New York University, http://www.nyu.edu/about/policies-guidelines-compliance/policies-and-guidelines/anti-harassment-policy-and-complaint-procedures.html.

28. Holy Cross College, *College of the Holy Cross Student Handbook and Planner*, http://www.holycross.edu/assets/pdfs/student_handbook.pdf.

29. "Policy Statement on Harassment," University of Connecticut, http://web2.uconn.edu/dde/docs/Harassment%20Policy%20Dec%202011.pdf.

30. Virginia State University, *Virginia State University Student Handbook, 2012–2013*, "Section 8–Fighting, Assault, Threats of Physical Abuse, and Verbal Abuse," 76, http://vsu.edu/files/docs/student-activities/student-handbook.pdf.

31. University of Wisconsin-Stout, "Information Technology Acceptable Use Policy," March 10, 2009, https://www.uwstout.edu/parq/upload/09-66-2.pdf.

32. Fordham University, "Information Technology Usage," updated August 11, 2014, http://legacy.fordham.edu/student_affairs/office_of_substance_/student_handbook/rose_hill_student_ha/university_regulatio/information_technolo_70917.asp.

33. Lafayette College, Division of Campus Life, "Bias Response Team (BRT)," http://studentlife.lafayette.edu/student-health-and-safety/bias-%20response-team-brt/.

34. In fact, it would be helpful if our colleges and universities consulted a dictionary and recognized that to "perceive" something means to see it accurately. I perceive that these speech codes are violations of free speech.

35. Northwestern University, "Reporting Bias or Hate Incidents," Division of Student Affairs, http://www.northwestern.edu/inclusion/respectnu/reporting-bias-hate-incidents/index.html.

36. Microaggression definition from D. W. Sue et al., "Racial Microaggressions in Everyday Life: Implications for Clinical Practice," *American Psychologist* 62, no. 4 (2007), 271–86; Douglas Ernst, "Princeton Students Start 'Microaggressions' to Combat 'Papercuts of Oppression,'" *Washington Times*, December 11, 2014, http://www.washingtontimes.com/news/2014/dec/11/princeton-students-start-microaggressions-page-com/.

37. Heather MacDonald, "The Microaggression Farce," *City Journal*, November 19, 2014, http://www.city-journal.org/2014/24_4_racial-microaggression.html.

38. Susan Kruth, "UCLA Report Suggests Chilling Speech Is the Answer to Offensive 'Microaggressions,'" FIRE, January 8, 2014, http://www.thefire.org/ucla-report-suggests-chilling-speech-is-the-answer-to-offensive-microaggressions/.

39. Omar Mahmood, "Do the Left Thing," *Michigan Review*, http://www.michiganreview.com/do-the-left-thing/.

40. Susan Kruth, "U. of Michigan Student Forced to Quit Student Publication Following Satirical Article," FIRE, December 3, 2014, http://www.thefire.org/u-michigan-student-forced-quit-student-publication-following-satirical-article/.

41. Omar Mahmood, "Read the 'Hostile' Column That Got Student Writer Suspended by Campus Newspaper," *College Fix*, November 23, 2014, http://www.thecollegefix.com/post/20236/.

42. Oberlin College, Office of Equity Concerns, "Sexual Offense Resource Guide: Support Resources for Faculty," http://web.archive.org/web/20131222174936/http:/new.oberlin.edu/office/equity-concerns/sexual-offense-resource-guide/prevention-support-education/support-resources-for-faculty.dot.

43. Lisa Leff, "Trauma Warning Move from Internet to Ivory Tower," AP The Big Story, April 26, 2014, http://bigstory.ap.org/article/trauma-warnings-move-internet-ivory-tower.

44.   Justin Peligri, "Why We Need Trigger Warnings on Syllabi," *GW Hatchet*, April 16, 2014, http://www.gwhatchet.com/2014/04/16/justin-peligri-why-we-need-trigger-warnings-on-syllabi/.

45.   Philip Wythe, "Trigger Warnings Needed in Classroom," *Daily Targum*, February 18, 2014, http://www.dailytargum.com/article/2014/02/trigger-warnings-needed-in-classroom.

46.   Hamilton Nolan, "'Triggered' College Professor Argues for Right to Tear Up Protest Signs," *Gawker*, March 24, 2014, http://gawker.com/triggered-college-professor-argues-for-right-to-tear-1550250284.

47.   Jessy Diamba, "A.S. Resolution Policy Aims to Protect Students from PTSD Triggers," *Daily Nexus*, March 7, 2014, http://dailynexus.com/2014-03-07/a-s-resolution-policy-aims-to-protect-students-from-ptsd-triggers/.

48.   Harvey Silverglate, "Liberals Are Killing the Liberal Arts," *Wall Street Journal*, November 9, 2014, http://online.wsj.com/articles/harvey-silverglate-liberals-are-killing-the-liberal-arts-1415573959.

49.   "Petition: Move the 'Sleepwalker' Inside the Davis Museum," Change.org, February 5, 2014, https://www.change.org/petitions/president-h-kim-bottomly-move-the-sleepwalker-inside-the-davis-museum.

50.   Lisa Fischman, "Response to Petition," Change.org, February 4, 2014, https://www.change.org/p/president-h-kim-bottomly-remove-the-uncomfortable-and-potentially-triggering-statue-put-up-without-student-consent/responses/10205.

CHAPTER FIVE: INTOLERANCE 201

1.   "University of Cincinnati: Speech Code Litigation," FIRE, http://www.thefire.org/cases/university-of-cincinnati-speech-code-litigation/.

2.   Ibid.; "Federal Court Delivers Final Blow to U. of Cincinnati 'Free Speech Zone,'" FIRE, August 22, 2012, http://www.thefire.org/federal-court-delivers-final-blow-to-u-of-cincinnati-free-speech-zone-2/.

3.   "Speech Zones," Center for Campus Free Speech, http://www.campusspeech.org/page/cfs/speech-zones.

4.   Section 4. Code of Student Conduct, 2014–2015 Student Guide, Boston College, http://www.bc.edu/publications/studentguide/behavioralpolicies.html.

5. Rachel S. Stuart, "UCF Students Protest Shrinking Free-Speech Zones," Central Florida Future, September 18, 2014, http://www.centralfloridafuture.com/story/news/2014/09/18/ucf-free-speech-zones/15839401/.

6. "University of Cincinnati: Speech Code Litigation," FIRE.

7. Greg Lukianoff, interview with author.

8. "California College Forbids Passing Out Constitutions . . . on Constitution Day," FIRE, September 19, 2013, http://www.thefire.org/california-college-forbids-passing-out-constitutions-on-constitution-day/.

9. Ibid.

10. Clarke Reilly, "Hawaiian University Sued for Blocking Students from Passing Out Copies of the Constitution," Huffington Post, April 26, 2014, http://www.huffingtonpost.com/2014/04/26/hawaii-constitution-lawsuit-university-students_n_5216705.html.

11. Kevin Horne, "[Video] YAF Meets HUB Bureaucrats," Onward State, September 18, 2014, http://onwardstate.com/2014/09/18/video-yaf-meets-hub-bureaucrats/; "Penn State Revises Speech Policies," Daily Collegian, August 8, 2006, http://www.collegian.psu.edu/archives/article_5ee8bf5b-6faf-5dbe-8ded-b347242801f1.html.

12. Horne, "[Video] YAF Meets HUB Bureaucrats."

13. Jennifer Kabbany, "Conservative Activist Kicked Off Campus after Asking if 'Big Government Sucks?,'" College Fix, October 18, 2014, http://www.thecollegefix.com/post/19760/.

14. Lauren Cooley, "Remove the Free Speech Zone at Broward College by Making the Entire Campus Open for Free Speech and Expression, as Protected by the First Amendment," Change.org, https://www.change.org/p/broward-college-remove-the-free-speech-zone-at-broward-college-by-making-the-entire-campus-open-for-free-speech-and-expression-as-protected-by-the-first-amendment.

15. Kristina Sgueglia, "Condoleezza Rice Declines to Speak at Rutgers after Student Protests," CNN, May 5, 2014, http://www.cnn.com/2014/05/04/us/condoleeza-rice-rutgers-protests/.

16. Douglas Belkin, "IMF's Lagarde Won't Speak at Smith, Part of a Growing List," *Wall Street Journal*, May 12, 2014, http://www.wsj.com/articles/SB10001424052 70230385180457955839003535958.

17. "Statement of Protest against HGSE's 2014 Alumni Convocation Speaker, Mike Johnston," ConvocationProtest2014.wordpress.com, http://convocationprotest2014. wordpress.com/statement-and-endorsers/

18. Dottie Lamm, "Kudos to Michael Johnston for Making Commencement Speech," *Denver Post*, June 6, 2014, http://www.denverpost.com/opinion/ci_25912244/ kudos-michael-johnston-making-commencement-speech.

19. Ari Cohn, Foundation for Individual Rights in Education, February 24, 2015.

20. Susan Snyder, "Haverford Commencement Speaker Backs Out," Philly.com, May 13, 2014, http://www.philly.com/philly/blogs/campus_inq/Haverford-commencement-speaker-backs-out.html#7Ampz6tWT5qJBzzi.99.

21. Ibid.

22. Isabel Knight, Martin Froger-Silva, and Eduard Saakashvili, "Students Share Mixed Responses to George/West Collection," *Daily Gazette*, February 13, 2014, http://daily.swarthmore.edu/2014/02/13/students-share-mixed-responses-to-georgewest-collection/.

23. Ellie Sandmeyer, "George Will's Offensive Rape Comments Alienate Another Institution (Updated)," Media Matters for America, October 7, 2014, http:// mediamatters.org/blog/2014/10/07/did-george-wills-offensive-rape-comments-aliena/201043.

24. George F. Will, "Colleges Become the Victims of Progressivism," *Washington Post*, June 6, 2014, http://www.washingtonpost.com/opinions/george-will-college-become-the-victims-of-progressivism/2014/06/06/e90e73b4-eb50-11e3-9f5c-9075d5508f0a_story.html.

25. Tyler Kingkade, "Nearly 1,000 Students, Faculty Demand Miami University Cancel George Will Speech," Huffington Post, October 21, 2014, http://www. huffingtonpost.com/2014/10/21/miami-university-george-will_n_6017292.html.

26. Joe Strupp, "Professors Slam George Will Campus Appearance after 'Hate Speech' Rape Column," Media Matters for America, October 17, 2014, http:// mediamatters.org/blog/2014/10/17/professors-slam-george-will-campus-appearance-a/201212.

27. Beth Dalbey, "MSU Defends George Will as Commencement Speaker," Royal
     Oak Patch, December 3, 2014, http://patch.com/michigan/royaloak/msu-
     defends-george-will-commencement-speaker.

28. Zack Budryk, "A Speaker Withdraws at Swarthmore," Inside Higher Ed, April 8,
     2013, https://www.insidehighered.com/news/2013/04/08/swarthmore-
     commencement-speaker-withdraws-over-controversy.

29. Pervaiz Shallwani, "Kelly Booed off Stage during Talk," *Wall Street Journal*,
     October 29, 2013, http://www.wsj.com/articles/SB10001424052702303471004579
     166202578075932; Connor McGuigan and Corky Siemaszko, "Brown University
     Students Shout Commissioner Kelly off the Stage as He Attempted Lecture on
     Policing," *Daily News*, updated October 30, 2013, http://www.nydailynews.com/
     news/national/brown-students-shout-commish-kelly-talk-article-1.1500618.

30. Amy Taxin, "Muslim Students Protest Michael Oren, Israeli Ambassador: Free
     Speech or Criminal Act?," Huffington Post, September 7, 2011, updated
     November 7, 2011, http://www.huffingtonpost.com/2011/09/07/muslim-
     students-protest-michael-oren_n_952207.html.

31. Jeff Greer, "Olmert Heckled at University of Chicago," *U.S. News & World Report*,
     October 19, 2009, http://www.usnews.com/education/blogs/paper-
     trail/2009/10/19/olmert-heckled-at-university-of-chicago.

32. "Southern California—This Just In," *Los Angeles Times*, February 9, 2010, http://
     latimesblogs.latimes.com/lanow/2010/02/11-students-arrested-for-disrupting-
     israeli-ambassadors-speech-at-uc-irvine-.html.

33. Greer, "Olmert Heckled at University of Chicago."

34. "Making Sense of Simcox," *Hoya*, November 7, 2006, http://www.thehoya.com/
     making-sense-of-simcox/.

35. Eliana Johnson, "At Columbia, Students Attack Minuteman Founder," *New York
     Sun*, October 5, 2006, http://www.nysun.com/new-york/at-columbia-students-
     attack-minuteman-founder/41020/.

36. Charles B. Reed, Memorandum regarding Student Activities—Executive Order
     1068, California State University, December 21, 2011, https://www.calstate.edu/
     eo/EO-1068.html.

37. Shane Morris, "One-Way Diversity," Summit, October 17, 2014, http://www.
     summit.org/blogs/summit-announcements/one-way-diversity/.

38. Carla Rivera, "Christian Group Fights for Identity against Cal State Policy," *Los Angeles Times*, October 24, 2014, http://www.latimes.com/local/education/la-me-calstate-clubs-20141024-story.html#page=1.

39. Rod Dreher, "A Response from Vandy's Misfit Christian," American Conservative, August 27, 2014, http://www.theamericanconservative.com/dreher/vanderbilt-misfit-christian-tish-harrison-warren/.

40. Harvey A. Silverglate, "A Campus Crusade against the Constitution," *Wall Street Journal*, September 18, 2014, http://www.wsj.com/articles/harvey-a-silverglate-a-campus-crusade-against-the-constitution-1411081302.

41. "Buffalo Chapter Regains Status," InterVarsity, August 8, 2012, http://www.intervarsity.org/news/buffalo-chapter-regains-status.

42. Tish Harrison Warren, "The Wrong Kind of Christian," *Christianity Today*, August 27, 2014, http://www.christianitytoday.com/ct/2014/september/wrong-kind-of-christian-vanderbilt-university.html?share=HEM3rHy3NoDHiyDTDefd4lNjZn9ixdLt&start=1.

43. Michael Paulson, "Colleges and Evangelicals Collide on Bias Policy," *New York Times*, June 10, 2014, http://www.nytimes.com/2014/06/10/us/colleges-and-evangelicals-collide-on-bias-policy.html?_r=1.

44. Warren, "The Wrong Kind of Christian."

45. Paulson, "Colleges and Evangelicals Collide."

46. Tish Warren, interview with author, January 2015.

47. Ibid.

48. Peter J. Gomes, "Staff's View of Christian Group Backward," *Harvard Crimson*, April 16, 2003, http://www.thecrimson.com/article/2003/4/16/staffs-view-of-christian-group-backward/; *Crimson* Staff, "A Discriminatory Clause," *Harvard Crimson*, April 15, 2003, http://www.thecrimson.com/article/2003/4/15/a-discriminatory-clause-last-week-the/.

49. Bob Smietana, "Foes of School's Nondiscrimination Policy Look to Harvard," *USA Today*, May 3, 2012, http://usatoday30.usatoday.com/news/education/story/2012-05-03/vanderbilt-harvard-nondiscrimination-christian-groups/54732314/1.

50. Peter J. Gomes, "Homophobic? Re-Read Your Bible," *New York Times*, August 17, 1992, http://www.nytimes.com/ref/opinion/op-classic-gomes.html?pagewanted=all.

51. Peter J. Gomes, "Staff's View of Christian Group Backward," *Harvard Crimson*, April 16, 2003, http://www.thecrimson.com/article/2003/4/16/staffs-view-of-christian-group-backward/.

52. Gomes, "Homophobic? Re-Read Your Bible."

53. Jennifer Kabbany, "Conservative Muslim Student Vandalized with Eggs, Hot Dogs; Told 'Shut the F*ck Up,'" *College Fix*, December 12, 2014, http://www.thecollegefix.com/post/20486/.

54. Gloria Steinem, Commencement Address 2007, Smith College, May 20, 2007, http://www.smith.edu/events/commencement_speech2007.php.

CHAPTER SIX: THE WAR ON FOX NEWS

1. "Remarks by the President at the White House Correspondents' Association Dinner," WhiteHouse.gov, April 29, 2012, https://www.whitehouse.gov/the-press-office/2012/04/29/remarks-president-white-house-correspondents-association-dinner.

2. "Remarks by the President at White House Correspondents' Association Dinner," WhiteHouse.gov, May 10, 2009, https://www.whitehouse.gov/the-press-office/remarks-president-white-house-correspondents-association-dinner-592009.

3. Peter Drivas, "Obama Hits Fox News: They're 'Entirely Devoted to Attacking My Administration'—Fox News Responds," Huffington Post, July 17, 2009, updated May 25, 2011, http://www.huffingtonpost.com/2009/06/16/obama-hits-fox-news-theyr_n_216574.html.

4. Joan Shorenstein Center, "The Invisible Primary—Invisible No Longer," Project for Excellence in Journalism, October 29, 2007, http://www.journalism.org/files/legacy/The%20Early%20Campaign%20FINAL.pdf.

5. Ibid.

6. David Bauder, "Study: Media Coverage Has Favored Obama Campaign," Huffington Post, December 1, 2008, updated May 25, 2011, http://www.huffingtonpost.com/2008/10/31/study-media-coverage-has_n_139916.html?; Alexander Burns, "Halperin at Politico/USC conf.: 'extreme pro-Obama' press bias," Politico, November 22, 2008, http://www.politico.com/news/stories/1108/15885.html.

7.   FoxNews.com, "White House Escalates War of Words with Fox News," Fox News, October 12, 2009, http://www.foxnews.com/politics/2009/10/12/white-house-escalates-war-words-fox-news/#ixzz2IYNOAqI1.

8.   Petition, "It's Time to Take on Fox," MoveOn.org, http://bit.ly/146eUuP.

9.   "Democratic Party Dumps Fox," MoveOn.Org, March 9, 2007, http://bit.ly/1xEuXNG.

10. Kate Phillips, "Stung by Remarks, Nevada Democrats Cancel Debate on Fox," *New York Times*, March 10, 2007, http://nyti.ms/146gj4g.

11. Matt Stoller, "Republican Propaganda Is Not News," *Politico*, March 13, 2007, http://www.politico.com/news/stories/0307/3109.html.

12. CNN Reliable Sources, Transcript, "Interview with White House Communications Director; Obama Wins Nobel Peace Prize," CNN, October 11, 2009, http://transcripts.cnn.com/TRANSCRIPTS/0910/11/rs.01.html.

13. Jim Rutenberg, "Behind the War Between White House and Fox," *New York Times*, October 22, 2009, http://www.nytimes.com/2009/10/23/us/politics/23fox.html?_r=0.

14. Michael Scherer, "Calling 'Em Out: The White House Takes on the Press," *Time*, October 8, 2009, http://content.time.com/time/magazine/article/0,9171,1929220,00.html.

15. Brian Stelter, "Fox's Volley With Obama Intensifying," *New York Times*, October 11, 2009, http://www.nytimes.com/2009/10/12/business/media/12fox.html?pagewanted=all&_r=0.

16. Mike Allen, "Fox 'Not Really News,' Says Axelrod," *Politico*, October 18, 2009, http://www.politico.com/news/stories/1009/28417.html#ixzz2IYVABVlp.

17. Ibid.

18. Rutenberg, "Behind the War Between White House and Fox."

19. Mark Jurkowitz, "Is MSNBC the place for opinion?" Pew Research Center, June 5, 2013, http://www.pewresearch.org/fact-tank/2013/06/05/is-msnbc-the-place-for-opinion/.

20. Ibid.

21. Brent Baker, "CBS Takes Up White House Quest to 'De-Legitimize' Fox News, 'Irony' FNC Enabled Attack," MRC NewsBusters, October 23, 2009, http://

newsbusters.org/blogs/brent-baker/2009/10/23/cbs-takes-white-house-quest-de-legitimize-fox-news-irony-fnc-enabled-at.

22. "CBS News' Chip Reid on Fox News and the Administration," YouTube, uploaded on October 23, 2009, https://www.youtube.com/watch?v=qnMiqIW5e1Q#t=162.

23. David Martosko, "Left-wing Foundations Lavish Millions on Media Matters," Daily Caller, February 17, 2012, http://dailycaller.com/2012/02/17/left-wing-foundations-lavish-millions-on-media-matters/.

24. Capital Research Center, "Organization Trends," CapitalResearch.org, https://capitalresearch.org/wp-content/uploads/2014/12/OT1214-1.pdf.

25. Media Matters, "About Us," Media Matters for America, http://mediamatters.org/about.

26. Maureen Dowd, "Call Off the Dogs," *The New York Times*, February 14, 2015, http://www.nytimes.com/2015/02/15/opinion/sunday/maureen-dowd-call-off-the-dogs.html?_r=0.

27. Ben Smith, "Media Matters Coordinates Campaign Against 'Lethal' Fox," *Politico*, October 23, 2009, http://www.politico.com/blogs/bensmith/1009/Media_Matters_coordinates_campaign_against_lethal_Fox.html.

28. Ibid.

29. Steve Krakauer, "Tipping Point? White House Press Pool Stands Up for Fox News," *Mediaite*, October 23, 2009, http://www.mediaite.com/tv/tipping-point-white-house-press-pool-stands-up-for-fox-news/.

30. Tommy Christopher, "Treasury Department Denies It Tried to Exclude Fox News From Interviews," *Mediaite*, October 23, 2009, http://www.mediaite.com/online/treasury-denies-it-tried-to-exclude-fox-news-from-interviews/.

31. Christina Bellantoni, "WH: We're Happy To Exclude Fox, But Didn't Yesterday With Feinberg Interview," Talking Points Memo, October 23, 2009, http://talkingpointsmemo.com/dc/wh-we-re-happy-to-exclude-fox-but-didn-t-yesterday-with-feinberg-interview.

32. "Documents Show Obama White House Attacked, Excluded Fox News Channel," Press Room, Judicial Watch, July 14, 2011, http://www.judicialwatch.org/press-room/press-releases/documents-show-obama-white-house-attacked-excluded-fox-news-channel/.

33. Jeff Greenfield, "President Obama's Feud with FOX News," CBS News, October 23, 2009, http://www.cbsnews.com/news/president-obamas-feud-with-fox-news/.

34. Steve Krakauer, "Fox News: White House Apologized for Pay Czar Interview Snub 'Mistake,'" *Mediaite*, October 24, 2009, http://www.mediaite.com/tv/white-house-admits-to-fox-news-pay-czar-interview-exclusion-a-mistake/.

35. Greta Van Susteren, "Obama Administration Has Some Explaining to Do," Fox News Insider, January 16, 2014, http://gretawire.foxnewsinsider.com/2014/01/16/obama-administration-and-new-york-times-have-some-explaining-to-do/.

36. Devin Dwyer, "Today's Q's for O's WH—10/20/2009," ABC News, October 20, 2009, http://abcnews.go.com/blogs/politics/2009/10/todays-qs-for-os-wh-10202009/.

37. Ibid.

38. Mike McCurry interview with author, January 2015.

39. Ibid.

40. Franklin Foer and Chris Hughes, "Barack Obama is Not Pleased," *New Republic*, January 27, 2013, http://www.newrepublic.com/article/112190/obama-interview-2013-sit-down-president.

41. Alexis Sobel Fitts, "And From the Left…Fox News," *Columbia Journalism Review*, http://www.cjr.org/feature/and_from_the_leftfox_news.php?page=all#sthash.P9SHaLy5.dpuf.

42. Lisa DePaulo, "How Joe Trippi Found Happiness at Fox News," *New Republic*, October 19, 2012, http://www.newrepublic.com/article/politics/magazine/108839/how-joe-trippi-found-happiness-fox-news?page=0,0.

43. Jim Rutenberg, "The Megyn Kelly Moment," *New York Times*, January 21, 2015, http://www.nytimes.com/2015/01/25/magazine/the-megyn-kelly-moment.html?_r=0.

44. Josh Feldman, "Time's Joe Klein Can't Stand Watching CNN, Would Rather Watch Fox," Mediaite, April 28, 2014, http://www.mediaite.com/tv/times-joe-klein-can't-stand-watching-cnn-would-rather-watch-fox/.

45. Brian Stelter, "Fox News Anchor Megyn Kelly Renews Contract," *New York Times*, May 7, 2013, http://www.nytimes.com/2013/05/08/business/media/fox-news-anchor-megyn-kelly-renews-contract.html.

46. Catherine Taibi, "Megyn Kelly, 'Attractive-Looking Blond' Anchorwoman, Leads the Pack at Fox News," Huffington Post, January 21, 2015, http://www.huffingtonpost.com/2015/01/21/megyn-kelly-new-york-time-attractive-fox-news-anchor_n_6516162.html.

47. Katie J. M. Baker, "Fox Newsbot Megyn Kelly Hands Misogynists Their Asses on a Plate," Jezebel, May 31, 2013, http://jezebel.com/fox-newsbot-megyn-kelly-hands-misogynists-their-asses-o-510710234.

48. Jim Romenesko, "MSNBC.com Adds Irin Carmon, Tim Noah and Others," JimRomenesko.com, June 17, 2013, http://jimromenesko.com/2013/06/17/msnbc-com-adds-irin-carmon-tim-noah-and-others/. Also, http://irincarmon.people.msnbc.com/#51.

49. Capital Staff, "The 60-Second Interview: Irin Carmon, National Reporter, MSNBC," Capital New York, January 16, 2015, http://www.capitalnewyork.com/article/media/2015/01/8560351/60-second-interview-irin-carmon-national-reporter-msnbc.

50. Jonathan Chait, "The Quintessential Fox News Image," New Republic, April 8, 2010, http://www.newrepublic.com/blog/jonathan-chait/the-quintessential-fox-news-image.

51. Lee Siegel, "The Right, Hot, and Bothered Blondes of Fox News," Men's Journal, February 2013, http://www.mensjournal.com/magazine/the-right-hot-and-bothered-blondes-of-fox-news-20130205#ixzz3PbCdcbE8.

52. Jonathan Chait, "The Fox News-iest Segment in Fox News History," New York, March 6, 2013, http://nymag.com/daily/intelligencer/2013/03/fox-newsiest-segment-in-fox-news-history.html.

53. Jon Greenberg, "Image of 9 White, Blond Women Shows 'Amazing Diversity of Fox News Anchors,'" PolitiFact, July 9, 2014 http://www.politifact.com/punditfact/statements/2014/jul/09/facebook-posts/facebook-post-blondes-fox-news/.

54. Ben Smith, "Media Matters' War Against Fox," Politico, March 26, 2011, http://www.politico.com/news/stories/0311/51949.html.

55. Jacob Weisberg, "The O'Garbage Factor," Newsweek, October 26, 2009, https://www.questia.com/article/1G1-210217914/the-o-garbage-factor.

56. Ibid.

57.   Howell Raines, "Why Don't Honest Journalists Take On Roger Ailes and Fox News?," *Washington Post*, March 14, 2010, http://www.washingtonpost.com/wp-dyn/content/article/2010/03/11/AR2010031102523.html.

58.   CNN/ORC Poll, July 23 2014, http://i2.cdn.turner.com/cnn/2014/images/07/22/rel7c.pdf.

59.   Angie Drobnic Holan, "Lie of the Year: 'If You Like Your Health Care Plan, You Can Keep It,'" PolitiFact, December 12, 2013, http://www.politifact.com/truth-o-meter/article/2013/dec/12/lie-year-if-you-like-your-health-care-plan-keep-it/.

60.   Dan Froomkin, "Why Journalists Shouldn't Be Defending Fox News," Huffington Post, March 18, 2010, updated May 25, 2011, http://www.huffingtonpost.com/2009/10/23/why-journalists-shouldnt_n_331748.html.

61.   Joseph Heath, "'Straight-Up Propaganda': Fox News, Charlatans, Conspiracy Theorists and the Religious Fanatics Endangering Democracy," Salon.com, September 28, 2014, http://www.salon.com/2014/09/28/straight_up_propaganda_fox_news_charlatans_conspiracy_theorists_and_the_religious_fanatics_endangering_democracy/.

62.   Tom Dickinson, "How Roger Ailes Built the Fox News Fear Factory," *Rolling Stone*, May 25, 2011, http://www.rollingstone.com/politics/news/how-roger-ailes-built-the-fox-news-fear-factory-20110525?page=3.

63.   Eddie Scarry, "*Salon*'s Joan Walsh: Fox News Would Have Considered Slave Owners 'Job Creators,'" *Mediaite*, September 8, 2014, http://www.mediaite.com/online/salons-joan-walsh-fox-news-would-have-considered-slave-owners-job-creators/.

64.   Richard Prince, "MSNBC to Apologize for Cinco de Mayo Segment," Maynard Institute for Journalism Education, May 5, 2014, http://mije.org/richardprince/millions-changed-race-or-ethnicity-2010-census#MSNBC.

65.   Teresa Mull, "Sharyl Atkisson: Don't Give Up," *Human Events*, November 7, 2014, http://humanevents.com/2014/11/07/sharyl-attkisson-dont-give-up/.

66.   Amanda Terkel, "Media Matters Declares Victory: 'The War on Fox Is Over,'" Huffington Post, January 23, 2014, http://www.huffingtonpost.com/2013/12/13/media-matters-fox_n_4433207.html.

67. Rick Kissell, "Fox News Dominates Cable News Ratings in 2014; MSNBC Tumbles," *Variety*, December 30, 2014, http://variety.com/2014/tv/news/fox-news-dominates-cable-news-ratings-in-2014-msnbc-tumbles-1201386523/.

68. Ibid.

69. David Zurawik, "New Level of Fox News Dominance Demands Analysis, Not Dismissal," *Baltimore Sun*, November 18, 2014, http://www.baltimoresun.com/entertainment/tv/z-on-tv-blog/bal-fox-news-ratings-dominance-demands-analysis-20141117-story.html.

70. Pamela Engel, "POLL: Fox Is the Most Trusted TV News Source In America," Business Insider, June 10, 2014, http://www.businessinsider.com/chart-fox-is-the-most-trusted-tv-news-source-in-america-2014-6.

CHAPTER SEVEN: MUDDY MEDIA WATERS

1. Andrew Holowchak, *Thomas Jefferson's Philosophy of Education: A Utopian Dream* (New York: Routledge, 2014), 173.

2. Lynn Sweet, "Sweet Blog Special: Obama Transparency Speech," *Chicago Sun-Times*, September 4, 2007, http://blogs.suntimes.com/sweet/2007/09/sweet_blog_special_obama_trans.html.

3. GLASSBOOTHdotORG, "Barack Obama on Government Transparency," YouTube, November 3, 2008, http://www.youtube.com/watch?v=CU0m6Rxm9vU.

4. Macon Phillips, "Change Has Come to WhiteHouse.gov," WhiteHouse.gov, January 20, 2009, http://www.whitehouse.gov/blog/change_has_come_to_whitehouse-gov.

5. Donovan Slack, "Obama ends term with fewer pressers than Bush or Clinton," *Politico*, January 15, 2013, http://www.politico.com/politico44/2013/01/obama-ends-term-with-fewer-pressers-than-bush-or-clinton-154233.html.

6. Jim VandeHei and Mike Allen, "Obama, the Puppet Master ," *Politico*, February 18, 2013, http://www.politico.com/story/2013/02/obama-the-puppet-master-87764_Page2.html.

7. Ibid.

8. Letter from news organizations hand-delivered to White House Press Secretary Jay Carney, November 21, 2013, available at the Associated Press blog, http://

corpcommap.files.wordpress.com/2013/11/white-house-photo-letter-final-00591175.pdf.

9.   Brian Montopoli, "Elena Kagan White House 'Interview' Riles Reporters," CBS News, May 12, 2010, http://www.cbsnews.com/news/elena-kagan-white-house-interview-riles-reporters/.

10. Paul Farhi, "Obama Keeps Newspaper Reporters at Arm's Length," *Washington Post*, February 10, 2013, http://articles.washingtonpost.com/2013-02-10/lifestyle/37025955_1_newspaper-group-interviews-obama-campaign.

11. "Steve Kroft on Why Obama Appears on 60 Minutes: 'I Think He Knows That We're Not Going to Play Gotcha with Him," RealClearPolitics, January 29, 2013, http://www.realclearpolitics.com/video/2013/01/29/steve_kroft_on_why_obama_appears_on_60_minutes_i_think_he_knows_that_were_not_going_to_play_gotcha_with_him.html.

12. "Letter Urges President Obama to Be More Transparent," Society of Professional Journalists, July 8, 2014, http://www.spj.org/news.asp?ref=1253.

13. Paul Farhi, "Reporters Say White House Sometimes Demands Changes to Press-Pool Reports," *Washington Post*, September 23, 2014, http://www.washingtonpost.com/lifestyle/style/reporters-say-white-house-sometimes-demands-changes-to-press-pool-reports/2014/09/23/e5e6fec8-42d9-11e4-9a15-137aa0153527_story.html.

14. Ann Marimow, "A Rare Peek into a Justice Department Leak Probe," *Washington Post*, May 19, 2013, http://www.washingtonpost.com/local/a-rare-peek-into-a-justice-department-leak-probe/2013/05/19/0bc473de-be5e-11e2-97d4-a479289a31f9_story.html; Michael Isikoff, "DOJ Confirms Holder OK'd Search Warrant for Fox News Reporter's Emails," NBC News, May 23, 2013, http://investigations.nbcnews.com/_news/2013/05/23/18451142-doj-confirms-holder-okd-search-warrant-for-fox-news-reporters-emails?lite.

15. Dylan Byers, "Report: DOJ Seized Phone Records of James Rosen's Parents," *Politico*, May 22, 2013, http://www.politico.com/blogs/media/2013/05/report-doj-seized-phone-records-of-james-rosens-parents-164541.html.

16. Tom McCarthy, "James Rosen: Fox News Reporter Targeted as 'Co-Conspirator' in Spying Case," *Guardian*, May 21, 2013, http://www.theguardian.com/world/2013/may/20/fox-news-reporter-targeted-us-government.

17.   "White House Escalates War of Words with Fox News," Fox News, October 12, 2009, http://www.foxnews.com/politics/2009/10/12/white-house-escalates-war-words-fox-news/.

18.   Michael Isikoff, "'Double Standard' in White House Leak Inquiries," NBC News, October 18, 2010, http://www.nbcnews.com/id/39693850/ns/us_news-security/t/double-standard-white-house-leak-inquiries/#.VMOTJC7F8YQ.

19.   Tal Kopan, "Eric Holder: James Rosen Probe 'Appropriate,'" *Politico*, June 20, 2013, http://www.politico.com/story/2013/06/eric-holder-james-rosen-93100.html.

20.   Olivier Knox, "Obama Administration Spied on Fox News Reporter James Rosen: Report," Yahoo!, May 20, 2013, http://news.yahoo.com/blogs/ticket/obama-admin-spied-fox-news-reporter-james-rosen-134204299.html.

21.   "Holder Says 'Subpoena' to Fox News Reporter Is His One Regret," Fox News, October 30, 2014 http://www.foxnews.com/politics/2014/10/29/holder-says-subpoena-to-fox-news-reporter-is-his-one-regret/.

22.   Charlie Savage and Lisa Kaufman, "Phone Records of Journalists Seized by U.S.," *New York Times*, May 13, 2013, http://www.nytimes.com/2013/05/14/us/phone-records-of-journalists-of-the-associated-press-seized-by-us.html?pagewanted=all.

23.   Leonard Downie, "Obama's War on Leaks Undermines Investigative Journalism," *Washington Post*, May 23, 2013, http://www.washingtonpost.com/opinions/leonard-downie-obamas-war-on-leaks-undermines-investigative-journalism/2013/05/23/4fe4ac2e-c19b-11e2-bfdb-3886a561c1ff_story.html.

24.   28 CFR Ch. 1 (7-1-10 Edition), U.S. Government Publishing Office, 44, http://www.gpo.gov/fdsys/pkg/CFR-2010-title28-vol2/pdf/CFR-2010-title28-vol2-sec50-10.pdf.

25.   Roger Yu, "Feds Seize AP Phone Records For Criminal Probe," *USA Today*, May 13, 2013, http://www.usatoday.com/story/news/2013/05/13/justice-department-associated-press-telephone-records/2156521/.

26.   Associated Press, "Justice Department Secretly Obtained AP Phone Records," Fox News, May 13, 2013, http://www.foxnews.com/politics/2013/05/13/justice-department-secretly-obtains-ap-phone-records/.

27.   Matt Apuzzo, "Times Reporter Will Note Be Called to Testify in Leak Case," *New York Times*, January 12, 2015, http://www.nytimes.com/2015/01/13/us/times-

reporter-james-risen-will-not-be-called-to-testify-in-leak-case-lawyers-say.
html?_r=0.

28.   Amy Calder, "*New York Times* reporter James Risen at Colby: 'Obama hates the
       press,'" *Portland Press Herald*, October 5, 2014, http://www.pressherald.
       com/2014/10/05/colby-college-honoring-new-york-times-reporter/.

29.   Glenn Greenwald, "Obama campaign brags about its whistleblower persecutions,"
       Guardian, September 5, 2012, http://www.theguardian.com/commentisfree/2012/
       sep/05/obama-campaign-brags-about-whistleblower-persecutions; Verbiage also
       available at Obama's president-elect website: http://change.gov/agenda/ethics_
       agenda/http://change.gov/agenda/ethics_agenda/.

30.   Leonard Downie Jr. and reporting by Sara Rafsky, "The Obama Administration
       and the Press," Committee to Protect Journalists, October 13, 2013, https://cpj.
       org/reports/2013/10/obama-and-the-press-us-leaks-surveillance-post-911.php.

31.   Rupert Allman, Arwa Gunja, and Jillian Weinberger, "'A New Level of Secrecy
       and Control': Jill Abramson and the Obama White House," The Takeaway, April
       10, 2014, http://www.thetakeaway.org/story/new-level-secrecy-and-control-
       nytimes-chief-jill-abramson-obama-white-house/.

32.   Juliet Eilperin, "How Obama's anti-leak policy has chilled the free press,"
       Washington Post, October 11, 2013, http://www.washingtonpost.com/blogs/
       the-fix/wp/2013/10/11/how-obamas-anti-leak-policy-has-chilled-the-free-
       press/.

33.   Carey Shenkman, interview with author, December 19, 2014.

34.   Leonard Downie Jr., "Obama's war on leaks undermines investigative
       journalism," *Washington Post*, May 23, 2014, http://www.washingtonpost.com/
       opinions/leonard-downie-obamas-war-on-leaks-undermines-investigative-
       journalism/2013/05/23/4fe4ac2e-c19b-11e2-bfdb-3886a561c1ff_story.html;
       Leonard Downie Jr., "In Obama's war on leaks, reporters fight back," *Washington
       Post*, October 4, 2013, http://www.washingtonpost.com/opinions/in-obamas-
       war-on-leaks-reporters-fight-back/2013/10/04/70231e1c-2aeb-11e3-b139-
       029811dbb57f_story.html.

35.   Leonard Downie Jr. with reporting by Sara Rafsky, "Leak Investigations and
       surveillance in post-9/11 America," Committee to Protect Journalists, http://cpj.
       org/reports/2013/10/obama-and-the-press-us-leaks-surveillance-post-911.

phphttp://cpj.org/reports/2013/10/obama-and-the-press-us-leaks-surveillance-post-911.php.

36. Downie Jr., "Obama's war on leaks undermines investigative journalism"; Downie Jr., "In Obama's war on leaks, reporters fight back."

37. Glenn Greenwald, "Obama Campaign Brags About Its Whistleblower Persecutions," *Guardian*, September 5, 2012, http://www.theguardian.com/commentisfree/2012/sep/05/obama-campaign-brags-about-whistleblower-persecutions.

38. "Media Bias Basics: Admissions of Liberal Bias," Media Research Center Archives, http://archive.mrc.org/biasbasics/biasbasics2.asp; Daniel Okrent, "The Public Editor: Is *The New York Times* a Liberal Newspaper?," *New York Times*, July 25, 2004, http://www.nytimes.com/2004/07/25/opinion/the-public-editor-is-the-new-york-times-a-liberal-newspaper.html.

39. Howard Kurtz, "Suddenly Everyone's A Critic," *Washington Post*, October 3, 2005, http://www.washingtonpost.com/wp-dyn/content/article/2005/10/02/AR2005100201296_2.html.

40. Thomas Edsall, "Journalism Should Own Its Liberalism," *Columbia Journalism Review*, October 8, 2009, http://www.cjr.org/campaign_desk/journalism_should_own_its_libe.php.

41. "Journalists Admitting Liberal Bias, Part One," Media Research Center, May 19, 2014, http://www.mrc.org/media-bias-101/journalists-admitting-liberal-bias-part-one.

42. David Weigel, "Kermit Gosnell: The Alleged Mass-Murderer and the Bored Media," *Slate*, April 12, 2013, http://www.slate.com/blogs/weigel/2013/04/12/kermit_gosnell_the_alleged_mass_murderer_and_the_bored_media.html.

43. Brandon Ambrosino, "What the Gay Rights Movement Should Learn from Martin Luther King, Jr.," *Time*, January 20, 2014, http://time.com/2332/what-the-gay-rights-movement-should-learn-from-martin-luther-king-jr/.

44. Luke Brinker, "Meet Brandon Ambrosino, Homophobes' Favorite Gay Writer and Vox's Newest Hire," Media Matters for America, March 12, 2104, http://mediamatters.org/blog/2014/03/12/meet-brandon-ambrosino-homophobes-favorite-gay/198461.

45. Gabriel Arana, "Ezra Klein's Queer New Hire," *American Prospect*, March 13, 2014, http://prospect.org/article/ezra-kleins-queer-new-hire.

46. Mark Joseph Stern, "*Vox*'s Unbelievably Terrible New Hire," *Slate*, March 13, 2014, http://www.slate.com/blogs/outward/2014/03/13/brandon_ambrosino_to_vox_he_s_unbelievably_terrible.html; Carlos Maza, "Ezra Klein: 'I Could've And Should've, Handled This Hire A Lot Better,'" Media Matters for America, March 14, 2014, http://mediamatters.org/tags/brandon-ambrosino.

47. Noah Michelson, "Ezra Klein, I'm Calling Bullsh*t on Your Defense of Hiring Brandon Ambrosino, and Here's Why," Huffington Post, May 14, 2014, http://www.huffingtonpost.com/noah-michelson/ezra-klein-im-calling-bul_b_4965557.html.

48. "110K Call on The *Washington Post* to End Climate Change Denial in its Editorial Page," Forecast the Facts, February 20, 2014, http://forecastthefacts.org/press/releases/2014/2/20/110k-call-washington-post-end-climate-change-denia/.

49. "About Forecast the Facts," Forecast the Facts, http://forecastthefacts.org/about/.

50. George Will, "Colleges Become the Victims of Progressivism," *Washington Post*, June 6, 2014, http://www.washingtonpost.com/opinions/george-will-college-become-the-victims-of-progressivism/2014/06/06/e90e73b4-eb50-11e3-9f5c-9075d5508f0a_story.html.

51. Andrew Johnson, "Will's Bout With Feminists," National Review Online, June 11, 2014, http://www.nationalreview.com/article/380156/wills-bout-feminists-andrew-johnson.

52. "Letter to George Will from Senators," June 12, 2014, available at the *Washington Post* website, http://www.washingtonpost.com/r/2010-2019/WashingtonPost/2014/06/13/Editorial-Opinion/Graphics/Letter-to-George-Will-from-Senators.pdf.

53. Michael Miner, "The *St. Louis Post-Dispatch* Conspicuously Dumps George Will," *Chicago Reader*, June 26, 2014, http://www.chicagoreader.com/Bleader/archives/2014/06/26/the-st-louis-post-dispatch-conspicuously-dumps-george-will.

54. Post Opinions Staff, "George Will Responds to Senators on His Sexual Assault Column," *Washington Post*, June 13, 2014, http://www.washingtonpost.com/blogs/post-partisan/wp/2014/06/13/george-will-responds-to-senators-on-his-sexual-assault-column.

55. "Tell the *Washington Post*: Fire George Will," UltraViolet, http://act.weareultraviolet.org/cms/sign/Fire_George_Will/.

56. National Organization for Women, "*Washington Post*: Dump George Will," NOW, http://now.org/take-action/washington-post-dump-george-will/.

57. Tony Messenger, "Editor's Note: Michael Gerson Replaces George Will," *St. Louis Post-Dispatch*, June 19, 2014, http://www.stltoday.com/news/opinion/columns/the-platform/editor-s-note-michael-gerson-replaces-george-will/article_4b645ed8-e70e-5357-a85b-d347e5802785.html.

58. Ellie Sandmeyer, "Backlash Against George Will's Offensive Rape Column Grows As Paper Drops Him," Media Matters for America, June 19, 2014, http://mediamatters.org/blog/2014/06/19/backlash-against-george-wills-offensive-rape-co/199797.

CHAPTER EIGHT: ILLIBERAL FEMINIST THOUGHT POLICE

1. Burwell v. Hobby Lobby Stores, Inc., et al., 573 U.S. (2014), http://www.supremecourt.gov/opinions/13pdf/13-354_olp1.pdf; See the brief for the respondents in Kathleen Sebelius v. Hobby Lobby Stories et al. at http://sblog.s3.amazonaws.com/wp-content/uploads/2013/10/No-13-354-Brief-for-Respondents.pdf; and Jayne O'Donnell, "Hobby Lobby Case; What Birth Control Is Affected?," *USA Today*, June 30, 2014, http://www.usatoday.com/story/news/nation/2014/06/30/morning-after-iuds/11768653/.

2. "Morning-After Pill (Emergency Contraception)," PlannedParenthood.org, http://www.plannedparenthood.org/health-info/morning-after-pill-emergency-contraception.

3. Jackie Seal, "MSNBC Guest Invokes Jim Crow, Apartheid in Reaction to Hobby Lobby Ruling," MRC NewsBusters, June 30, 2014, http://newsbusters.org/blogs/jackie-seal/2014/06/30/msnbc-guest-invokes-jim-crow-apartheid-reaction-hobby-lobby-ruling.

4. Tweet from Senator Harry Reid, June 30, 2014, https://twitter.com/senatorreid/status/483630584833773568.

5. Glenn Kessler, "Democrats on Hobby Lobby: 'Misspeaks,' 'Opinion,' and Overheated Rhetoric," *Washington Post*, July 14, 2014, http://www.washingtonpost.com/blogs/fact-checker/wp/2014/07/14/democrats-on-hobby-lobby-misspeaks-opinion-and-overheated-rhetoric/.

6.   Ruth Marcus, "Judging from Experience," *Washington Post*, July 1, 2014, http://
      www.washingtonpost.com/opinions/ruth-marcus-judging-from-
      experience/2014/07/01/78c51c30-0148-11e4-b8ff-89afd3fad6bd_story.html.

7.   Lydia Saad, "Contraception Debate Divides Americans, Including Women,"
      Gallup, February 24, 2012, http://www.gallup.com/poll/152963/contraception-
      debate-divides-americans-including-women.aspx.

8.   Kristina Arriaga, Executive Director, Becket Fund, interview with author, March
      6, 2015.

9.   The biography of Kristina Arriaga is available on the Becket Fund website at
      http://www.becketfund.org/staff-members/kristina-arriaga/.

10.   Lydia Saad, "Majority of Americans Still Support Roe V. Wade Decision," Gallup,
      January 22, 2013, http://www.gallup.com/poll/160058/majority-americans-
      support-roe-wade-decision.aspx.

11.   *Washington Post*–ABC News Poll National Politics, July 2013, http://www.
      washingtonpost.com/page/2010-2019/WashingtonPost/2013/07/25/National-
      Politics/Polling/question_11465.xml?uuid=bN9EXvUZEeKB-o6Ds4ZMNg.

12.   The amici curiae briefs are available online at http://www.becketfund.org/
      wp-content/uploads/2014/01/13-354-356-bsac-Womens-Policy-Groups-and-
      Coaltion-of-Female-State-Legislative-and-Executive-Branch-Officials.pdf;
      http://www.becketfund.org/wp-content/uploads/2014/01/13-354-bsac-Women-
      Speak-for-Themselves.pdf; http://www.becketfund.org/wp-content/
      uploads/2014/01/13-35413-356bsacIndependentWomen'sForum.pdf; and http://
      www.becketfund.org/wp-content/uploads/2014/01/bsac-13-354-and-13-356-
      Brief-of-Beverly-Lahaye-Institute-et-al.pdf.

13.   Ibid.

14.   Tweet from Jill Filipovic, June 30, 2014, https://twitter.com/jillfilipovic/
      status/483633989463592960.

15.   Tweet from CJ Werleman, September 8, 2014, https://twitter.com/cjwerleman/
      status/509063346092797952.

16.   Ibid.

17.   Seal, "MSNBC Guest Invokes Jim Crow."

18.   Ibid.

19. Paul Rosenberg, "This Is a Religious Civil War: Hobby Lobby Only the Beginning for New Religious Theocrats," Salon.com, July 8, 2014, http://www.salon.com/2014/07/08/this_is_a_religious_civil_war_hobby_lobby_only_the_beginning_for_new_religious_theocrats/.

20. Audio of Ed Schultz is available online at MRC NewsBusters, http://newsbusters.org/sites/default/files/2013/Schultz%20O%27Neill%20actual%20war%20on%20women.mp3. See also Peter Berkowitz, "The Left's Hollow Complaints about Hobby Lobby," RealClearPolitics, July 12, 2014, http://www.realclearpolitics.com/articles/2014/07/12/the_lefts_hollow_complaints_over_hobby_lobby__123293.html.

21. Tweet from Jimmy Williams, June 30, 2014, https://twitter.com/jimmyspolitics/status/483626621740789761.

22. Ibid.

23. Lincoln Mitchell, "How Hobby Lobby Undermines All Americans' Freedom," Huffington Post, July 6, 2014, http://www.huffingtonpost.com/lincoln-mitchell/how-hobby-lobby-undermine_b_5561501.html.

24. Mark Joseph Stern, "Of Course Hobby Lobby Discriminates against Trans Workers, Too," *Slate*, July 15, 2014, http://www.slate.com/blogs/outward/2014/07/15/hobby_lobby_discriminates_against_trans_workers_and_women.html.

25. Garance Franke-Ruta, "Rick Perry, Mansplainer in Chief," June 27, 2013, *Atlantic*, http://www.theatlantic.com/politics/archive/2013/06/rick-perry-mansplainer-in-chief/277308/.

26. Marin Cogan, "The Mittsplainer: An Alternate Theory of Mitt Romney's Gaffes," *GQ*, August 1, 2012, http://www.gq.com/news-politics/blogs/death-race/2012/08/the-mittsplainer-an-alternate-theory-of-mitt-romneys-gaffes.html.

27. Kat Stoeffel, "Watch Ted Cruz Mansplain the Second Amendment to Dianne Feinstein," *New York*, March 14, 2013, http://nymag.com/thecut/2013/03/watch-ted-cruz-mansplain-the-second-amendment.html.

28. Jillian Rayfield, "Sen. Ron Johnson Offers to Mansplain the Budget to Tammy Baldwin," Salon.com, November 8, 2012, http://www.salon.com/2012/11/08/sen_ron_johnson_offers_to_mansplain_the_budget_to_tammy_baldwin/.

29. Emily Swanson, "Poll: Few Identify as Feminists, but Most Believe in Equality of Sexes," Huffington Post, April 16, 2013, http://www.huffingtonpost.com/2013/04/16/feminism-poll_n_3094917.html.

30. Sue Owen, "Michelle Malkin Says Gloria Steinem Once Called Kay Bailey Hutchison a 'Female Impersonator,'" PolitiFact Texas, March 29, 2012, http://www.politifact.com/texas/statements/2012/mar/29/michelle-malkin/gloria-steinem-once-called-kay-bailey-hutchison-fe/.

31. Tom Humphrey, "Democrat on GOP's Female Lawmakers: 'Lift Their Skirts to Find Out If They Are Women,'" *Knoxville News Sentinel*, June 14, 2010, http://www.knoxnews.com/news/state/democrat-gops-female-lawmakers-lift-their-skirts-f.

32. "Just Plain Nut-ty," *Radio Equalizer*, August 10, 2010, http://radioequalizer.blogspot.com/2010/08/lefty-actress-threatens-rush-limbaugh.html; and Michelle Malkin, "The Vulgarity of Liberal Female 'Comedians,'" MichelleMalkin.com, August 12, 2010, http://michellemalkin.com/2010/08/12/the-vulgarity-of-liberal-female-comedians/.

33. "Ann Coulter Is a Man," *Fromtheleft*, https://fromtheleft.wordpress.com/2007/03/03/ann-coulter-is-a-man/; and Pam Spaulding, "Mann Coulter Is Crying That Her *Time* Cover Is Distorted," Firedoglake, April 18, 2005, http://pamshouseblend.firedoglake.com/2005/04/18/mann-coulter-is-crying-that-her-time-cover-is-distorted/.

34. Bennett Marcus, "Gloria Steinem: Sarah Palin and Michele Bachmann 'Are There to Oppose the Women's Movement,'" *New York*, August 11, 2011, http://nymag.com/daily/intelligencer/2011/08/gloria_steinem_sarah_palin_and.html.

35. Nico Pitney, "Sarah Palin: George Bush in Lipstick?," Huffington Post, October 8, 2008, http://www.huffingtonpost.com/2008/09/07/sarah-palin-george-bush-i_n_124654.html%22 %5Ct %22_blank.

36. Doniger is quoted in Michael Gaynor, "Sarah Palin IS a Woman and a Good Mom!," Renew America, September 17, 2008, http://www.renewamerica.com/columns/gaynor/080917.

37. Cintra Wilson, "Pissed about Palin," Salon.com, September 10, 2008, http://www.salon.com/2008/09/10/palin_feminism/.

38.   Caroline May, "Olbermann says S.E. Cupp Demonstrates the 'Necessity' of Planned Parenthood," Daily Caller, April 14, 2011, http://dailycaller.com/2011/04/14/olbermann-says-s-e-cupp-demonstrates-the-necessity-of-planned-parenthood/.

39.   Kirsten Powers, "Rush Limbaugh Isn't the Only Media Misogynist," Daily Beast, March 4, 2012, http://www.thedailybeast.com/articles/2012/03/04/rush-limbaugh-s-apology-liberal-men-need-to-follow-suit.html.

40.   Tommy Christopher, "Keith Olbermann Apologizes to SE Cupp and Michelle Malkin, Suspends Worst Persons Again," *Mediaite*, March 7, 2012, http://www.mediaite.com/tv/keith-olbermann-apologizes-to-se-cupp-and-michelle-malkin-suspends-worst-persons-again/.

41.   Peggy Noonan, "America's Real War on Women," *Wall Street Journal*, March 16, 2012, http://www.wsj.com/articles/SB10001424052702304459804577283841891275230.

42.   Nathan A. Heflick, "Sexualized Women Are Seen as Objects, Studies Find," *Psychology Today*, August 14, 2010, http://www.psychologytoday.com/blog/the-big-questions/201008/sexualized-women-are-seen-objects-studies-find.

43.   Ibid.

44.   Nina Burleigh, "The Best and the Rightest," *Elle*, August 12, 2011, http://www.elle.com/culture/career-politics/news/a12323/female-conservativism/.

45.   Ibid.

46.   Derek Hunter, "Progressives Make Sexist Twitter Smears about Combat Veteran Joni Ernst," Daily Caller, January 20, 2015, http://dailycaller.com/2015/01/20/progressives-make-sexist-twitter-smears-about-combat-veteran-joni-ernst/.

47.   Katie Glueck, "Tom Harkin: Joni Ernst as Pretty as Taylor Swift? So What?," *Politico*, November 2, 2014, updated November 3, 2014, http://www.politico.com/story/2014/11/2014-iowa-elections-tom-harkin-joni-ernst-taylor-swift-112433.html#ixzz3PgSeeW.

48.   Wilson, "Pissed about Palin."

49.   "Sarah Palin: Former Beauty Queen, Future VP? (Photos)," Huffington Post, October 21, 2008, http://www.huffingtonpost.com/2008/08/29/sarah-palin-former-beauty_n_122400.html?.

50. Rachel Slajda, "MSNBC Host Apologizes for Using Fake Palin Pics," Talking Points Memo, November 16, 2009, http://talkingpointsmemo.com/news/msnbc-host-apologizes-for-using-fake-palin-pics.

51. Gene Lyons, "Forget the Tea Party, What about the Crumpets?" Salon.com, September 22, 2010, http://www.salon.com/2010/09/23/gene_lyons_tea_party/.

52. Noah Rothman, "Russell Brand on the Reasons behind Sarah Palin's Broad Appeal: 'People Want to F**k Her,'" *Mediaite*, July 28, 2012, http://www.mediaite.com/online/russell-brand-on-the-reasons-behind-sarah-palins-broad-appeal-people-want-to-fk-her/.

53. Erin Gloria Ryan, "Kirsten Dunst Thinks Ladies in Relationships Should Wife the F— Out," Jezebel, April 3, 2014, http://jezebel.com/kirsten-dunst-thinks-ladies-in-relationships-should-wif-1557845533.

54. Hollie McKay, "Kirsten Dunst Sparks Debate over Support for Traditional Gender Roles," Fox News, April 7, 2014, http://www.foxnews.com/entertainment/2014/04/07/kirsten-dunst-sparks-debate-over-support-for-traditional-gender-roles/.

55. Burleigh, "The Best and the Rightest."

56. Karin Agness, "Conservative Women as 'Baby Palins,'" National Review Online, August 22, 2011, http://www.nationalreview.com/corner/275226/conservative-women-baby-palins-karin-agness.

57. Amy Gardner, "Sarah Palin Issues a Call to Action to 'Mama Grizzlies,'" *Washington Post*, May 14, 2010, http://www.washingtonpost.com/wp-dyn/content/article/2010/05/14/AR2010051402271.html.

58. Sarah Palin, "Remarks on Pro-Life Agenda," CSPAN, May 14, 2010, http://www.c-span.org/video/?293509-1/sarah-palin-remarks-prolife-agenda.

59. "Feminism Is Alive and Well…Even Sarah Palin Wants to Be One," transcript of interview with Katie Couric, Gloria Steinem, and Jehmu Greene, Alternet.org, July 8, 2010, http://www.alternet.org/story/147478/feminism_is_alive_and_well_..._even_sarah_palin_wants_to_be_one.

60. Chloe Angyal, "The Feministing Five; Amanda Marcotte," *Feministing*, May 5, 2010, http://feministing.com/2010/05/08/the-feministing-five-amanda-marcotte/comment-page-1/.

61. Jessica Valenti, "The Fake Feminism of Sarah Palin," *Washington Post*, May 30, 2010, http://www.washingtonpost.com/wp-dyn/content/article/2010/05/28/AR2010052802263.html.

62. Marcus, "Gloria Steinem: Sarah Palin and Michele Bachmann 'Are There to Oppose the Women's Movement."

63. Burleigh, "The Best and the Rightest."

64. Allie Jones, "Kaley Cuoco: I'm Not a Feminist and I Love Feeling like a Housewife," *Gawker*, December 30, 2014, http://gawker.com/kaley-cuoco-im-not-a-feminist-and-i-love-feeling-like-1676352429.

65. Some of the Twitter responses to Kaley Cuoco can be seen at https://twitter.com/MeleMallory/status/550407772735422465.

66. Associated Press, "Kaley Cuoco-Sweeting Apologizes for Comments on Feminism," *New York Times*, January 6, 2015, http://www.nytimes.com/aponline/2015/01/06/arts/ap-us-people-kaley-cuoco-sweeting.html.

67. Ann Romney, "Three Seasons of Motherhood," *USA Today*, May 10, 2012, http://usatoday30.usatoday.com/news/opinion/forum/story/2012-05-10/ann-romney-mitt-stay-home-work-mom-grandkids/54862378/1.

68. "Newsweek Columnist Likens 'Insufferable' Ann Romney to Hitler, Stalin," RealClearPolitics, May 14, 2012, http://www.realclearpolitics.com/video/2012/05/14/newsweek_columnist_likens_insufferable_ann_romney_to_hitler_stalin.html.

69. Michelle Goldberg, "Michelle Goldberg on the Ann Romney Hitler Tempest," Daily Beast, May 14, 2012, http://www.thedailybeast.com/articles/2012/05/14/michelle-goldberg-on-the-ann-romney-hitler-tempest.html.

70. Votes on HB 574 (2013) in the Pennsylvania House are available online at http://votesmart.org/bill/votes/35196#.VNtq0nQo4dk.

71. PoliticsPA Staff, "5/5 Morning Buzz," PoliticsPA.com, http://www.politicspa.com/55-morning-buzz/57539/.

72. John Kopp, "Davidson Takes Swipe at Dem Party Leaders," *Delco Times*, May 22, 2014, http://www.delcotimes.com/general-news/20140521/davidson-takes-swipe-at-dem-party-leaders.

73. "Davidson Sworn In to Third Term in House of Representatives," news release, Office of Representative Margo Davidson, January 6, 2014, http://www.pahouse. com/Davidson/InTheNews/NewsRelease/?id=60216.

74. Tweet from Cecile Richards, October 16, 2014, https://twitter.com/cecilerichards/ status/522781979893592064.

75. "Statement from Planned Parenthood of the Rocky Mountains CEO and President Vicki Cowart on the Indefinite Postponing of HB 1256," news release, PlannedParenthood.org, March 17, 2011, http://www.plannedparenthood.org/ planned-parenthood-rocky-mountains/newsroom/press-releases/statement-planned-parenthood-rocky-mountains-ceo-president-vicki-cowart-indefinite-postponing-h; and *Taking Control: The Ongoing Battle to Preserve the Birth Control Benefit in the Affordable Care Act*, Planned Parenthood, 2013, http://www. plannedparenthood.org/files/4913/9611/7011/BC_Report_062713_vF.PDF.

76. Lydia Saad, "U.S. Still Split on Abortion: 47% Pro-Choice, 46% Pro-Life," Gallup, May 22, 2014, http://www.gallup.com/poll/170249/split-abortion-pro-choice-pro-life.aspx.

77. See the bulletin from Planned Parenthood of Santa Barbara, Ventura and San Luis Obispo Counties, Inc., Autumn 2008, http://www.plannedparenthood.org/ files/8214/0302/5698/Fall_2008.pdf.

78. "Abortion," Gallup, no date, http://www.gallup.com/poll/1576/Abortion.aspx.

79. Norma Nyhoff, "Anti-Abortion Groups in a Tizzy over FDA's Approval of Ella," NOW.org, August 24, 2010, http://now.org/blog/anti-abortion-groups-in-a-tizzy-over-fda-s-approval-of-ella/.

80. "Ohio Governor Kasich Sides with Extremists, Signs Dangerous Anti-Choice Measures into Law," press release, NARAL, July 1, 2013, http://www. prochoiceamerica.org/media/press-releases/2013/pr07012013_ohio.html.

81. "Brownback Signs Extreme Anti-Choice Bill Banning Abortion in Almost All Cases," press release, NARAL, April 19, 2013, http://www.prochoiceamerica.org/ media/press-releases/2013/pr04192013_kansas.html.

82. Terry Moran, "Does John Edwards Condone Hate Speech?," ABC News, February 6, 2007, http://abcnews.go.com/blogs/headlines/2007/02/does_john_edwar/.

83.   Paige Winfield Cunningham, "SGR Senate Vote on Monday—Enrollment Hits
       6 Million—The Obamacare Report Card," *Politico*, March 28, 2014, http://www.
       politico.com/politicopulse/0314/politicopulse13441.html.

84.   Melinda Henneberger, "'Princess Nancy' Pelosi Calls Cain 'Clueless'; Vows to Do
       More for Child Care," *Washington Post*, November 17, 2011, http://www.
       washingtonpost.com/lifestyle/style/princess-nancy-pelosivows-to-do-for-child-
       care-what-we-did-for-health-care/2011/11/15/gIQACzY1VN_story_1.html.

85.   "Gillibrand, Maloney, Quinn, Gloria Steinem and Dozens of Women Leaders
       Join Together to Protest Anti-Choice Stupak Amendment in Health Reform Bill,"
       press release, Office of Kirsten Gillibrand, November 16, 2009, http://www.
       gillibrand.senate.gov/newsroom/press/release/gillibrand-maloney-quinn-gloria-
       steinem-and-dozens-of-women-leaders-join-together-to-protest-anti-choice-
       stupak-amendment-in-health-reform-bill.

86.   Katie McDonough, "Delusional National Review Writer Thinks 'Pro-Life'
       Efforts—Not Contraception—Reduce Abortion Rate," Salon.com, June 18, 2014,
       http://www.salon.com/2014/06/18/delusional_national_review_writer_thinks_
       pro_life_efforts_not_contraception_reduces_abortion_rate/.

87.   *Choice*, a publication of Planned Parenthood of the Southern Finger Lakes, Fall
       2010, http://www.plannedparenthood.org/files/2914/0546/1803/PPSFL_
       CHOICE_Fall_2010.pdf.

88.   Amanda Marcotte, "Anti-Choicers Drop the 'Life' Pretense, Increasingly Admit
       They're Angry about Sex," RH Reality Check, January 27, 2014, http://
       rhrealitycheck.org/article/2014/01/27/anti-choicers-drop-life-pretense-
       increasingly-admit-theyre-angry-sex/.

89.   Amanda Marcotte, "Civility? For the Anti-Choice Movement, It's an Alien
       Concept," RH Reality Check, September 25, 2011, http://rhrealitycheck.org/
       article/2011/09/25/impossibility-civility-0/.

90.   Michelle Goldberg, "Paul Ryan's Extreme Abortion Views," Daily Beast, August
       11, 2012, http://www.thedailybeast.com/articles/2012/08/11/paul-ryan-s-
       extreme-abortion-views.html.

91.   An image of the original press release appears in Andrew Johnson, "Emily's List:
       Selecting Iowa's First Female Senator to Respond to SOTU Just 'Window
       Dressing,'" National Review Online, January 16, 2015, http://www.

nationalreview.com/corner/396579/emilys-list-selecting-iowas-first-female-senator-respond-sotu-just-window-dressing.

92.   Hanna Rosin, "The Patriarchy Is Dead," *Slate*, September 11, 2013, http://www.slate.com/articles/double_x/doublex/2013/09/the_end_of_men_why_feminists_won_t_accept_that_things_are_looking_up_for.single.html.

93.   Nora Caplan-Bricker "'The End of Men' Author Mansplains," *New Republic*, September 12, 2013, http://www.newrepublic.com/article/114683/hanna-rosins-end-men-wrong-patriarchy-not-dead.

94.   See tweet from Janet D. Stemwedel, Steptember 13, 2013, https://twitter.com/docfreeride/status/378685999405989888.

95.   Caplan-Bricker "'The End of Men' Author Mansplains."

96.   Katie J. M. Baker, "Patriarchy Is Dead If You're a Rich White Lady," Jezebel, September 11, 2013, http://jezebel.com/patriarchy-is-dead-if-youre-a-rich-white-lady-1294793681.

97.   Kat Stoeffel, "39 Things We'll Miss about Patriarchy, Which Is Dead," *New York*, September 11, 2013, http://nymag.com/thecut/2013/09/39-things-well-miss-about-patriarchy.html.

98.   Jonathan Chait, "Not a Very P.C. Thing to Say: How the Language Police Are Perverting Liberalism," *New York*, January 27, 2015, http://nymag.com/daily/intelligencer/2015/01/not-a-very-pc-thing-to-say.html.

99.   Liesl Schillinger, "Endangered Species or Still the Enemy?," *New York Times*, July 13, 2008, http://www.nytimes.com/2008/07/13/fashion/13books.html.

100.   Cassy Fiano, "Breaking News: Jessica Valenti Is a Giant Coward," *NewsRealBlog*, November 12, 2010, http://www.newsrealblog.com/2010/11/12/breaking-news-jessica-valenti-is-a-giant-coward/2/.

101.   Ibid.

102.   Alan White, "Oxford Abortion Debate between Two Male Journalists Cancelled due to 'Security Concerns,'" Buzzfeed, November 18, 2014, http://www.buzzfeed.com/alanwhite/heres-what-happened-when-two-men-decided-to-debate-abortion#.axx825bD3.

103.   Tim Stanley, "Oxford Students Shut Down Abortion Debate. Free Speech Is under Assault on Campus," *Telegraph*, November 19, 2014, http://www.telegraph.co.uk/

news/politics/11239437/Oxford-students-shut-down-abortion-debate.-Free-speech-is-under-assault-on-campus.html.

104. White, "Oxford Abortion Debate."

105. Tom Calver, "Christ Church Refuses to Hold 'Abortion Culture' Debate," *Cherwell*, November 17, 2014, http://www.cherwell.org/news/college/2014/11/17/christ-church-refuses-to-hold-quotabortion-culturequot-debate.

106. Niamh McIntyre, "I Helped Shut Down an Abortion Debate between Two Men Because My Uterus Isn't Up for Their Discussion," *Independent*, November 18, 2014, http://www.independent.co.uk/voices/comment/i-helped-shut-down-an-abortion-debate-between-two-men-because-my-uterus-isnt-up-for-their-discussion-9867200.html.

107. Ibid.

108. Tim Black, "Oxford, Abortion and the Closing of the Western Mind," *Spiked*, February 2, 2015, http://www.spiked-online.com/freespeechnow/fsn_article/oxford-abortion-and-the-closing-of-the-western-mind#.VNvXsHQo4dk.

109. William Saletan, "Do Pro-Lifers Oppose Birth Control?," *Slate*, January 15, 2014, http://www.slate.com/blogs/saletan/2014/01/15/do_pro_lifers_oppose_birth_control_polls_say_no.html.

110. Scott Lemieux, "A Guide to Anti-Choice Concern Trolling," *American Prospect*, July 23, 2013, http://prospect.org/article/guide-anti-choice-concern-trolling.

111. Amie Newman, "Media Watch: Saletan in Slate," RH Reality Check, May 1, 2007, http://rhrealitycheck.org/article/2007/05/01/media-watch-saletan-in-slate/.

112. "DePaul Punishes Student for Exposing Vandals of Pro-Life Display," press release, TheFire.org, February 28, 2013, http://www.thefire.org/depaul-punishes-student-for-exposing-vandals-of-pro-life-display-2/.

113. Greg Lukianoff, "Vigilante Censorship Alive and Well in Kentucky," TheFire.org, April 14, 2006, http://www.thefire.org/vigilante-censorship-ali.

114. Geroge Will, "Pro-'Choice' Intolerance: A Johns Hopkins Anti-Abortion Group Is Denied Recognition," *Pittsburgh Post-Gazette*, April 8, 2013, http://www.post-gazette.com/stories/opinion/perspectives/george-f-will-pro-choice-intolerance-a-johns-hopkins-anti-abortion-group-is-denied-recognition-682514/#ixzz2PrwVbAHP.

115. Todd Starnes, "University Compares Pro-Life Students to White Supremacists," Fox News, no date, http://radio.foxnews.com/toddstarnes/top-stories/university-compares-pro-life-students-to-white-supremacists.html.

116. Yvonne Wenger, "Anti-Abortion Group Stirs Speech Debate at Hopkins," *Baltimore Sun*, April 8, 2013, http://www.baltimoresun.com/news/maryland/education/bs-md-voice-for-life-20130408,0,198981.story.

117. "National Survey of Healthcare Consumers: Abortion," Thomson Reuters, March 2011, https://web.archive.org/web/20110626152139/http://www.factsforhealthcare.com/pressroom/NPR_report_Abortion.pdf.

118. Robert P. Jones, Daniel Cox, and Rachel Laser, *Millenials, Religion, and Abortion Survey* (Washington, DC: Public Religion Research Institute, 2011), http://publicreligion.org/site/wp-content/uploads/2011/06/Millenials-Abortion-and-Religion-Survey-Report.pdf.

119. Alexa Coombs, "Johns Hopkins Denies Pro-Life Club, Equates Them to White Supremacists," LifeNews.com, March 29, 2013, http://www.lifenews.com/2013/03/29/johns-hopkins-denies-pro-life-club-equates-them-to-white-supremacists/.

120. Maria Wiering, "Johns Hopkins' Pro-Life Club Fighting for Official Recognition," *Catholic Review*, April 8, 2013, http://www.catholicreview.org/article/home/johns-hopkins-pro-life-club-fighting-for-official-recognition.

121. Maria Wiering, "Johns Hopkins' Pro-Life Club Fighting For Official Recognition, Abortion," *Free Republic*, April 8, 2013, http://www.freerepublic.com/focus/f-news/3005558/posts.

122. Foundation for Individual Rights in Education, "FIRE Letter to Schaefer Whiteaker, Chief Justice, Student Government Association Judiciary, Johns Hopkins University," FIRE, April 8, 2013, http://www.thefire.org/fire-letter-to-schaefer-whiteaker-chief-justice-student-government-association-judiciary-johns-hopkins.

123. Foundation for Individual Rights in Education, "John Hopkins Office of Institutional Equity Response to Voice for Life," FIRE, April 3, 2013, http://www.thefire.org/johns-hopkins-office-of-institutional-equity-response-to-voice-for-life/.

124. Alice Bell, "Why Women in Science Are Annoyed at Rosetta Mission Scientist's Clothing," *Guardian*, November 13, 2014, http://www.theguardian.com/science/2014/nov/13/why-women-in-science-are-annoyed-at-rosetta-mission-scientists-clothing.

125. Rose Eveleth, Tweet on November 12, 2014, Twitter, https://twitter.com/roseveleth/status/532538957490561024.

126. Chris Plante and Arielle Duhaime-Ross, "I Don't Care If You Landed A Spacecraft On a Comet, Your Shirt Is Sexist and Ostracizing," *Verge*, November 13, 2014, http://www.theverge.com/2014/11/13/7213819/your-bowling-shirt-is-holding-back-progress.

127. Ibid.

128. S.E. Smith, "A Philae Researcher Wore An Unbelievably Sexist Shirt on A Livefeed and Women in STEM Are Pissed," *xoJane*, November 12, 2014, http://www.xojane.com/issues/sexist-shirt-philae-matt-taylor.

129. Ibid.

130. Elly PriZeMaN, Tweet on November 13, 2014, Twitter, https://twitter.com/ellyprizeman/status/532927131098300416,

131. Tim Stanley, "Matt Taylor's Sexist Shirt and the Day Political Correctness Officially Went Mad," *Telegraph*, November 15, 2014, http://www.telegraph.co.uk/news/science/space/11232986/Matt-Taylors-sexist-shirt-and-the-day-political-correctness-officially-went-mad.html.

132. Lakeidra Chavis, "UAF Announces Plans for New Kameel Toi Henderson Building in Honor of 59 Percent Female Demographic," *University of Alaska Fairbanks' The Sun Star*, March 26, 2013, https://web.archive.org/web/20131114174408/http://www.uafsunstar.com/archives/22309.

133. Will Creeley, Letter to Chancellor Brian Rogers, FIRE, January 15, 2014, http://www.thefire.org/fire-letter-to-university-of-alaska-fairbanks/.

134. Samantha Sunne, "University of Alaska Fairbanks student newspaper under investigation following sexual harassment claims," Student Press Law Center November 26, 2013, http://www.splc.org/article/2013/11/university-of-alaska-fairbanks-student-newspaper-under-investigation-following-sexual-harassment-cla.

135. Interview with author, November 2014.

136. Pauline W. Chen, "Sexism Charges Divide Surgeons' Group," *New York Times*, April 15, 2011, http://well.blogs.nytimes.com/2011/04/15/sexism-charges-divide-surgeons-group/?_r=1.

137. Ian Tucker, "The Uses of Semen? One: Reproduction. Two: Best Not Mentioned, Really ... ," *Guardian*, May 7, 2011, http://www.theguardian.com/lifeandstyle/2011/may/08/lazar-greenfield-semen-antidepressant-women.

138. Chen, "Sexism Charges Divide Surgeons' Group."

139. Ibid.

140. Ibid.

141. Michael Smerconish, "Lazar Greenfield's 'Semengate' Stuns Scientific Community," Huffington Post, April 25, 2011, http://www.huffingtonpost.com/michael-smerconish/semengate-stuns-scientifi_b_853164.html.

142. Jacquelyn C. Campbell et. al, "Risk Factors for Femicide in Abusive Relationships: Results from a Multisite Case Control Study," *American Journal of Public Health*, July 2003, http://www.ncbi.nlm.nih.gov/pmc/articles/PMC1447915/#rl.

143. "Intimate Partner Homicide," National Institute of Justice Journal, U.S. Department of Justice, https://www.ncjrs.gov/pdffiles1/jr000250.pdf.

144. Bureau of Justice Statistics Factbook, "Violence by Intimates," U.S. Department of Justice, http://bjs.gov/content/pub/pdf/vi.pdf.

145. Glenn Kessler, "Holder's 2009 Claim That Intimate-Partner Homicide Is the Leading Cause of Death for African American Women," *Washington Post*, December 18, 2013, http://www.washingtonpost.com/blogs/fact-checker/wp/2013/12/18/holders-2009-claim-that-intimate-partner-homicide-is-the-leading-cause-of-death-for-african-american-women/.

146. Christina Hoff Sommers, "Domestic Violence Myths Help No One," *USA Today*, February 4, 2011, http://usatoday30.usatoday.com/news/opinion/forum/2011-02-03-sommers04_st_N.htm.

147. Kessler, "Holder's 2009 Claim That Intimate-Partner Homicide Is the Leading Cause of Death for African American Women."

148. "Incomes vs. Earnings," United States Census Bureau Blog, September 23, 2010, http://blogs.census.gov/2010/09/23/income-vs-earnings/.

149. Carrie Lukas, "It's Time That We End the Equal Pay Myth," *Forbes*, April 16, 2012, http://www.forbes.com/sites/realspin/2012/04/16/its-time-that-we-end-the-equal-pay-myth/.

150. Glenn Kessler, "President Obama's Persistent '77-Cent' Claim on the Wage Gap Gets a New Pinocchio Rating," *Washington Post*, April 9, 2014, http://www.washingtonpost.com/blogs/fact-checker/wp/2014/04/09/president-obamas-persistent-77-cent-claim-on-the-wage-gap-gets-a-new-pinocchio-rating/.

151. Mark J. Perry and Andrew G. Biggs, "The '77 Cents on the Dollar' Myth About Women's Pay," *Wall Street Journal*, April 7, 2014, http://www.wsj.com/articles/SB10001424052702303532704579483752909957472.

152. See, e.g., *Forbes*, supra at 16.

153. CONSAD Research Corporation, "An Analysis for the Disparity in Wages Between Men and Women," CONSAD, January 12, 2009, http://www.consad.com/content/reports/Gender%20Wage%20Gap%20Final%20Report.pdf.

154. Louis Jacobson, "Barack Obama Ad Says Women Are Paid '77 Cents on the Dollar For Doing the Same Work As Men,'" PolitiFact, June 21, 2012, http://www.politifact.com/truth-o-meter/statements/2012/jun/21/barack-obama/barack-obama-ad-says-women-are-paid-77-cents-dolla/.

155. Hanna Rosin, "The Gender Wage Gap Lie," *Slate*, August 30, 2013, http://www.slate.com/articles/double_x/doublex/2013/08/gender_pay_gap_the_familiar_line_that_women_make_77_cents_to_every_man_s.html.

156. Meghan Casserly, "The Gender Pay Gap Got Worse, Not Better, in 2012—And It's Great for Women," *Forbes*, February 14, 2014, http://www.forbes.com/sites/meghancasserly/2013/02/14/gender-pay-gap-wider-2012-and-its-great-for-women/.

157. Sarah Jane Glynn, "Explaining the Gender Wage Gap," Center for American Progress, May 19, 2014, https://www.americanprogress.org/issues/economy/report/2014/05/19/90039/explaining-the-gender-wage-gap/.

CHAPTER NINE: FEMINISTS AGAINST FACTS, FAIRNESS, AND THE RULE OF LAW

1. Eliana Dockterman, "When Enforcing School Dress Codes Turns Into Slut Shaming," *Time*, March 25, 2014; http://time.com/36997/when-enforcing-

school-dress-codes-turns-into-slut-shaming/; Christine Wolf, "Haven Middle School Bans Leggings & Yoga Pants – Too Distracting for Boys," Evanston Patch, March 23, 2014, http://patch.com/illinois/evanston/leggings—yoga-pants-banned-at-haven-middle-school.

2.   Rebecca Rose, "Confusing School Ban Over 'Distracting' Leggings Ignites Controversy," Jezebel, March 19, 2014, http://jezebel.com/confusing-school-ban-over-distracting-leggings-ignite-1547616678.

3.   Maya Dusenberry, "Quick Hit: #Rapecultureiswhen….," *Feministing*, March 25, 2014, http://feministing.com/2014/03/25/quick-hit-rapecultureiswhen/.

4.   Charles Bartling, "Middle school dress code clarified," Evanston Now, March 26, 2014, http://evanstonnow.com/story/education/charles-bartling/2014-03-26/62445/middle-school-dress-code-clarified.

5.   Ibid.

6.   Rachel Raczka, "Students in Ill. Are protesting legging ban," Boston.com, March 25, 2014, http://www.boston.com/lifestyle/fashion/2014/03/25/students-ill-are-protesting-legging-ban/rPifhOXhTfntj1Ok6MPC1O/story.html.

7.   "What Is Rape Culture?," Women Against Violence Against Women, http://www.wavaw.ca/what-is-rape-culture/.

8.   Kaelyn Polick-Kirkpatrick, "Man Up and WOW Factor! perpetuate sexism and rape culture," The State Press, October 8, 2014, http://www.statepress.com/2014/10/08/man-up-and-wow-factor-perpetuate-sexism-and-rape-culture/.

9.   Tara Culp-Ressler, "Why Rape Prevention Activists Don't Like the New Nail Polish That Can Detect Roofies," *ThinkProgress*, August 25, 2014, http://thinkprogress.org/health/2014/08/25/3475190/date-rape-nail-polish/.

10.   Ibid.

11.   Katrin Bennhold, "Abuse Cases in British City Long Ignored, Report Says," *New York Times*, August 26, 2014, http://www.nytimes.com/2014/08/27/world/europe/children-in-rotherham-england-were-sexually-abused-report-says.html.

12.   June Thomas, "At Least 1,400 Children Sexually Exploited in One English Town. How Could This Possibly Happen?," *Slate*, September 2, 2014, http://www.slate.com/blogs/xx_factor/2014/09/02/rotherham_sexual_abuse_1400_children_exploited_in_one_english_town_and_authorities.html; "1,400 Kids Sexually

Abused in U.K. Town," Daily Beast, August 26, 2014, http://www.thedailybeast.com/cheats/2014/08/26/1-400-kids-sexually-abused-in-rotterham.html; Isha Aran, "New Details Emerge in Case of Horrifying British Sex Abuse Ring," Jezebel, September 2, 2014, http://jezebel.com/new-details-emerge-in-case-of-horrifying-british-sex-ab-1629539480; "Muslims react with outrage at UK sex abuse report," Salon.com, August 27, 2014, http://www.salon.com/2014/08/27/muslims_react_with_outrage_at_uk_sex_abuse_report/; Maya Dusenberry, "Daily Feminist Cheat Sheet," Feministing, http://feministing.com/?s=rotterham.

13.   Celeste Katz, "Sen. Kirstin Gillibrand, colleagues, push for more federal funding to investigate college sexual assaults," New York Daily News, April 7, 2014 http://www.nydailynews.com/blogs/dailypolitics/sen-kirsten-gillibrand-colleagues-push-federal-funding-investigate-college-sexual-assaults-blog-entry-1.1748384.

14.   Christopher P. Krebs, Ph.D., Christine H. Lindquist, Ph.D., Tara D. Warner, M.A., Bonnie S. Fisher, Ph.D., Sandra L. Martin, Ph.D., "The Campus Sexual Assault (CSA) Study," National Institute of Justice, December 2007, https://www.ncjrs.gov/pdffiles1/nij/grants/221153.pdf.

15.   Ibid.

16.   Glenn Kessler, "One in five women in college sexually assaulted: an update on this statistic," Washington Post, December 17, 2014, http://www.washingtonpost.com/blogs/fact-checker/wp/2014/12/17/one-in-five-women-in-college-sexually-assaulted-an-update/; Caroline Kitchens, "The Rape 'Epidemic' Doesn't Actually Exist," U.S. News & World Report, October 24, 2013, http://www.usnews.com/opinion/blogs/economic-intelligence/2013/10/24/statistics-dont-back-up-claims-about-rape-culture.

17.   Jake New, "One in Five?," Inside Higher Ed, December 15, 2014, https://www.insidehighered.com/news/2014/12/15/critics-advocates-doubt-oft-cited-campus-sexual-assault-statistic.

18.   Emily Yoffe, "The College Rape Overcorrection," Slate, December 7, 2014, http://www.slate.com/articles/double_x/doublex/2014/12/college_rape_campus_sexual_assault_is_a_serious_problem_but_the_efforts.html.

19.   Dana Goldstein, "The Dueling Data on Campus Rape," The Marshall Project, December 11, 2014, https://www.themarshallproject.org/2014/12/11/the-dueling-data-on-campus-rape.

20. George F. Will, "George Will: Colleges become the victims of progressivism," *Washington Post*, June 6, 2014, http://www.washingtonpost.com/opinions/george-will-college-become-the-victims-of-progressivism/2014/06/06/e90e73b4-eb50-11e3-9f5c-9075d5508f0a_story.html; Hannah Groch-Begley, "A Guide to George Will's Decades of Attacks On Sexual Assault Victims And 'Rape Crisis Feminists,'" Media Matters for America, October 15, 2014, http://mediamatters.org/research/2014/10/15/a-guide-to-george-wills-decades-of-attacks-on-s/201166.

21. Joe Strupp, "EXCLUSIVE: NOW President Calls On *Washington Post* to Drop George Will Over Rape Column," Media Matters for America, June 10, 2014, http://mediamatters.org/blog/2014/06/10/exclusive-now-president-calls-for-george-wills/199666.

22. "Tell The *Washington Post*: Fire George Will," We Are UltraViolet, http://act.weareultraviolet.org/cms/sign/Fire_George_Will/.

23. Ibid.

24. "Letter to George Will from Senators," *Washington Post*, June 12, 2014, http://www.washingtonpost.com/r/2010-2019/WashingtonPost/2014/06/13/Editorial-Opinion/Graphics/Letter-to-George-Will-from-Senators.pdf.

25. "George Will responds to senators on his sexual assault column," *Washington Post*, June 13, 2014, http://www.washingtonpost.com/blogs/post-partisan/wp/2014/06/13/george-will-responds-to-senators-on-his-sexual-assault-column/.

26. Emily Yoffe, "The College Rape Overcorrection."

27. Bonnie S. Fisher, Francis T. Cullen, Michael G. Turner, "The Sexual Victimization of College Women," National Institute of Justice, December 2000, https://www.ncjrs.gov/pdffiles1/nij/182369.pdf.

28. Emily Yoffe, "The College Rape Overcorrection."

29. Fisher, Cullen, and Turner, "The Sexual Victimization of College Women."

30. @MDRSWRJ, tweet, December 8, 2014, https://twitter.com/MDRSWRJ/status/541989076162052097.

31. Alexandra Brodsky, "7 Things You Should Know About Evidence in Campus Rape Proceedings," *Feministing*, December 8, 2014, http://feministing.com/2014/12/08/7-things-you-should-know-about-evidence-in-campus-rape-proceedings/.

32.   Alexandra Brodsky, tweet, December 8, 2014, https://twitter.com/azbrodsky/
      status/541995401201848321.

33.   Christopher P. Krebs, Ph.D., Christine H. Lindquist, Ph.D., Tara D. Warner, M.A.,
      Bonnie S. Fisher, Ph.D., Sandra L. Martin, Ph.D., "College Women's Experiences
      with Physically Forced, Alcohol- or Other Drug-Enabled, and Drug-Facilitated
      Sexual Assault Before and Since Entering College," *Journal of American College
      Health*, August 7, 2010, http://www.tandfonline.com/doi/abs/10.3200/
      JACH.57.6.639-649#.VLGQx2TF_oF.

34.   "The Left's Top 25 Journalists," Daily Beast, http://www.thedailybeast.com/
      galleries/2010/02/16/the-left-s-top-25-journalists.html.

35.   Jessica Valenti, tweet, October 16, 2013, https://twitter.com/JessicaValenti/
      status/390501900484747264.

36.   Kim LaCapria, "Slate's Prudie, Emily Yoffe, Thinks Drunk Girls Cause Rape in
      Infuriating Piece," Inquisitr, October 16, 2013, http://www.inquisitr.com/995747/
      slates-prudie-emily-yoffe-thinks-drunk-girls-cause-rape-in-infuriating-piece/.

37.   Thomas, "Emily Yoffe's Rape Apologism: Some Very Quick Thoughts," *Yes Means
      Yes*, October 16, 2013, https://yesmeansyesblog.wordpress.com/2013/10/16/
      emily-yoffes-rape-apologism-some-very-quick-thoughts/; Katie McDonough,
      "Sorry, Emily Yoffe: Blaming assault on women's drinking is wrong, dangerous
      and tired," Salon.com, October 16, 2013, http://www.salon.com/2013/10/16/
      blaming_assault_on_womens_drinking_is_tired_dangerous_rape_apology/.

38.   Emily Yoffe, "Emily Yoffe Responds to Her Critics," *Slate*, October 18, 2013,
      http://www.slate.com/blogs/xx_factor/2013/10/18/rape_culture_and_binge_
      drinking_emily_yoffe_responds_to_her_critics.html.

39.   Jonah Goldberg, "*Rolling Stone* Crumbles," National Review Online, December
      5, 2014, http://www.nationalreview.com/corner/394084/rolling-stone-crumbles-
      jonah-goldberg.

40.   Anna Merlan, "'Is the UVA Rape Story a Gigantic Hoax?' Asks Idiot," Jezebel,
      December 1, 4014, http://jezebel.com/is-the-uva-rape-story-a-gigantic-hoax-
      asks-idiot-1665233387.

41.   Amanda Marcotte, tweet, December 5, 2014, https://twitter.com/
      amandamarcotte/status/540935488576978945.

42.   Katie McDonough, "'It makes me really depressed': From UVA to Cosby, the rape denial playbook that won't go away," Salon.com, December 4, 2014, http://www.salon.com/2014/12/04/it_makes_me_really_depressed_from_uva_to_cosby_the_rape_denial_playbook_that_wont_go_away/.

43.   "Thomas Jefferson and Sally Hemings: A Brief Account," Monticello, http://www.monticello.org/site/plantation-and-slavery/thomas-jefferson-and-sally-hemings-brief-account.

44.   Bonnie Gordon, "The UVA Gang Rape Allegations Are Awful, Horrifying, and Not Shocking at All," *Slate*, November 25, 2014, http://www.slate.com/blogs/xx_factor/2014/11/25/uva_gang_rape_allegations_in_rolling_stone_not_surprising_to_one_associate.html.

45.   Will Dana, "A Note to Our Readers," *Rolling Stone*, December 5, 2014, http://www.rollingstone.com/culture/news/a-note-to-our-readers-20141205.

46.   Jessica Valenti, "Who is Jackie? Rolling Stone's rape story is about a person – and I believe her," *Guardian*, December 8, 2014, http://www.theguardian.com/commentisfree/2014/dec/08/who-is-jackie-rolling-stone-rape-story.

47.   Andrew Elliott, "Being Phi Psi: fraternity looks forward," *Cavalier Daily*, January 26, 2015, http://www.cavalierdaily.com/article/2015/01/interviewing-phi-psi-on-aftermath-of-rolling-stone-article-at-uva.

48.   Jonathan H. Adler, "Does the University of Virginia owe its fraternities an apology?," *Washington Post*, December 31, 2014, http://www.washingtonpost.com/news/volokh-conspiracy/wp/2014/12/31/does-the-university-of-virginia-owe-its-fraternities-an-apology/.

49.   Craig Silverman, "The Year in Media Errors and Corrections 2014," Poynter, updated December 19, 2014, http://www.poynter.org/news/mediawire/306801/the-year-in-media-errors-and-corrections-2014/.

50.   Craig Silverman, "The year in media errors and corrections 2014," Poynter, December 18, 2014, http://www.poynter.org/news/mediawire/306801/the-year-in-media-errors-and-corrections-2014/.

51.   Zerlina Maxwell, "No matter what Jackie said, we should generally believe rape claims," *Washington Post*, December 6, 2014, http://www.washingtonpost.com/posteverything/wp/2014/12/06/no-matter-what-jackie-said-we-should-automatically-believe-rape-claims/.

52. "Harvard University: Denial of Due Process for Student Acquitted of Criminal Charges," FIRE, January 4, 2004, http://www.thefire.org/cases/harvard-university-denial-of-due-process-for-student-acquitted-of-criminal-charges/.

53. Dana Cimulluca, "Accused Former Duke Lax Player Lands Morgan Stanley Job," *Wall Street Journal*, April 18, 2007, http://blogs.wsj.com/deals/2007/04/18/accused-former-duke-lax-player-lands-morgan-stanley-job/.

54. Michael Dwyer, "The Duke Lacrosse Player Still Outrunning His Past," *Vanity Fair*, March 24, 2014, http://www.vanityfair.com/society/2014/03/duke-lacrosse-rape-scandal-ryan-mcfadyen#.

55. Chelsea Allison, "Lax lawsuit targets Duke, Durham," *Chronicle*, February 21, 2008, http://www.dukechronicle.com/articles/2008/02/22/lax-lawsuit-targets-duke-durham#.VJnWz7APMIA .

56. Complaint, "Case Summary," February 2008 (see above) http://dig.abclocal.go.com/wtvd/dukeplayers38_casesummary.pdf.

57. Cathy Young, "Last Call for 'Rape-Crisis' Feminism?," *Reason*, April 16, 2007, http://reason.com/archives/2007/04/16/last-call-for-rape-crisis-femi ; Howard Kurtz, "A Blogger for Edwards Resigns After Complaints," *Washington Post*, February 13, 2007, http://www.washingtonpost.com/wp-dyn/content/article/2007/02/12/AR2007021201632.html.

58. Good Lt. "My Liberalism Says You're Guilty of Rape (Updated)," *Jawa Report*, January 12, 2007, http://mypetjawa.mu.nu/archives/186032.php.

59. "Potbangers protest Part II," YouTube, https://www.youtube.com/watch?v=g_RVCA5bl1E.

60. Kurt Andersen, "Rape, Justice, and the 'Times,'" *New York*, October 16, 2006, http://nymag.com/news/imperialcity/22337/.

61. Wahneema Lubiano, "A Social Disaster : Voices from Durham," NewBlackMan (in Exile) The Digital Home for Mark Anthony Neal, April 13, 2006, http://newblackman.blogspot.com/2006/04/social-disaster-voices-from-durham.html.

62. Karla FC Holloway, "Coda: Bodies of Evidence," *Scholar and Feminist*, Summer 2006, http://sfonline.barnard.edu/sport/printkho.htm.

63. Karla FC Holloway, bio, http://english.duke.edu/people?Gurl=&Uil=39&subpage=profile.

64.   Peter Lange, "Provost Responds to Faculty Letter Regarding Lacrosse," Duke
      University, April 3, 2006, http://today.duke.edu/showcase/mmedia/features/
      lacrosse_incident/lange_baker.html.

65.   The Situation with Tucker Carlson, June 5, 2006, http://www.nbcnews.com/
      id/13165471/ns/msnbc-the_ed_show/t/situation-tucker-carlson-june/#.
      VOIjRO85CM8.

66.   "Member of Duke Lacrosse Team Breaks the Silence," CNN, May 3, 2006, http://
      edition.cnn.com/TRANSCRIPTS/0605/03/lt.01.html.

67.   "'The Situation with Tucker Carlson' for June 5," NBC News, June 5, 2006. http://
      www.nbcnews.com/id/13165471/ns/msnbc-the_ed_show/t/situation-tucker-
      carlson-june/#.VOIjRO85CM8http://durhamwonderland.blogspot.
      com/2006/12/wendy-murphy-file.html.

68.   Lara Setrakian, "Charges Dropped in Duke Lacrosse Case," ABC News, April 11,
      2007, http://abcnews.go.com/US/LegalCenter/story?id=3028515.

69.   Farai Chideya, Waler Fields, Julianne Malveaux, and Ron Christie, "Roundtable:
      Imus, Duke Charges, Iraq Tours," NPR, April 12, 2007, http://www.npr.org/
      templates/story/story.php?storyId=9536095.

70.   Michael Winerip, "Revisiting a Rape Scandal That Would Have Been Monstrous
      if True," *New York Times*, June 3, 2013, http://www.nytimes.com/2013/06/03/
      booming/revisiting-the-tawana-brawley-rape-scandal.html.

71.   Robert D. McFadden, "BRAWLEY MADE UP STORY OF ASSAULT, GRAND
      JURY FINDS," *New York Times*, October 7, 1988, http://www.nytimes.
      com/1988/10/07/nyregion/brawley-made-up-story-of-assault-grand-jury-finds.
      html?pagewanted=all&src=pm.

72.   Winerip, "Revisiting a Rape Scandal That Would Have Been Monstrous if True."

73.   Assistant Secretary for Civil Rights Russlynn Ali, "Dear Colleague" Letter on
      Title IX, April 4, 2011, http://www2.ed.gov/about/offices/list/ocr/letters/
      colleague-201104.html.

74.   Robert Shibley, "Due Process, Clarity Suffer As Feds Tackle Campus Sexual
      Assault," WGBH News, May 1, 2014, http://wgbhnews.org/post/due-process-
      clarity-suffer-feds-tackle-campus-sexual-assault.

75.   Assistant Secretary for Civil Rights Russlynn Ali, "Dear Colleague" Letter on
      Title IX.

76.   Ibid.

77.   Ibid.

78.   Brett A. Sokolow, "Sex and Booze," *ATIXA*, April 24, 2014, https://www.atixa. org/wordpress/wp-content/uploads/2012/01/ATIXA-Tip-of-the- Week-04_24_141.pdf.

79.   Joe Palazzolo, "Harvard Law Professor: Feds' Position on Sexual-Assault Policies Is 'Madness,'" *Wall Street Journal*, December 31, 2014, http://blogs.wsj.com/ law/2014/12/31/harvard-law-professor-feds-position-on-sexual-assault-policies- is-madness/.

80.   Judith Shulevitz, "Accused College Rapists Have Rights, Too," *New Republic*, October 11, 2014, http://www.newrepublic.com/article/119778/college-sexual- assault-rules-trample-rights-accused-campus-rapists.

81.   "Rethink Harvard's sexual harassment policy," *Boston Globe*, October 15, 2014, http://www.bostonglobe.com/opinion/2014/10/14/rethink-harvard-sexual- harassment-policy/HFDDiZN7nU2UwuUuWMnqbM/story.html.

82.   Ibid.

83.   Jeannie Suk, "The Trouble with Teaching Rape Law," *New Yorker*, December 15, 2014, http://www.newyorker.com/news/news-desk/trouble-teaching-rape-law.

84.   Jed Rubenfeld, "Mishandling Rape," *New York Times*, November 15, 2014, http:// www.nytimes.com/2014/11/16/opinion/sunday/mishandling-rape.html?_r=3.

85.   Ibid.

86.   Jessica Valenti, "If you can't talk about rape without blaming victims, don't talk about rape," *Guardian*, November 17, 2014, http://www.theguardian.com/ commentisfree/2014/nov/17/rape-blaming-victims-talk.

87.   Alexandra Brodsky, "7 Things You Should Know About Evidence I Campus Rape Proceedings," *Feministing*, December 8, 2014, http://feministing. com/2014/12/08/7-things-you-should-know-about-evidence-in-campus-rape- proceedings/.

88.   David Siders, "Jerry Brown signs 'affirmative consent' sex assault bill," *Sacramento Bee*, September 28, 2014, http://www.sacbee.com/news/politics-government/ capitol-alert/article2614723.html.

89. "FIRE Statement on California 'Affirmative Consent' Bill," FIRE, February 13, 2014, http://www.thefire.org/fire-statement-on-california-affirmative-consent-bill/.

90. Shikha Dalmia, "California's Sexual Consent Law Will Ruin Good Sex for Women," *Reason*, October 7, 2014, http://reason.com/archives/2014/10/07/ruining-sex-in-california.

91. Kaili Joy Gray, "Some Dumb Lady: Consent Will Ruin Good Sex, Boo Hoo," *Wonkette*, October 8, 2014, http://wonkette.com/562741/some-dumb-lady-consent-will-ruin-good-sex-boo-hoo#6aH0pqCWhQedjvmv.99.

92. Erin Gloria Ryan, "Consent Laws Are Ruining Sex, Says Writer Who Probably Has Awful Sex," Jezebel, October 8, 2014, http://jezebel.com/consent-laws-are-ruining-sex-says-writer-who-probably-1643987479/.

93. Jill Filipovic, tweet, October 7, 2014, https://twitter.com/JillFilipovic/status/519603875293040640.

EPILOGUE

1. Debate, "LIBERALS ARE STIFLING INTELLECTUAL DIVERSITY ON CAMPUS," Intelligence Squared, February 24, 2015, http://intelligencesquaredus.org/debates/past-debates/item/1310-liberals-are-stifling-intellectual-diversity-on-campus.

2. Bruce L.R. Smith, Jeremy D. Mayer, A. Lee Fritschler, "Closed Minds?: Politics and Ideology in American Universities," Brookings Institution Press, August 11, 2008, http://www.amazon.com/Closed-Minds-Politics-Ideology-Universities/dp/0815780281#.

3. Transcript, "Liberals are stifling intellectual diversity on campus," Intelligence Squared, February 24, 2015, http://intelligencesquaredus.org/images/debates/past/transcripts/022415%20Liberal%20Stifling.pdf.

INDEX

273

M

N